HORSES

THEIR ROLE IN THE HISTORY OF MAN

HORSES

THEIR ROLE IN THE HISTORY OF MAN

Based on the original screenplay by Jan Darnley-Smith

Elwyn Hartley Edwards

A Channel 4/Scottish Television Book

WILLOW BOOKS
Collins
8 Grafton Street, London
1987

Willow Books
William Collins Sons and Co. Ltd.
London · Glasgow · Sydney
Auckland · Toronto · Johannesburg

First published in Great Britain 1987
© Scottish Television 1987 with acknowledgements to Jan Darnley-Smith

BRITISH LIBRARY CATALOGUING IN PUBLICATION DATA
Hartley Edwards, Elwyn
Horses.
1. Horses – History
I. Title
636.1'009   SF283

ISBN 0 00 218216 5

Filmset in Bembo by CG Graphic Services
Aylesbury, Bucks.
Made and printed in Great Britain by
Butler & Tanner Ltd, Frome

CONTENTS

'He serves without servility, he has fought without enmity. There is nothing so powerful, nothing less violent; there is nothing so quick, nothing more patient. England's past has been borne on his back. All our history is his industry. We are his heirs, he our inheritance.'

(From *To The Horse* by Ronald Duncan, lines spoken each year to close the final performance at the Horse of the Year Show, London)

ACKNOWLEDGEMENTS

My thanks are due to Alison Dawes, the instigator of my involvement with the Scottish Television series; Jan Darnley-Smith, the director of the series who also wrote the working script and whose enthusiasm and highly developed sense of humour were a great encouragement; Irene Black of Scottish Television, an incredibly efficient administrator, who researched much of the book's illustrative content; Louise Haines, commissioning editor of Collins Publishers, who was both helpful and tactful in every sort of situation. Finally, I have to thank my wife Mary who put up with me so patiently during the writing of this book, as, indeed, she has done throughout our married life.

E.H.E.
Chwilog

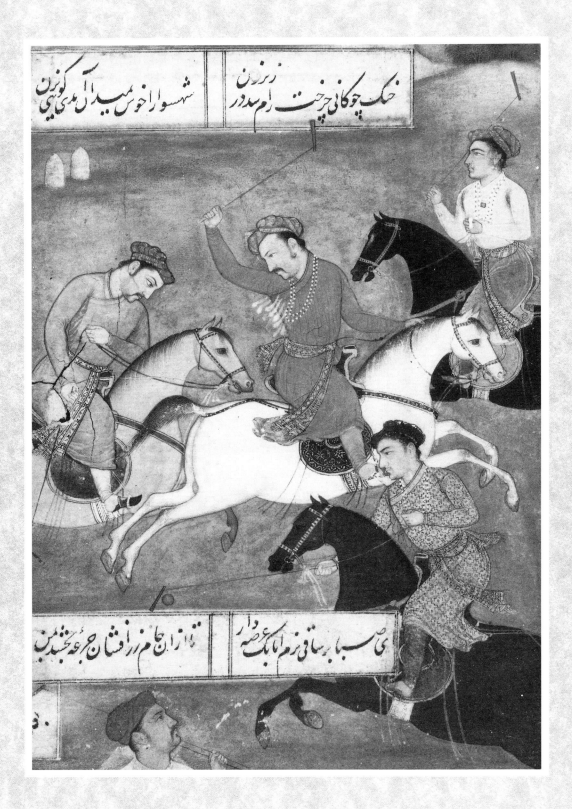

Chapter 1

SETTING THE SCENE

Sometime during the next century space travel is likely to become commonplace, with planetary cruises regarded as no more unusual than today's sea-board excursions to the Greek Islands or the Norwegian fjords. If, however, we were to pause in what may yet be a Gadarene flight to the stars, we might just experience a brief sense of wonder, even perhaps a twinge of humility, on reflecting that the human race has been brought within sight of the conquest of new worlds largely because of its association with a creature which inhabited 'our' Earth long before the human race had achieved any recognisable form.

That creature is the horse, and mankind was brought to within virtually fifty years of lift-off to the constellations on account of its exertions on our behalf.

Up to the end of the nineteenth century and well into the first part of this one, human progression over something like five thousand years had depended on the use and exploitation of the world's horse-power. Today there are still parts of Eastern Europe where the horse remains an essential element in agriculture and transport, while in some of the eastern republics of the USSR herds are still kept in what is virtually the modern equivalent of the systems employed to form the economy of the early nomadic Mongol and Euro-Asian tribes.

The first association between man and horse was between the hunter and the hunted. In the later stages of the Ice Age, primitive man used wild horse herds as a convenient larder on the hoof. Early cave drawings illustrate the use of the horse as a source of food. Huge depositories of horse bones found in France in Solutré, Lascaux, La Madeleine, Langerie and Les Eyzies de Tayac are evidence of man's reliance upon horse herds for his survival. A favoured way of killing the horses was to drive a group of them over a cliff – a method with obvious advantages over individual pursuit.

In time there came domestication, the herds being used to supply meat, hides for clothing and shelters, milk – and, quite quickly, that particular potent brew made from fermented mare's milk (*kummis*) which originated with the horsemen of the steppes and is still made at Russian horse factories today. Quickly, too, the horse must have been pressed into service as a pack animal, enabling nomadic peoples to cover greater distances.

Polo is one of the oldest and fastest sports known to man. The Mogul Emperor Jahangir (1605–27) is seen here playing with his sons Parviz and Kurram.

Through the medium of television and picture magazines, we seem to be returning to the picturate societies of over twenty thousand years ago. Cave drawings represent one of the earliest forms of human communication. This one indicates the presence of horses, which was important information for nomadic hunters.

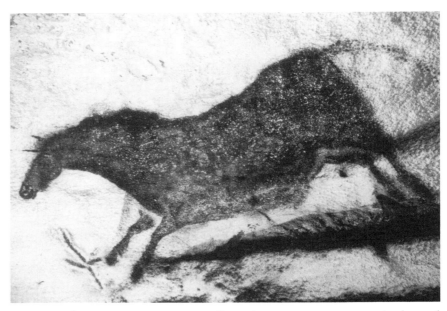

It was, however, as a means of waging war more extensively and effectively that the horse – first harnessed to the war chariot and then becoming the mount of the more widely-ranging cavalryman – began to exert his inexorable influence upon human progress. The nomadic herdsman became the mounted warrior to hold his newly gained pasture lands; then, as his stock increased, he needed to make war upon his neighbours to obtain more pasture, more stock and even more possessions.

A tremendous cross-fertilisation of peoples and cultures occurred as the horse peoples surged back and forth over the Asiatic steppes and the Ukraine, sweeping outwards into western Europe; into Asia Minor and the countries we now term Iran and Iraq; spreading over the Mediterranean countries and onwards to India and China. Empires rose and fell, civilisations were created and destroyed – for five thousand years the horse was inherent in this process. Transport, communication, war and, in time, agriculture were all dependent upon horse-power.

It was, in fact, only in those areas where the domestic horse existed that cultural and physical advances could take place at all. With the notable exceptions of the Inca and Aztec empires, which themselves fell ultimately to an army possessed of cavalry, there was no significant power in the world that was created, maintained, or enlarged without the horse.

Alongside horses at work and at war, there were those used from the earliest times for sport. Evidence of chariot racing occurs almost as soon as horses were put to a chariot pole; hunting for pleasure, as

much as for the pot, was practised by all the horse peoples of the world while the need to decide whose was the fastest horse by matching the animals against each other must go back to the time when men first sat astride horses. Polo, for example, has its origins in central Asia. The earliest record of the game is from Persia in the sixth century BC, and the related games of *bagai* and *buzkashi* are still played in Afghanistan, Turkestan and adjacent states today.

Much later, equitation rose above the basic needs of the cavalry soldier and approached an art-form as the nobility of Renaissance Europe, inspired by the rediscovered works of the Greek general, Xenophon, rode their carousels in the baroque schools of Italy and France. Their *pirouettes*, *levades*, awe-inspiring leaps and parade paces of *piaffe* and *passage* provided the basis for classical equitation which continues today in Grand Prix dressage.

Hunting, with hounds pursuing a quarry by scent, was also practised in the pre-Christian era. First among the medieval beasts of venery was the stag, but the boar was also a highly-regarded and legitimate quarry. In Europe and the Mediterranean countries, the hare was hunted extensively.

The consuming passion of the British sportsman, fox hunting, in which the quarry runs straight rather than circling like the hare, was not introduced until the eighteenth century. With the increasing enclosures of land, the erection of fences and banks, and the growing of thick hedges to confine cattle, jumping and galloping became a necessity for those who would hunt across English country with hounds bred for their speed and drive.

Raised in the image of war, the horse soon became the partner of man. This relief from the Great Temple at Abu Simbel shows the Pharaoh Rameses II and his sons storming a mountain fortress.

In the USA, another and older school of horsemanship flourishes. The skill and agility of the Western horseman and his horse in the rodeo has its roots deep in the Iberian Peninsula.

The popular modern sports of showjumping and horse trials are relative newcomers. They did not really enter the sporting calendar until the turn of this century, although 'leaping competitions' were first included in the programmes of British agricultural shows in the 1870s, and competitions for 'wide' and 'high' leaps were held at the Royal Dublin Society's Show in 1865. France, a pioneer in the sport, Russia and Germany were also holding competitions at about the same time.

Horse trials or 'combined training', another and more accurate synonym for eventing, originated with the cavalry as an all-round test of horse and rider. France staged the *Championnat du Cheval d'Armes* outside Paris in 1902; in 1912 the event became part of the Olympic Games. The first British horse trials were held at Badminton in 1949, following the London Olympics of the previous year. Badminton, held as an annual event ever since, is now one of the most prestigious fixtures in the world's horse trials calendar.

Steeplechasing, a derivation of the hunting field, has its first recorded race over constructed fences at Bedford in 1810, but the honour of staging the first recorded match belongs to Ireland. In 1752 O'Callaghan and Blake rode across country from Buttevant Church to St Leger Church: church steeples, always prominent landmarks, made convenient starting and finishing points.

In a superficial study of an association that goes back to the very dawning of our history, it may seem to be a very one-sided affair with the horse being continuously and unfeelingly exploited. In mankind's incessant, impatient struggle to shape his destiny, he seems to be moulding, conquering and sometimes destroying the environment and whatever inhabits it. Certainly, the use of the horse by man has resulted frequently in misuse and abuse. But there are still the elements of a strong partnership, a relationship, which in an extraordinary fashion, works both ways.

The natural factors influencing the evolution of any species are, first, the environment in which it has its existence and, secondly, the law of natural selection under which only the fittest and the best equipped survive to reproduce their kind. But the third and most powerful factor is the intervention of man to accelerate evolution at a rate which would be impossible under the natural law. By culling, selective breeding and cross-breeding, by careful management of the most suitable stock-raising land, and by the practice of supplementary feeding he is able to produce types suitable for a variety of purposes and to do so in a matter of generations.

All in all, this human intervention in the development of the horse has been beneficial to the species. There is no equine equivalent of the Boxer dog with its grotesquely misshapen face and jaw, nor do we encounter the failings that occur in other dogs as a result of excessive in-breeding.

The early horses harnessed to chariots were neither strong enough

Fox hunting was described by R. S. Surtees as being raised, 'In the image of war but without its guilt and only 25 per cent of its danger.' Perhaps the percentage of danger is rather greater in hunt racing. The Maryland Cup, unlike most European steeplechases, is run over timber.

nor large enough to carry riders, yet in a matter of just hundreds of years the Persian cavalry were mounted on horses of appropriate size and of obvious strength and spirit. From that point on, groups of horses having common characteristics become apparent. The Romans developed horses for specialised purposes – they had travelling animals, pack and draught horses, circus performers, racers, amblers, general utility geldings and so on. *Venaticus* was a hunter; *celer equus*, the racehorse; *bellator equus*, the charger or warhorse; *itinerarius* and *manuus*, the draught and harness horse; *cantherius*, the parade horse; *gradarius* or *ambulator*, the much prized and very comfortable ambling or pacing horse. Least popular of all, since the Romans had neither stirrups nor much in the way of saddles, must have been the trotting horse, called either *concussator*, *succusator*, or even more tellingly, *cruciator*. A recent standard work on modern horse and pony breeds lists as many as one hundred and fifty breeds and types.

Not surprisingly, perhaps, in view of the horse's contribution to the world, he occupies a unique position in the regard of men and women, whether they are themselves concerned with him or not. He inspires respect and admiration above all other domestic animals. The horse cannot have the same relationship with man as the dog which shares his master's home, sometimes takes over the favourite chair and may even insinuate himself into the bed. He is too big to be allowed into the house (although the desert Bedouin shared his tent with his mare as a regular thing), nor is he really equipped to express affection. A dog's wagging tail is a sure indication of affection or greeting. If the horse should swish his tail, wise horsemen take evasive action, knowing it expresses irritation and may presage some violent movement.

Yet, although preserving their independence, most horses can be affectionate to a horseman or woman sufficiently versed in their ways to activate the response. There is no rapport so deep as that possible between the horse and the rider. It is the truest partnership possible, since each when it comes to the 'moment of truth' – the huge fence, the instant of ultimate effort – is dependent upon the other and each is a source of encouragement and courage to the other. The horse has to trust the rider, the rider has to trust his mount. And what other animal is able to confer such authority, even majesty, upon its rider?

More remarkable and less easily understood is the horse's adaptability, which has enabled him to serve man in ways often alien to his nature almost since the world began. In essence the horse is a highly strung, nervous animal whose defensive system is based on acutely developed senses, a particular type of vision, and the physical ability to flee swiftly when danger, or apparent danger, threatens. Unlike the dog, the horse is not an aggressor. He may use teeth and heels in occasional acts of aggression and as a means of establishing a 'pecking order' among his fellows, but the prime purpose of his teeth is to enable him to graze efficiently. Yet this timorous creature has fought and laboured on every battlefield of the world. Now, mercifully superseded by the tank and the missile, he performs for his rider with an amazing willingness in some of the world's toughest sports.

At the juncture in his shared history with man when the horse had outlived his usefulness as a partner in human aspirations, he took on another role. In the world's increasingly affluent societies he became a powerful factor in the recreational pursuits made possible by greater wealth and more leisure time. He is the central figure in sports which have a world-wide following. A whole industry still revolves round the horse, giving employment on a large scale. Yet at the end of the Second World War it would not have been unreasonable to suppose that the horse was about to enter a period of real decline. He now flourishes as never before, underlining not only the extraordinary adaptability of the animal but also the peculiar strength of the man–horse relationship.

It is thought that thousands of years before the horse's domestication there was some form of religious significance connected with the animal. Cave drawings suggest something of the kind, and in parts of the world the horse remains a symbol of fertility. Certainly, it was accepted as an image of power and majesty, horsemen always being considered, and considering themselves, superior to unmounted men. The horse was immortalised from the beginning of time in every art form; he was buried with kings and, though so highly esteemed, was sometimes given up as the ultimate, perfect sacrifice to the gods. At times in the world's history men deified the horse.

Monarchs and captains even in our own time use horses as the proper accompaniment to the pomp and pageantry of a great occasion. And when they die their cortèges are followed by chargers carrying on their saddles the reversed boots of the deceased.

Today, horses are for the most part better treated than at any other time in their history. They are not exactly deified but horsey households pay tribute to the descendants of the Dawn Horse, Eohippus, the first direct ancestor of the modern horse, in numerous painted likenesses and with images graven from silver and fine china. Teenage bedrooms are made into veritable temples of Equus, and more and more young ladies vie yearly with each other to become hand-maidens to man's most faithful servant. Has the wheel turned full circle?

This book does not attempt to define or to explain the strange and powerful bonds forged between man and horse in the former's long journey to the stars. It seeks only to reveal the framework within which the relationship grew and flourished, and perhaps to put man's oldest ally into the perspective he deserves.

As a partner of man, the horse soon entered into partnership with the gods. Pegasus, the winged horse, was seen as a symbol of speed.

EVOLUTION

'After creating the Heavens, the birds of the air and the fishes of the sea, God found it good to bestow on Man a supreme mark of his favour. He created the Horse. In the magnificent sequence of creation the last phase, that of perfection, was reserved for this beautiful creature . . .' The Book of Genesis puts it a little differently, but not with any more lyricism than this eighteenth-century French author, who continued: 'Man, encompassed by the elements which conspired to destroy him, by beasts faster and stronger than himself, would have been a slave, had not the horse made him a King.'

The Emir Abd-el-Kadr (1808–83) carried on a lengthy correspondence with the French General Melchior Daumas, author of *Horses of The Sahara* (1850), and answered his question about the origin of the Arabian horse: 'Know then that amongst us it is accepted that God created the horse from the wind, as He created Adam from clay . . .'

Neither of them was familiar with Charles Darwin's *The Origin of the Species by Means of Natural Selection*, which did not appear until 1859, but even if they had been it is unlikely that they would have changed their views. Clerics, and not only those of the fundamentalist school, were still thundering their condemnation of what they deemed a heretical theory, if not an outright blasphemy, from pulpits all over Europe almost up to Darwin's death in 1882. Even in the twentieth century the arch-priestess of the Arabian horse, the late Lady Wentworth – a publicist of the first order – was preaching the gospel of a separate creation for her chosen race.

In fact, it was only a hundred and twenty years ago, in 1867, that a remarkably complete horse skeleton was found in Eocene rock structures in the southern part of the USA. From this it was possible to show a progression on that continent over a period of sixty million years which culminated, about one million years ago, in the emergence of Equus Caballus, the forbear of the modern horse.

The scientific name for the animal whose skeleton provided the scientists with so large a field of study is *Hyracotherium* (viz. *Hyrax*, a genus of rabbit-like mammals). It had been first given by a leading anatomist, Sir Richard Owen, to the remains of a primitive animal found some years before at Studd Hill in Kent, England. But since these remains comprised no more than incomplete parts of a skull, it is

The Akhal-Teke, 'the Golden Horse of Samarkand', is one of the oldest breeds in the world.

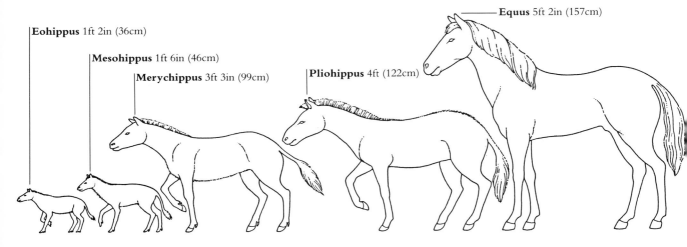

Equus 5ft 2in (157cm)

Eohippus 1ft 2in (36cm)

Mesohippus 1ft 6in (46cm)

Merychippus 3ft 3in (99cm)

Pliohippus 4ft (122cm)

It took fifty-five million years for the horse to progress from a multi-toed browsing animal, no larger than a Labrador, to the modern Derby winner. Man developed in something like one five-hundredth of this time.

not surprising that Owen found nothing to suggest that they belonged to the equine species. Only in 1932 did Sir Charles Forster-Cooper discover that the Studd Hill fossils were genetically inseparable from those found in the USA.

The American scientists, displaying a nicely romantic touch, called their animal Eohippus, the Dawn Horse, which is the name used commonly today for the first ancestor of Equus Caballus.

Eohippus can be traced to a member of an extinct group comprising the Condylarth family, which lived on earth some seventy five million years ago and were the far-off ancestors of all hoofed creatures. These prehistoric animals would have varied in size, none being larger than a middle-sized dog, but the principal point of interest about them in relation to the horse was the formation of the feet. These were each equipped with five toes ending in very strong, horny nails of some thickness. Fifteen million years later the feet of the Condylarth descendant, Eohippus, were equipped with four toes on the forelimbs and three toes behind.

Another skeleton of Eohippus, remarkably explicit, was found in 1931 in the Big Horn Basin, Wyoming, and skilfully mounted by palaeontologists at the California Institute of Technology. Along with other remains, it has enabled us to achieve a fairly accurate reconstruction of the Dawn Horse.

It would have weighed about 12lb (5.4kg) and stood about 14in (36cm) at the shoulder – the size of a fox or middle-sized dog. No one knows what colour it was, but experts consider that its coat would have consisted of light spots or blotches on a darker background, a characteristic camouflage of animals inhabiting the sort of forest surroundings natural to early horses.

The feet indicate that its environment included the kind of soft soil found in jungle areas and at the edges of pools and streams. Behind the toes was a pad like those found in dogs and tapirs, animals that are closely related to the horse. It enabled the animal to cross wet, soft ground easily; today, the vestige of this pad may still be seen on the modern horse as the ergot, a now superfluous horny growth on the back of the fetlock.

The eyes were in the middle of the head (lateral vision evolved much later). The teeth, short-crowned like those of monkeys or pigs, were quite unlike those of the modern horse: they were adapted for a diet of soft leaves, found on low-growing succulent shrubs, and were in no way suitable for grazing – but then there was no grass.

Of course, there were numerous variations of shape and size within the species. Professor George Gaylord Simpson considers that animals measuring 10in (25cm) at the shoulder were possibly the smallest, and those of 20in (50cm) the largest, implying that the latter were approximately eight times as heavy as their smaller contemporaries. It is possible that even larger types existed in Europe, but became extinct.

The Euro-Asian version, or versions, of Eohippus, which spread from the cradle of the New World both westward and eastward over the landbridges which then existed, are held to have become extinct in the early Oligocene period, some forty million years ago. There then occurred a pronounced hiccup in the evolutionary process which led to Equus Caballus in the Old World. On the American continent, the story and the development continued, albeit in no ordered fashion of steady growth and change in size and physical characteristics.

In evolution there is no overall constancy nor a single constant factor. Short bursts of development are followed by millions of years in which change seems imperceptible. Additionally, in one area there may be advances while elsewhere progress is dormant. And then there is the complication of numerous strains or lines, only a very few of which led ultimately to the emergence of the single-hoofed equine.

In very general terms we can say that Eohippus was followed by a three-toed creature, Mesohippus, which had a somewhat more advanced dental arrangement. Mesohippus was succeeded by Merychippus, which still had three toes but used only the central one. At last there came, in the Pliocene period, the first single-hoofed animal, Pliohippus, which is the direct link to Equus Caballus.

Within the Eocene period, the American Eohippus developed in two relatively defined stages: Orohippus and Epihippus. This was not the case in Europe, where wide and confusing divergences occurred.

The changes that took place in the offshoots of the New World's Eohippus are concerned primarily with improvements in the teeth. A more powerful chopping action was made possible with more complex pre-molars, or incisors, and this allowed for the consumption of a greater variety of leaf foliage.

Mesohippus and then his close successor Miohippus (which might well have overlapped) come onto the scene in the Oligocene period, forty to twenty five million years ago. Changes in the teeth were taken a stage further to the point where efficient browsing on a whole variety of soft plant growth was possible. But the teeth were still not suitable for eating the tough, wiry grasses which were to contribute to the strength and stamina of future generations.

Both fore and hind feet were now three-toed, and more weight was being taken by the centre one of the trio. These changes correlated with the existing environment of wooded, scrub areas covered with brush, and the soft soil for which the purchase possible with a three-toed foot is necessary.

There were alterations, too, in the structure of the head, to correspond with the change in the teeth, and in the leg, particularly in regard to its length. By the time of Miohippus, the leg movement was limited to the fore-and-aft motion reminiscent of that of the modern horse. As a result the animal was able to move at greater speed – though not, of course, at a speed anything like that of the modern horse.

There was also an increase in size as a result of the demands of an altered environment and the ability to obtain a more nutritious diet, although an increase in physical stature was probably not general. It would have depended on the degree of change in a particular environment, and the existence within it of larger quantities of nutritious vegetation.

To complicate matters yet further, there existed less advanced types alongside those which had made or were making these adaptations. By the beginning of the Miocene period, for instance (twenty five to ten million years ago), Eohippus and his early derivatives had long been extinct in the Old World and had been replaced by browsing animals from the American continent. Among these was Anchitherium, a contemporary of Merychippus, the forerunner of the first single-hoofed horse, Pliohippus, and the larger Hypohippus. An even larger contemporary – far, far bigger than the modern horse – was the mammoth Megahippus, which may have survived in both worlds almost up to the end of the Miocene period, while Anchitherium and Hypohippus, still retaining the three-toed foot, were about up to perhaps seven million years ago.

The great watershed in the development of the horse occurred during the Miocene period, albeit gradually and over a period of many million years. This was due to the evolution of plains or steppe-lands, virtually treeless and supporting a low growth of wiry grasses. Jungle and forest had provided for browsing, multi-toed animals; now this environment compelled adaptations which became the prime characteristics of Equus, the grazing horse.

The teeth became stronger, higher-crowned, covered in protective enamel and with a heavy filling of cement, a substance unnecessary in the teeth of browsing animals. Such teeth, used in a grinding action, were able to withstand the constant wear caused by the consumption of abrasive grasses. Similarly, in order to feed from ground level, the neck became longer, and the head could then be raised higher. The eyes changed to a position nearer the sides of the head, permitting what was virtually all-round vision. These two changes formed part of the horse's defensive system, providing the animal with the ability to become aware quickly of the approach of possible attackers. It is interesting that the modern horse, although unlikely to be able to see its feet or the contents of its manger, can yet cover the area almost immediately to its rear when its head is lowered in the act of grazing.

With the passing of more years, legs increased in length, more use was made of the central toe, and the dog-like pads became smaller and eventually disappeared. The lateral toes remained but much reduced in size. Flexing leg ligaments contributed to the running action which was fast approaching that of the modern horse. Equipped with the physical means to flee swiftly from carnivorous predators, the horse then began to develop that heightening of the senses which completed its defence mechanism and resulted in the naturally highly-strung character of the domestic horse.

Even today, when the domestic horse is separated by millions of years from the time when its early grass-eating ancestors were adapting to life on the Miocene grasslands, the defensive system which then evolved remains integral to its character, even though it is largely irrelevant to modern conditions. There are no predators lurking in our hedgerows, but the rustle of a scrap of paper in the wind produces the same swift reaction – the quick shying away, even perhaps the attempt to turn and run – reminding us that despite all the implications of domestication the horse remains essentially the same. And modern horse-management, aimed at producing the super-fit horse with generous heating and high protein foodstuffs, actually accentuates the animal's highly-strung nature and increases the sensitivity of its defensive mechanisms.

By the end of the Miocene period, it is probable that at least six distinct groups existed on the prairies of the American continent. At the beginning of the Pliocene era, one of these, Hipparion, had moved into Asia and from thence had spread rapidly throughout Europe. It achieved in the course of this quiet conquest the distinction of being the first horse, so far as is known, to become established in Africa.

In America, the final prototype for Equus was beginning to emerge. This was Pliohippus, which made its entrance somewhere around six million years ago. A recognisable version of Equus, though smaller, Pliohippus had the first single, ligament-sprung hoof and its teeth closely resembled those of Equus. From this type descends the true horse – and also zebras, asses and hemionids.

Some five million years after Pliohippus, about one million years ago, Equus Caballus had become established. The first examples may not have conformed very closely to the modern horse, but they were certainly single-hoofed with the triangular anti-concussion and anti-slip device called the frog extending into the sole of the foot in place of the erstwhile pad. The last toe had become the ergot on the point of the fetlock, and the dental development was complete. The animal was not, however, very much bigger than the average Shetland and had yet to develop the freedom of movement of the modern equine.

Equus spread rapidly into South America, where previously there had been no horses, into Asia and Europe and finally into Africa. Once that had occurred, Hipparion, the last of the three-toed prototypes, ceased to exist. From that point onwards, our concern is really limited to the development of the single species, Equus.

For perhaps a quarter of a million years the interchange of horses between America, Asia and Europe continued. It seems likely to have continued during the greater part of the eight hundred thousand-year

The most influential of the primitive breeds was the Tarpan. The original Tarpan is extinct but the ingenuity of man has preserved sufficient elements to produce this modified form.

duration of the Ice Age, which began in the Pleistocene period and extended up to about ten thousand years ago.

When massive packs of ice, originating in the polar regions, engulfed the earth in successive waves, feeding grounds were destroyed, with the inevitable consequence that the horse population was pushed southwards. In the process, the remaining landbridges joining the American continent to Europe and Asia disappeared. We were left with four closely-related types of Equus: the horse, the ass, the zebra and the onager. These were roughly distributed as follows: horses in Europe and the nearer parts of Asia; asses and zebras in the north and south of Africa respectively; onagers in the Middle East.

Any student of the works of the most eminent palaeontologists of the past century is bound to encounter differences of opinion and interpretation, as well as what amount at times to quite contradictory theories. David P. Willoughby, the American authority, points to the existence of 'at least twenty different forms of the true horse, Equus Caballus, existing in the Ice Age, most of which were heavily built types approaching the present-day draught horse, but with relatively longer legs', while others were of the 'slender build of the racehorse'.

In all examinations of the development of the horse continuous reference is made to migrations from the American continent into Asia and Europe. Rather less reference is made to any contra-flow from the Old World to what we term the New. At least one authority holds that migration, across the Bering Strait and over the landbridges that once linked America with Asia, cannot have happened.

But one point which appears not to be in contention is that about eight to ten thousand years ago the horse became extinct in the American continent, which may be regarded as the very cradle of the species. With it there disappeared also the sloths and mastodons. No substantiated explanation exists for this disappearance. Perhaps it was the result of some severe climatic change or, more likely, of some fatal disease, produced possibly by a virulent insect such as the African tsetse fly. It remains one of the world's great unsolved mysteries.

The species was not re-introduced until the early sixteenth century when Cortes brought a complement of sixteen horses to Havana, Cuba, prior to his conquest of Mexico. Thereafter the development of Equus in the Americas, in terms of variety and size of population, was both unique and extraordinarily swift.

In the Old World, temperate zones with the availability of suitable foodstuffs produced larger horses. Soils rich in minerals and vitamins also contributed to their growth and strength.

In areas of high rainfall, where there was lush, succulent herbiage, a heavier type of horse evolved, possibly disposed as much to browsing as to grazing. Dry regions produced lighter-boned specimens, capable

The stripes of the zebra are a form of camouflage, which can be seen in different forms in all the primitives.

of greater speed in movement but not achieving great size. In mountainous regions and in climatic extremes where vegetation was sparse, small, hardy ponies evolved which were well equipped to cope with the harsh rigours of their habitat.

Notable within the category Equus Caballus, and excluding the ass, zebra and onager, are three defined types from which it is thought that the present domestic stock descended.

From Asia came the steppe horse, known as the Asiatic Wild Horse but also as Equus Przewalskii Przewalskii Poliakov, after a Polish colonel who discovered a wild herd existing in Mongolia in 1881. This primitive horse still exists in zoos throughout the world, but has probably been hunted to extinction in its Asian habitat.

Evolving much further to the west was the plateau horse, Equus Przewalskii Gmelini Antonius, the Tarpan of forest and steppe varieties. This horse inhabited areas of Eastern Europe and the Ukrainian steppes and it too has been hunted to virtual extinction, although it continues to exist in a re-constituted environment, in the famous herd maintained at Popielno in Poland.

The third primitive type, now certainly extinct, was Equus Przewalskii Silvaticus, a heavy, slow-moving horse living in the wet, marsh-type lands of northern Europe. It is sometimes called the Forest horse (Silvaticus) or the Diluvial horse, since it may have ceased to exist, at least in its early constituted form, during the Diluvial period.

It is not unreasonable to conjecture in the most general sense that the population of light horses descends from primitive Tarpan and Asiatic Wild Horse stocks via their subsequent derivatives, modern horses probably having their origin in a mixture of the two. The Forest horse, probably a variant of the Asiatic Wild Horse, is thought to be the far-off ancestor of the heavy draught horses of Europe.

The Asiatic Wild Horse displays characteristics not found in the domestic or 'tame' horse and additionally it has a chromosome count of 66 as opposed to the domestic horse's 64. The body colour of the Wild Horse is a sand dun with the usual accompaniment of black legs, mane and tail and a cream underbelly. The mane is a notable feature in these 'primitive' horses. About 8in (20cm) long, it grows upright in contrast to the mane of the domestic horse which, if not shortened by pulling and trimming, grows full and falls over one side of the neck. The head is long with a straight profile, and is made to look even longer because of the high setting of the eyes. The hair round the eyes and on the muzzle is lighter in colour than the remainder of the coat. The height of these horses is about 13 hands. (The measurement of a hand's width is taken to be 4in (10.2cm) and horses are measured from the highest part of the wither, the juncture of the shoulder and top line of the neck, to the ground.)

The Tarpan is about the same height but is of a lighter build. Originally it, too, would have had the characteristic upright mane of the 'primitive', with the pronounced eel stripe of the Tarpan running from the tail and continuing along the full length of the mane. The Popielno herd, however, does not display this characteristic. The Tarpan's coat is blue dun with a texture resembling that of a deer. The dark eel stripe along the back is always very prominent. As usual with any form of dun colouring the 'points' (legs, mane and tail) are black but often the legs show 'zebra' bar markings. The eye setting is the same as that found in the domestic horse but the profile tends towards being slightly concave.

In winter the Tarpan's coat turns white, as do the coats of other truly wild animals when they are subjected to Arctic conditions. The Asiatic Wild Horse is the exception, its dun coat becoming significantly paler but not actually white. It is held that the Tarpan is ultimately at the root of the Arabian horse, the oldest of the 'modern' world breeds.

The appearance of the Forest horse is less easy to determine; it has to depend upon reconstructions of remains and, to some degree, on cave drawings made by ancient man. Traces of what was clearly a heavy, slow-moving animal have been discovered in Scandinavia and have been dated as being ten thousand years old. More recent findings in north-west Germany show a marked resemblance to the massive

The most primitive of all the genus Equus was the Przewalskii, the Asiatic Wild Horse. Unlike the Tarpan, it has survived in its pure form. British, American and Russian breeders are collaborating to return this horse to its original habitat in Outer Mongolia.

Swedish Heavy Horse, a discovery which seems to indicate the existence of a domesticated horse about three thousand years ago.

The Forest horse would have stood about 15 hands. Thick-legged and massive-bodied with broad, large feet suitable for a swamp environment, it would have been covered in thick, coarse hair, the mane and tail growing long and luxuriantly. The coat was dark and probably dappled to provide camouflage in the light and shade of woodlands.

There is also evidence of a fourth wild horse to provide yet another unsolved mystery in the history of the equine. This is the Tundra horse, remains of which, as well as those of mammoths, have been found in the valley of the Yana in north-east Siberia, where winter temperatures are below those at the North Pole. Sightings of groups of wild white horses have been reported from here as recently as 1964. Soviet scientists believe the local Yakut ponies to be direct descendants of the Tundra horse. About the horse itself there is an unusual uniformity of opinion among scholars. It is acknowledged that it did exist but, in the words of Professor F. N. Zeuner, 'it has almost certainly not contributed to the domestic stock of horses'.

On the whole, there is a large degree of agreement about the

One of the closest of modern day breeds to the primitive Forest or Diluvial horse of north west Europe is the Ardennes, a Belgian heavy draught breed. A subject of considerable debate among anthropologists today is whether man had a hand in the evolution of the Forest horse.

The primitive-looking Yakut pony, which still can be seen in the Soviet Union today, is not unlike what is believed to have been his historic forefather, the Tundra horse.

development of the earliest horses. But this is not the case when we come to the more immediate ancestry of the domestic horse.

Some of the problems arise on account of the variety of names employed, one type going under possibly two or three different names depending upon the choice of the individual scientist. So J. U. Duerst talks about a 'desert' type while Dr J. C. Ewart, former Regius Professor of Natural History at Edinburgh University, calls it 'plateau'. There are, indeed, areas where the experts express entirely contrary opinions. The Russian zoologist B. F. Rumjahcev, for instance, stated categorically, and possibly unwisely, that 'Przewalskii's horse has played no part in the evolution of the domestic horse'. On the other hand, the very able Hellmut Antonius, one time Director of the Schönbrunn Zoological Garden, was equally adamant in holding the opposite view.

Dr Ewart attributed the modern breeds of horse to three sub-species: Equus Caballus Celticus, the Plateau or Celtic horse, presently represented by the Icelandic ponies, the Irish Connemara, the Shetlands and the dun Norwegian or Fjord pony; the Asiatic or Mongolian Wild Horse which he calls the Steppe horse; and finally the Forest horse of which the Gudbrandsdal of Norway is a modern example.

This is no more than a variant of the theory already put forward of the basic trio of founding fathers. Duerst, some years after Ewart, alters the nomenclature and introduces an oriental, 'desert' type; other authorities introduce further variations on the central theme. But by far the most favoured and publicised theory of immediate domestic ancestry is that formulated jointly by J. G. Speed of Edinburgh, Edward Skorkowski of Cracow and F. Ebhardt of Stuttgart. It is really a more specific extension of the basic premise.

Their detailed analyses of bone structure, teeth, etc., brought them to conclude that four sub-species existed immediately prior to the domestication of the horse by humans.

Pony Type 1 Height between 12 and 12.2 hands; broad forehead, straight profile and small ears. It approximates to the present day Exmoor pony and eventually became established in north-west Europe. Like the Exmoor it was resistant to wet and thrived in harsh environments. The present day Exmoor has the same jaw formation and the beginnings of a seventh molar tooth as did the fossilised remains of a prehistoric pony found in Alaska, points not found in any other equine. Additionally the Exmoor is equipped with a protective 'toad' eye and an 'ice' tail characterised by a fan-like growth at the top.

Pony Type 2   Heavily built, coarse and heavy-headed with a profile inclining to the convex. Height between 14 and 14.2 hands, it inhabited northern Eurasia and was very resistant to cold. Of the modern breeds the Highland Pony would most resemble this type.

Horse Type 3   Taller, at around 14.3 hands. Long and narrow in the body, goose-rumped with a long neck and long ears, it inhabited central Asia. The Akhal-Teke of Turkmenistan, sometimes known as the Turkmene, is reminiscent of it and is likewise resistant to great heat.

Horse Type 4   Offered as the Arab prototype, it was much smaller than the others but had greater refinement with a concave profile and a high-set tail. It lived in western Asia and had a very close equivalent in the Caspian pony of Iran which only recently has been re-discovered. (The Caspian is termed a 'pony' on account of its size although it has the characteristics of a horse.)

Many say the Exmoor is the oldest European breed. It retains characteristics not found in other equines. The mouth, for instance, is unique and the Exmoor also has the distinctive features of toad eyes and an 'ice-fan' tail.

So when did domestication take place? Domestication and the initial uses made of the horse are the subject of Chapter 4, but once more there is no real agreement about the date of this momentous occurrence.

There is evidence of domestication in the third millenium, probably about 2700 BC, by a nomadic Aryan people who spoke an Indo-European language and ranged the steppe lands bordering the Black and Caspian Seas. They kept no records, but clay tablets of their southern neighbours make mention of them and of their horse herds.

This is possibly the first definitive record of domestication, but that does not mean that horses were not domesticated elsewhere prior to this date. Semi-domestic herds certainly would have existed far earlier and it seems probable that domestication could have occurred, again by nomadic steppe people, perhaps as much as a thousand years earlier.

What is certain is that at the point of domestication there existed several types of equine. Over the centuries man, seeking to improve the horse stock so that it should fulfil his needs more closely, intervened in the natural order, practising selective breeding and encouraging growth by artificial feeding. As a result, recognisable breeds sharing common characteristics were eventually created. Today there are about a hundred and fifty recognised horse and pony breeds as well as a number of horse types which are the product of a variety of crosses. A long road, indeed, from the multi-toed Eohippus.

THE FIRST
PROGENITOR

There can be little doubt that of all the horse breeds the Arab has exerted the greatest influence on the world's equine population. To what extent that influence extended to the stock of the ancient horse is not certain nor, of course, is there much in the way of documentation. But the more one can see of the horse in early art forms of, say, 2000–2500 BC and later in Egypt, the Nejd and Syria, for instance, the more one becomes aware of the debt that early horsemen, as well as those of much later civilisations, owe to the up-grading capacity of what is now called the Arabian horse.

For a long time it was sufficient to regard the Tarpan as the most likely origin for the Arabian or Oriental horse, and there is still support for this view. Those embracing the later theory of Speed, Ebhardt and Skorkowski tend to think that the small Horse Type 4 of western Asia, with an admixture of Type 3 of central Asia, is the probable prototype. Horse Type 4 is certainly recognisable as Arabian, and no great stretch of imagination is needed to perceive a possible relationship between the Arab horse and the rediscovered Caspian pony of Iran which, though described as a pony, has horse characteristics and should more accurately be termed a small horse. It is rather more difficult to see any resemblance between the unprepossessing Horse Type 3 and the modern Arabian of today, with its refinement, beauty, high carriage of the tail, dished face, great luminous eye and flared nostril.

Horse Type 3 on the other hand is exemplified fairly accurately in horses like the Akhal-Teke, which has its origin in Turkmenistan; and those Turkoman horses of the Altai plains and Kazakstan which today still roam in a semi-wild state in Iran and along the Russian borders from Beshahr in the west to the northern steppes.

But not all Arabian strains resemble the popular image. The Muniqi (Munaghi), the racing strain, looks very like both Akhal-Teke and Turkoman. The first imports from Arabia – made by Wilfrid Scawen Blunt and his wife Lady Anne when they founded their Crabbet Stud in Sussex in 1878–79 – would be considered by today's show ring standards to be lacking in type, if the photographs are to be believed. On their appearance alone it is quite possible to accept the presence of Horse Type 3 in the Arab horse.

It has been claimed that the spread of Islam was written in the 'hoofprints of the Arabian horse'. Initially, however, the Muslim armies were more concerned with the camel. Here the Prophet Mohammed is entering Medina on a camel.

Lucinda Green and the modern equivalent of the Nisean-type horse.

Wilfred and Lady Anne Blunt, the saviours of the modern Arabian, imported desert Arabs to their Crabbet stud in Sussex.

There is then no reason to suppose that the Arab did not have its influence on the Nisean horse raised in the grass country of western Iran by the Medes. Geographically it is entirely possible. The Nisean horse was foremost of the horses of the ancient Orient, Oppian describing them as 'the handsomest, fit only for mighty rulers. They are splendid, running swiftly under the rider, obeying the bridle willingly, with ram-nosed heads carried high and streaming golden manes'. Ram noses are not, of course, associated with Arabian horses but there are strains with straight profiles, like the Munaghi, and there was of course much wild steppe blood, coming from further north, in the Nisean make-up which would account for those convex profiles.

Similarly, the Bactrian horses, originating further to the east, hard up against what we know as Afghanistan in the area of the Oxus river, would have benefited from Arab/Oriental infusions. Alexander's horse Bucephalus was without much doubt of the 'Oriental breed'. Bucephalus means 'ox-head', the charger having the broad forehead, large eyes and concave profile which belongs to the Arabian horse, but would suggest bovine rather than equine features to European eyes unused to the distinctive conformation.

The exact origin of the wild Oriental-type horse, developing into the Arabian, remains to be definitively established. There is some evidence from excavations in the Acacus Mountains of the Fezzan in southern Libya, in west Iran and even in Japan of wild horses that are unmistakably Arabian in appearance.

Wentworth, Raswan, Seydel and Upton all subscribed to the theory of a race of wild horses in central and southern Arabia which was in times past 'a land of trees and rivers', conducive to supporting a horse population. That no remains of an early horse have been found in Arabian desert lands is no argument against the existence of equines there. The sands and the extremes of climate would long since have effaced all traces of living things and, in any case, there has been little or no archaeological activity. What is certain is that evidence of Arabian-type horses exists in, through and round the cockpit of the ancient world – those intersecting highways of civilisation which allowed such remarkable degrees of cross-fertilisation.

The Bedouin are the people associated indelibly with the 'desert horse,' and their traditions, passed by word of mouth, are therefore important. Their belief corresponds with that of the Wentworth school and is recorded, if sometimes more allegorically than factually, by the Arab historian El Kelbi who, in about the year AD 786, towards the end of the Islamic conquests which threatened to engulf Europe, recorded the history and pedigrees of the Arabian horse strains.

El Kelbi, in accordance with Bedouin belief, traced the Arabian horse from around 3000 BC to the mare Baz, the horse captured by

The first habitat of the Dawn Horse was in primeval forest conditions such as this.

Right: Early scrub terrain caused the first horses to develop browsing characteristics. *Above:* Once grasslands appeared the horses became grazing animals and developed defensive mechanisms to cope with their new environment.

An ancient breed, the golden Akhal-Teke derives from the blending of blood lines which in their day represented the world's best horse stock.

Peter Tillemans Pinxit.

To the most Noble and Puissant Lord JAMES STANLEY Earl of DARBY, Viscount KINTON, Baron STANLEY, &c. Lord MOHUN, &c. Lord

MAN & the Isles, & Lord Lieutenant of the County of LANCASTER.

This View of the Round Course or Plate Course, with divers Jockeys & Horses in different Actions & Postures, going to Start for the King's

is most humbly Dedicated by Y.r Lordships most humble & most obedient Servant

Peter Tillemans. 1723.

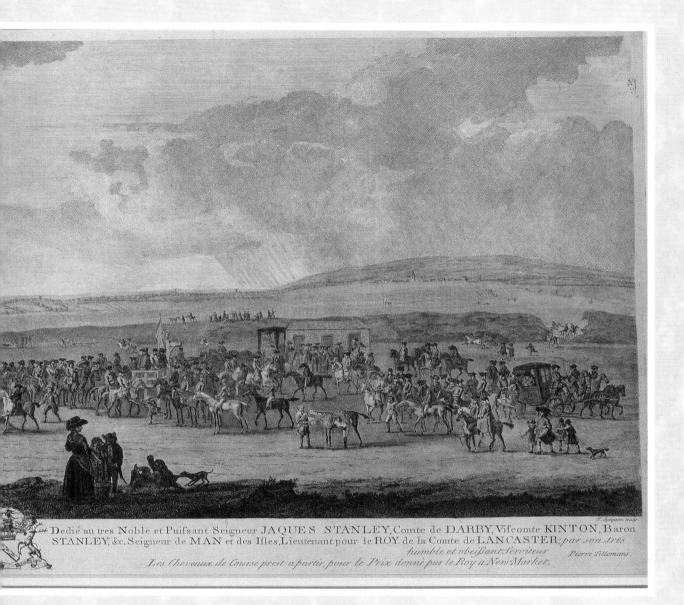

Dedié au tres Noble et Puissant Seigneur JAQUES STANLEY, Comte de DARBY, Vicomte KINTON, Baron STANLEY, &c. Seigneur de MAN et des Isles, Lieutenant pour le ROY de la Comte de LANCASTER, par son tres humble et obeissant Serviteur.

Pierre Tillemans

T. Jayson sculp

Les Cheveaux de Course prest a partir, pour le Prix donné par le Roy a New Market.

Under the Stuart kings, Newmarket quickly became the centre of Thoroughbred racing and today is the home of the sport's governing body, the Jockey Club.

The characteristic head of the Barb remains a basic feature in the breeds which were influenced by the North African horse. The bridle is similarly typical and is virtually the same as that used a thousand years ago.

Opposite page: The Barb, toughened by the hard desert conditions, made a notable contribution to the world's horse population through its influence on Spanish stock during the long occupation of the Iberian Peninsula by the Moors. This painting is by Henri Rousseau.

Mohammed, unifier of the Arab
people and the inspiration of the
Moorish invasions, ascends to
Paradise in a manner befitting the
Prophet of Islam.

Baz, great-great grandson of Noah and the first to attempt domestication of the wild horses of the Yemen. The detailed pedigrees produced
by El Kelbi trace the Arabian horse families, each associated with one
or other of the numerous Bedouin tribes, to the produce of Baz and the
stallion Hoshaba.

The Emir Abd-el-Kadr had this to say: 'When God wanted to create
the horse, he said to the South Wind, "I want to make a creature of
you. Condense." And the Wind condensed. Archangel Gabriel
immediately appeared and took a handful of the stuff and presented it
to God, who made a brown bay or burnt chestnut [*Koummite* – red
mixed with black] upon saying, "I call you Horse [*frass*]; I make you
Arabian and I give you the chestnut colour of the ant; I have hung
happiness from the forelock which hangs between your eyes; you shall
be the lord [*sid*] of the other animals. Men shall follow you wherever
you go; you shall be as good for pursuit as for flight; you shall fly
without wings; riches shall be on your back and fortune shall come
through your mediation." Then He put on the horse the mark of glory
and happiness [*ghora*], a white mark in the middle of the forehead.'
'*Ghora*', interestingly, is also the Hindi word for 'horse'.

In the record of Abd-el-Kadr the history of the Arabian horse was
divided into four eras: Adam to Ishmael, the son of Abraham and first
ancestor of the desert Bedouin, who was reputed to be the first man to
ride a desert horse; Ishmael to Solomon; Solomon to Mohammed, and
then from the Prophet onwards.

Ishmael, of whom the angel speaking to Hagar said, 'He shall be a
fierce man. He shall lift his hand against all men and they shall lift their
hands against him', was the outcast who became the personification of
the fierce desert tribes. The association of Ishmael and his followers
with the horse allowed them to create a place for themselves in the
world which had rejected them, inspiring awe and respect among
their fellows. Their desert-bred horses, tough, amenable and
courageous, were as hardy and enduring as themselves; with them
these early Bedouin established a special relationship.

After the break-up of the desert tribes following the death of
Ishmael, the great King Solomon continued the saga of the desert-
bred horse. Solomon, indeed, was the archetypal horse-dealer and in
that capacity has never been exceeded. In his stables, in defiance of the
Judaic law which forbade the keeping of horses as a form of idolatry,
Solomon had as many as forty thousand chariot horses and between
1,200 and 2,000 riding horses.

But it is on account of Islam, its Prophet Mohammed and the
superiority of the Arabian race of horses that one of the great
watersheds in human history took place. Mohammed united the tribes
in a religious brotherhood dedicated to the prosecution of *Jihad*, the

Holy War, to be waged not so much for the material expansion of Islam as for its spiritual extension. It was a war of religious conversion, its object being to bring the world to the worship and acceptance of Allah, the One True God.

Mohammed, while keeping an eye on Paradise, had both feet firmly on the desert sands. He was a practical, pragmatic politician as well as a soldier of no mean order. Essential to the furtherance of his evangelical mission was the power of swift, decisive movement by large bodies of troops. This could be achieved only by possession of a mounted host, making the most effective use of its horse-power. To fulfil the immense ambitions of Islam that horse-power had to be both sufficient and of the highest quality.

Astutely, Mohammed incorporated the management and well-being of the horse into the very heart of Muslim belief. In a sense, it was a revival of that part of the old Arabian religion which had worshipped the horse through the idols Ya'uk and Ya'bub. Islam, of course, forbade idolatry, which is why neither pictures nor any sort of art forms survive to illustrate for us the Arab way of life. The care of horses as a tenet of the faith was, however, entirely acceptable, and was scrupulously observed by the fanatical warriors who welcomed death in battle as the passport to the eternal joys of Paradise.

Mohammed avoiding the fire on the day of resurrection.

In the Koran the horse is called 'the supreme blessing' and the recorded sayings of the Prophet about their treatment were powerful stimuli to the management, improvement and maintenance of the horses that contributed so much to two centuries of Islamic conquest.

'Happiness in this world,' says the Prophet, 'rich booty and eternal reward are attached to the horse's forelock'; 'Who feeds the horse for the triumph of religion makes a magnificent loan to God'; 'A horse scrupulously bred for the Holy War will save his master from the fire on the Day of Resurrection'; 'Money spent on horses is, in the eyes of God, like giving alms'; 'Each grain of barley given to a horse is inscribed in the ledger of good works.' 'Love horses and look after them,' exhorted the Prophet's companion Sidi-Aomar, 'for they deserve your tenderness; treat them as you do your children; nourish them as you do friends of the family and blanket them with care. For the love of God do not be negligent for you will regret it in this life and the next.'

The Bedouin kept their horses either in or near their tents, hand-feeding them with grain, milk, dates, even fish and balls of meat, the latter supposedly inducing courage. This sort of care was a matter of necessity since desert lands do not produce any plenitude of grass or other edible herbage. As a result, however, the horses became enormously docile with their handlers. The sale of horses to infidels was forbidden and though pedigrees, until the time of El

Kelbi, were handed down by word of mouth, breeding was carefully selective. The circumstances in which the horses were kept created a superlative breed of horse, enormously tough and enduring and, most importantly, of a fixed type.

After the death of Mohammed in AD 632 the Islamic hosts burst out of their desert lands in a series of conquests which took the green standards up to the very walls of China in the east and to the ramparts of Europe in the west. They overran the provinces of the Byzantine Empire, Syria, Palestine, Mesopotamia and Armenia and by 643 had occupied north Africa. They had taken the Indus Valley by 664 and fifty years later were masters of central Asia. From north Africa they crossed into Spain, took possession of the whole of the Iberian Peninsula and pressed upwards into Gaul. There their advance was halted when they were defeated by Charles Martel and the Frankish knights at Poitiers in 732.

Throughout these conquests, their incomparable horses were inevitably brought into contact with horses already inhabiting the conquered territories, and from that point they became the principal influence on the greater part of the world's equine population. The Arabian horse presence in Europe reached its climax in the evolution, during the late seventeenth and early eighteenth centuries, of the world's super-horse, the English Thoroughbred, which in a remarkably short space of time outstripped its progenitor in terms of size and speed, though not in stamina, hardiness or hereditary soundness.

To understand a little more about why horses bred in such inhospitable lands became so important an element in universal breeding one must appreciate that of all breeds the Arabian has been kept the most pure. It is, so far as anyone knows, uncontaminated by any other breed. This purity of stock and pedigree produces the prepotency which enables the Arab to stamp so indelibly the progeny of both pure and cross matings, and to 'nick' (i.e. cross successfully) with so many different types of equine, always refining and upgrading the subsequent offspring.

In the breeding of the desert Arabian, the Bedouin recognised certain superlative strains from which stemmed many hundreds of sub-strains. Each of these belonged to particular tribes and their purity was jealously guarded. In the time of the Mameluke Sultan El Nasser (1291–1341) and later it was customary for the mating of a pure-bred mare to be witnessed by a committee and the foaling to be similarly attended. El Nasser had records kept, even if the 'pedigrees' were not much more than a statement that a horse had been bred within a particular tribe. Otherwise, pedigrees were passed from mouth to mouth, from generation to generation.

That may sound a very haphazard practice by European standards, and one open to error. Without much doubt the early purchases of Arab horses by Europeans did result in confusion, largely because the vendor, still bound by the law forbidding the sale of horses to Christians, attempted to mitigate his transgression by being deliberately vague, concealing the true pedigree in a flow of verbiage.

Within the tribes, however, breeding records were extraordinarily accurate. This is not so surprising: the Koran, after all, was memorised by devout Muslims from the spoken, not the written, word.

A number of main strains were, and are still, recognised, among them Seglawi, Hadban, Munaghi, Nowak, Dahman, Krush, Abeyan, Wadnan, Jilfan, Jellabi and Hamdani. But names were rarely spelt the same way twice, and no two authorities seem to agree entirely on which are the main strains.

Inevitably, too, the student will come up against the *Khamsa*, the corporate word for the principal or foundation strains. It is thought to comprise five strains: Kehilan, literally 'pure-bred' but always qualified by the addition of the word Ajuz, which is claimed as the oldest of the strains; Seglawi, the pure strain being called Seglawi Jedran; Abeyan; Hadban and Hamdani. Munaghi and many others were excluded from the foundation or principal strains.

The Kehilan is said to descend from the line of the mare Baz and from the stallion Zad er Rakib, a horse given to the tribe of Ben Zad by no less than King Solomon in about the year 1000 BC. From this line descended Sabal, who was the dam of the mare Ajuz whose name completes the title Kehilan Ajuz.

The idea of the *Khamsa*, dismissed by Lady Wentworth as a 'pious fairy tale', has its adherents, including the late Henry Wynmalen and Reginald Summerhays. Arab tradition has it that when God had made the gift of a hundred horses to Ishmael or, alternatively, when he had acquired them in human fashion, he resolved upon a sort of selection test. He withheld water from the herd for eight days and then set them free near to the seashore. All the thirst-maddened animals stampeded into the sea and drank the salt water, except one. This was the mare Ajuz, who stood at the sea's edge looking out over the water, from which arose a great and beautiful stallion who mated with her. In due course Ajuz gave birth to a colt foal which was called Kehilan Ajuz.

In another version, the test was made by the Prophet himself under slightly different circumstances. Mohammed released the thirsty herd to water and at the last moment called them back. Five mares obeyed his call, the five founding dams of the *Khamsa*, and the Prophet signified their special worth by placing his thumb on the neck of each one. Where the imprint was made a whorl of hair was left. The mark is still known as the Prophet's Thumbmark and horses today bearing the strange whorl of hair are supposed to be of especial merit.

Feats by horses regarded as extraordinary by European standards were often considered commonplace by the Bedouin. But then the Bedouin life in itself constitutes a pretty rigorous survival test. One exceptional ride was described by General Daumas, corroborated by witnesses who did not view it as being unusual. Si-ben-Zyam was ordered by his father to take a favourite mare to Algiers to prevent her being requisitioned by the Turks. He rode through the night resting for an hour by some dwarf palms, the fronds of which were eaten by the mare while her rider slept. The journey was then continued with just one stop to allow the mare to drink. She was fed when they reached their destination, Leghrouat, 80 leagues (240 miles) from their home. The pair had completed the trip in twenty four hours, and Si-ben-Zyam stated that had it been necessary he could have continued on to Ghardaia, another 45 leagues away.

The General also instanced the races held between Europeans and Arabs, each on their own horses. The Arabs were surprised when the Europeans asked for six weeks in which to prepare their horses, their own being kept always in a condition fit to race. They were even more bemused when they understood that the Europeans were thinking of a race over three miles – their own races went on for three days! After an agreement on miles, not days, the Arabs won easily.

Possibly one of the greatest records of sustained endurance is provided by the Arab stallion Maidan, born in the Nejd in 1869 and sold by the most notable dealer of the day, Abd-er-Rahman, in Bombay two years later. He was raced successfully on the flat and over

The Trakehner, together with most of the modern breeds of light horse, has a strong Arabian background.

The Arab horse was an essential factor in the government of British India. It was the customary mount of officers of the Indian Army.

fences and became a great pig-sticking horse, his owner Captain Johnstone winning with him the blue riband of that highly dangerous and demanding sport, the Kadir Cup. Maidan's next owner was Lt-Colonel Brownlow, who raced him and then took him as his charger during the Afghan campaign of 1879–80.

Then, with Captain Vesey, he returned to Europe, stopping off at Suez to take part in the relief of Suakin. Despite the sea voyage the pair marched from Port Said to Massawa on the Red Sea and then made the return journey. The distance as the crow flies is 866 miles (1,394km) but the line of march would have been longer than that. Continuing the journey, Maidan was disembarked at Marseilles to race over the banks in the Pau country. At twenty years of age, in England, he won three point-to-point races against Thoroughbreds, and at 22 he won a three-mile steeplechase. The next year he broke a leg and had to be destroyed. His most famous son, Jamrood, figures prominently in the pedigree of notable Arabians in England and abroad.

Much of Europe's cavalry employed Arab horses, in particular the Poles and Hungarians, while the Indian cavalry kept them until the advent of the cheaper Australian Waler in the last quarter of the nineteenth century. To the British Raj the horse was an essential adjunct to government and the Arab was the favourite. Napoleon made extensive use of the breed to found studs to supply his cavalry; the French Anglo-Arab (the Thoroughbred/Arab cross in which at least 25 per cent must be pure Arab) became one of the world's toughest and most enduring sports horses.

Nearly every European breed of the present day, and therefore most if not all of the American ones, have benefited from the Arabian infusion. The Lippizaner, of Vienna's Spanish School, has its Seglawi strain; the Trakehner studs had an Arab base herd. There is Arabian blood in everything from a Percheron to a Welsh Pony and from the Tirolese Haflinger to the French Trotters.

But the greatest achievement of the Arabian horse is undoubtedly the English Thoroughbred. The world's super-horse, it owes its existence to three Eastern or Oriental horses, all of which were indubitably Arabian, although at the time imported Oriental horses were often loosely termed Turk (possibly having come from Turkish sources) or Barb (although they were unlikely to have been that) as well as Arabian.

First of the three founding fathers was the Byerley Turk, captured by Captain Robert Byerley at the Battle of Buda during the last campaign against the Turkish invaders of Hungary. In July 1690, Byerley, by then commanding the 6th Dragoon Guards, rode him at the Battle of the Boyne. This very beautiful Arabian horse then returned to England to stand at stud first at Middridge Hall in Co. Durham and later at Goldsborough Hall, near York. Through his son, Jigg, and his great-grandson Tartar, he was the ancestor of Herod, from whom were descended twentieth century stallions such as The Tetrarch and Tourbillon. Herod's progeny won over a thousand races and established him as one of the most important sires in the history of the Thoroughbred.

The Darley Arabian, notable for exceptional symmetry of form and a distinctive large white blaze on his long head (he was of the Munaghi strain) was foaled in 1700, being bred by the Anazeh tribe living on the edge of the Syrian desert. He was bought in 1704 by Thomas Darley, British Consul in Aleppo, from Sheik Mirza for three hundred sovereigns. He stood at Darley's home, Aldby Park in East Yorkshire, where he was immensely successful as a sire. Mated with Betty Leedes, whose dam was of the Leedes Arabian line, the Darley Arabian produced Flying Childers, the first really great top-class racehorse. His full brother, Bartlett's Childers, though unable to race

THE THOROUGHBRED LINE

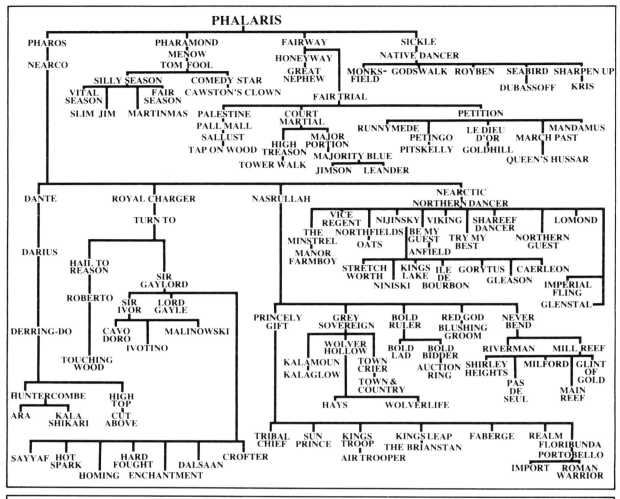

PHALARIS

PHAROS
NEARCO
PHARAMOND
MENOW
TOM FOOL
SILLY SEASON
VITAL SEASON
FAIR SEASON
COMEDY STAR
CAWSTON'S CLOWN
SLIM JIM
MARTINMAS
FAIRWAY
HONEYWAY
GREAT NEPHEW
FAIR TRIAL
SICKLE
NATIVE DANCER
MONKS-FIELD
GODSWALK
ROYBEN
SEABIRD
SHARPEN UP
DUBASSOFF
KRIS
PALESTINE
PALL MALL
SALLUST
TAP ON WOOD
COURT MARTIAL
HIGH TREASON
MAJOR PORTION
MAJORITY BLUE
TOWER WALK
JIMSON
LEANDER
PETITION
RUNNYMEDE
PETINGO
PITSKELLY
LE DIEU D'OR
GOLDHILL
MANDAMUS
MARCH PAST
QUEEN'S HUSSAR

DANTE
ROYAL CHARGER
TURN TO
NASRULLAH
NEARCTIC
NORTHERN DANCER
VICE REGENT
THE MINSTREL
MANOR FARMBOY
NIJINSKY
NORTHFIELDS
OATS
VIKING
BE MY GUEST
ANFIELD
SHAREEF DANCER
TRY MY BEST
LOMOND
NORTHERN GUEST
DARIUS
HAIL TO REASON
SIR GAYLORD
STRETCH WORTH
NINISKI
KINGS LAKE
ILE DE BOURBON
GORYTUS
GLEASON
CAERLEON
IMPERIAL FLING
ROBERTO
SIR IVOR
LORD GAYLE
MALINOWSKI
GLENSTAL
CAVO DORO
IVOTINO
DERRING-DO
PRINCELY GIFT
GREY SOVEREIGN
WOLVER HOLLOW
BOLD RULER
RED GOD
BLUSHING GROOM
NEVER BEND
TOUCHING WOOD
KALAMOUN
KALAGLOW
TOWN CRIER
TOWN & COUNTRY
BOLD LAD
BOLD BIDDER
AUCTION RING
RIVERMAN
SHIRLEY HEIGHTS
PAS DE SEUL
MILFORD
MILL REEF
GLINT OF GOLD
MAIN REEF
HUNTERCOMBE
ARA
KALA SHIKARI
HIGH TOP
CUT ABOVE
HAYS
WOLVERLIFE
SAYYAF
HOT SPARK
HARD FOUGHT
HOMING
ENCHANTMENT
DALSAAN
CROFTER
TRIBAL CHIEF
SUN PRINCE
KINGS TROOP
AIR TROOPER
KINGS LEAP
THE BRIANSTAN
FABERGE
REALM
FLORIBUNDA
PORTOBELLO
IMPORT
ROMAN WARRIOR

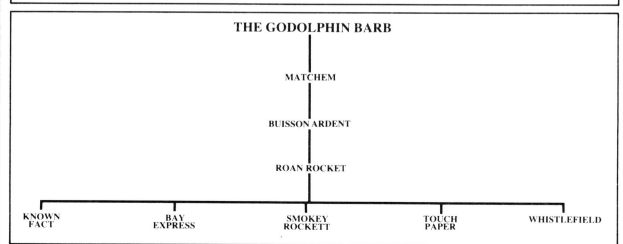

THE GODOLPHIN BARB

MATCHEM

BUISSON ARDENT

ROAN ROCKET

KNOWN FACT
BAY EXPRESS
SMOKEY ROCKETT
TOUCH PAPER
WHISTLEFIELD

THE THOROUGHBRED LINE

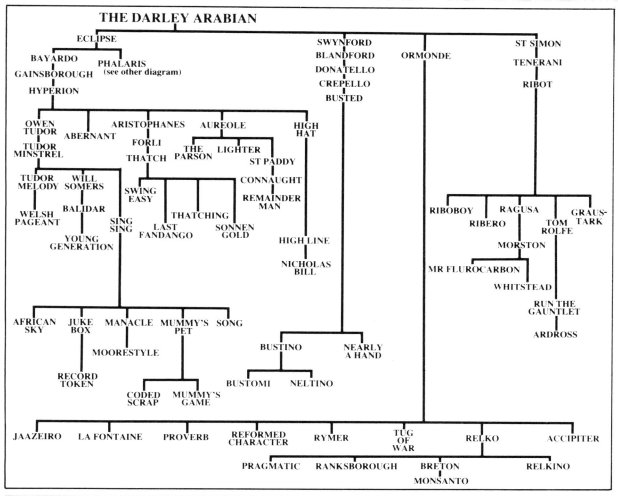

THE DARLEY ARABIAN

ECLIPSE

BAYARDO
GAINSBOROUGH   PHALARIS
(see other diagram)

HYPERION

SWYNFORD
BLANDFORD   ORMONDE
DONATELLO
CREPELLO
BUSTED

ST SIMON

TENERANI

RIBOT

OWEN
TUDOR   ABERNANT
TUDOR
MINSTREL

ARISTOPHANES   AUREOLE
FORLI   HIGH
THATCH   THE   LIGHTER   HAT
PARSON   ST PADDY

CONNAUGHT

TUDOR   WILL
MELODY   SOMERS
BALIDAR
WELSH
PAGEANT   SING
SING

SWING
EASY   REMAINDER
MAN
THATCHING

YOUNG
GENERATION   LAST   SONNEN
FANDANGO   GOLD

HIGH LINE

NICHOLAS
BILL

RIBOBOY   RAGUSA   GRAUS-
RIBERO   TARK
TOM
ROLFE

MORSTON

MR FLUROCARBON

WHITSTEAD

RUN THE
GAUNTLET

ARDROSS

AFRICAN   JUKE   MANACLE   MUMMY'S   SONG
SKY   BOX   PET

MOORESTYLE

BUSTINO   NEARLY
A HAND

RECORD
TOKEN

CODED   MUMMY'S
SCRAP   GAME

BUSTOMI   NELTINO

JAAZEIRO   LA FONTAINE   PROVERB   REFORMED   RYMER   TUG   RELKO   ACCIPITER
CHARACTER   OF
WAR

PRAGMATIC   RANKSBOROUGH   BRETON   RELKINO
MONSANTO

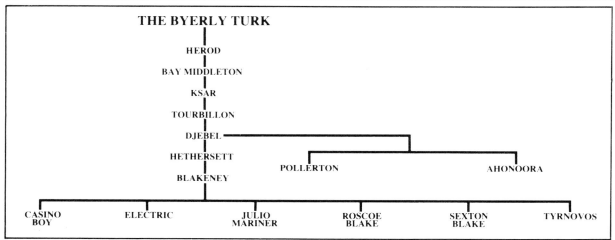

THE BYERLY TURK

HEROD

BAY MIDDLETON

KSAR

TOURBILLON

DJEBEL

HETHERSETT   POLLERTON   AHONOORA

BLAKENEY

CASINO   ELECTRIC   JULIO   ROSCOE   SEXTON   TYRNOVOS
BOY   MARINER   BLAKE   BLAKE

The founding fathers of the Thoroughbred. *Top left:* Byerly Turk; *Top right:* Darley Arabian; *Above left:* Godolphin Barb; *Above right:* The Godolphin line produced arguably the greatest racehorse of all time, Eclipse, whose line in turn is present in over eighty per cent of all modern Thoroughbreds.

because of a propensity to break blood vessels, sired Squirt, the sire of Marske, the sire of one of the greatest horses of all time – Eclipse. The modern lines of St Simon, Gainsborough and Blandford are traced to the Darley Arabian.

Last of the trio was the Godolphin Arabian, born in the Yemen in 1724, exported to Tunis via Syria and given as a gift to Louis XIV by the Bey of Tunis. The story goes that he was degraded to pulling a Paris dust-cart but no one is too sure of that. What is certain is that he was bought in 1729 by Edward Coke of Longford Hall, Derbyshire, and after Coke's death in 1733 passed into the hands of Lord Godolphin who sent him to his stud at Gog Magog, near Cambridge. It is said that he was first used as a 'teaser' (a horse used to test whether the mare

The ultimate racing machine, The Tetrarch.

is in season before she is mated with the stud stallion), and that he asserted himself by fighting another stallion to mate with the mare Roxana. Roxana's foal, Cade, born in 1834, became the sire of Matchem, whose line had a profound influence on racing stock, producing such horses as Hurry On and Precipitation. Five years after the birth of Cade, the Godolphin sired Regulus who was to be the sire of Spiletta, the dam of the illustrious Eclipse.

And so three of the four great tail-male lines of the modern Thoroughbred – Herod, Eclipse and Matchem – were established by these Oriental horses. The fourth was Highflyer, a son of Herod. It is largely because it is possible to trace *direct* descent through the male lines to this predominant trio that the Byerley Turk, the Darley and the Godolphin are recognised as the foundation sires of the breed. That is not to say, however, that no other Oriental horses were involved. There were indeed several Arabian sires who played an important part in the Thoroughbred's development. The Unknown Arabian, D'Arcy's Chestnut Arabian, D'Arcy's White Arabian, the Leedes Arabian, the Helmsley Turk and the Lister Turk all figure prominently in Thoroughbred pedigrees. The indefatigable Lady Wentworth, in a monumental work, calculated that the pedigree of Bahram, winner in 1935 of the English Triple Crown (Two Thousand Guineas, the Derby and the St Leger), contained tens, and sometimes hundreds, of thousands of crosses of each of those horses.

However, it takes two to breed, and in Britain there was a tradition of 'running horses', many of them of Oriental origin. These provided suitable mates for the later Arabian imports. Henry VIII founded the Royal Paddocks at Hampton Court, where racing stock was produced, his daughter Elizabeth I had a stud at Tutbury in Staffordshire, and it was James I who put Newmarket on the map as the headquarters of racing and who was instrumental in the importing of Oriental horses. There were several Arabians at the Royal Studs, including the Markham Arabian, imported by Sir Thomas Esmond. Charles I encouraged racing at Newmarket and so, after the Restoration, did Charles II who was very fond of the place and of the 'sport of Kings'.

There is little doubt that much of the racing stock from fairly early times was of Eastern origin, although there would have been numerous outcrosses and part may well have been influenced by the Barb of north Africa. Two Oriental horses, the mare Truncefice and the stallion Arundel, raced at the court of King Edgar in the tenth century for an astronomical purse, about a thousand pounds.

Thoroughbred pedigrees are recorded in the *General Stud Book* which first appeared in 1808 after some preliminary editions, the first of which was published in 1791. Up to the late 1960s a section of the Stud Book was reserved for Arabs, although by then, of course, their relevance to the Thoroughbred had long since passed. Today the Arab horse has its own stud book in every country in which it is bred; an international body, the World Arab Horse Organisation, acts centrally to ensure the acceptance of individual stud book entries between the various countries and to promote and maintain the purity of the breed.

The Thoroughbred quickly found its way to America, Europe and to every country of the old British Empire. In fact it was very soon established in every country in the world where it was possible to race. Furthermore, it was used extensively to cross with indigenous stock. Like its forbear, the Arab, it appears in the background of nearly every breed and is, indeed, more involved in the production of the modern competition horse than any other.

From the racing field the Arab is virtually excluded. For a period Arabs were raced in competition with the embryo Thoroughbred; Maidan, for instance, won just such a race. The last serious attempt to race Arabs in England, prior to the revival of the 1980s, was in 1884, with another somewhat abortive attempt being staged in 1923. Currently, however, Arab racing in England is enjoying a boom and it is the only form of flat racing in which an individual may own, train and ride his horse as an amateur.

But as a racehorse the pure-bred Arab cannot hope to compete with the Thoroughbred. While it can jump, it has neither the size nor scope for the modern sports of show-jumping and eventing. Part-breds, on the other hand, do very well and so do the Anglo-Arabs. It is as a long-distance riding horse that the Arab reigns supreme.

Today, the desert horse is still bred in astonishingly large numbers throughout the world, the USA having the largest Arab horse population. Enthusiasm is generally on the increase and, if anything, the stock produced now is more beautiful than ever. The esteem in which the horse is held is quite as high as that given it by the old desert Bedouin, even if the modern Arab is cared for in purpose-built stables rather than in one corner of a black tent pitched by a desert oasis.

Racing of purebred Arabs is enjoying a revival in Britain.

Chapter 4

DOMESTICATION AND EARLY USAGE

The first relationship between man and the horse was that between hunter and hunted. The cave drawings at Lascaux in France, and Santander in Spain, which are possibly fifteen thousand years old, illustrate that relationship vividly. Long before actual domestication took place, men would have been at least conversant with the character of the species they pursued. Nonetheless, largely because of the size of the horse, the unpredictability of its temperament, and the difficulties of capturing and herding it, the horse comes at the bottom of the domestication charts.

At the top by a significant interval of probably as much as three thousand years is the dog, whose domestication is thought to have come about around 12,000 BC. In the life of primitive man, whose social structure and very survival depended upon hunting, the dog was the obvious subject for domestication. Not only are puppies easily tamed and infinitely appealing, but dogs, like men, are hunters and carnivores and became the natural auxiliary in hunting forays. Even today the dog fulfils this role. Hounds are bred to hunt by scent; some, such as greyhounds and whippets, hunt their quarry by sight. There are terriers which will go to ground, hounds which are bred to hunt men and, of course, the gun-dog.

Somewhere about 9000 BC sheep were kept in domestic flocks by pastoral people and some two thousand years after that goats, pigs and cattle were added to the list of domestic animals. By then the nomadic existence was in certain areas giving way to more settled communities. In the river valleys of the Tigris and Euphrates, for instance, cultivation of crops was possible and man the hunter was beginning to make the transition to man the farmer, and beginning, too, the practice of enclosing his animals, or at least of operating on what might be termed semi-open or restricted range.

It can be argued that such people, having learnt the ways of enclosure, would be well fitted to add the horse to their domestic stock. In time, of course, they did, after a short dalliance with the more easily available but even less tractable onager. But in this transitional period it is difficult to see what would have been the advantage in possessing a horse herd if, indeed, horses were available to them. The animals they had provided food and by-products and

In both East and West, the horse provided the means for man to overcome the restrictions of his environment.

were more tractable and therefore more easily managed than the horse. There were certainly enough of them to propitiate the gods in sacrificial ritual (poultry, it is suggested, were first kept and developed for purposes of religious divination, rather than for their eggs and flesh, and that might also have been an incentive for the husbandry of goats, sheep and even cattle). Cattle could be made to perform adequately enough for the needs of the community as load-carriers or in the early forms of draught.

It has been postulated that the first domestication of the horse was made by the American aboriginal, prior to the horse becoming extinct on the American continent. It is an interesting thought, but lacks corroboration and has no relevance to the ensuing progress of the man/horse relationship unless it somehow accounts for the relationship that was so quickly established between the latter-day American Indian and the horse.

The consensus of informed opinion and a considerable bulk of evidence places the early domestication of the equine as occurring in Eurasia among nomadic steppe people some five to six thousand years ago, towards the end of the Neolithic period.

Probably, they were Aryan tribes speaking Indo-European languages who moved about the steppes bordering the Caspian and Black Seas, but it could well be that domestication was taking place

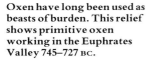

Oxen have long been used as beasts of burden. This relief shows primitive oxen working in the Euphrates Valley 745–727 BC.

simultaneously in various parts of Eurasia. These Asian nomads would have acquired basic herding techniques very early in their existence. Initially, herding was probably more a matter of 'following' the movement of wild or semi-wild flocks of animals like sheep, goats, cattle and, important for our hypothesis, reindeer – migratory animals rather than wandering ones, whose movement is governed by the incidence of the 'reindeer moss' on which they feed.

Familiarity results in acceptance, particularly in the animal context. In time, even wild creatures, particularly those of a gregarious nature, would have accepted the presence of the accompanying humans and fairly soon they would allow themselves to be driven from one pasture area to another and to be moved to winter quarters in more sheltered regions which would at least offer a subsistence diet.

In the harsh environment of the steppe lands the possession of horse herds was a far more attractive proposition than in more clement regions. Horses were better equipped than other animals to find food in difficult climatic conditions and could manage perfectly well in the snow which created problems for smaller beasts.

It seems likely that it would be the smaller, and therefore more easily handled, horses which would first be herded, the group being led by an old mare. Where horses are kept in herd conditions today – as, for instance, in Argentina – the leader is often an old bell mare. It is

The steppe pony can still provide all the needs of the nomadic herdspeople.

The Asian Nomadic people still rely on the horse for dairy products.

unlikely that stallions would have been included initially. Breeding would have been effected by tying out the in-season female, who would attract a wild stallion to mate with her. This practice is still carried out in parts of the world where wild or semi-wild stock exists. Neolithic wall pictures and drawings from Ferghana, in Bactria, and also from the eastern parts of Egypt, substantiate this theory of early horse-keeping.

The male products of such matings would either be eaten when young, before they posed behavioural problems, or possibly gelded to ensure greater amenability. But even geldings can be a nuisance when mares are in season, and if the herd was large enough there would seem to have been little object in the retention of any great number of males after weaning. Once systematic methods of breeding were practised and the management of horses became further advanced, geldings were used increasingly as saddle horses. Fillies were pretty easily managed; furthermore, in course of time, they become milk producers and mothers.

So far as the wild horse is concerned, the initial impact of domestication is retrograde. The stock becomes smaller because of the primary selection of small animals, which are more manageable. The brain, too, diminishes in size and one must conclude that the animal becomes less intelligent as it becomes more reliant upon the herds-man. It loses some of the natural ability to fend for itself, once the initiative for finding new grazing areas and new sources of food passes to its human keeper. The modern horse, groomed, clothed in rugs after his coat has been clipped off, fed at regular intervals, stabled and provided with a deep bed of straw, is almost entirely dependent upon the human agency and would make a poor job of survival if he was turned out in the wild.

Once the tribe learned to ride its horses, its mobility and speed greatly increased, gaining access to a greater range of feeding grounds. The animals could then be better fed and thus grow larger in succeeding generations. And when men learned to cultivate crops and to hand-feed their animals, this also encouraged an increase in stature. The animals would not become any more intelligent, however, and their dependence on the human may well increase.

In time the horse herd became the very staff of life for the nomads, providing for every basic need. Hides and hair were converted to tents and clothes, and dung dried to make fires. Mares supplied milk, which could be fermented to make *Kummis*, and fresh meat was always available. The tame, quieter horses were used to transport goods – the fixing of a load on the back of an old mare would not have been a difficulty and it is then a short step to a primitive form of draught, which would allow the movement of even bigger loads. Before the acquisition of the wheel, a form of sled or a *travois*, as used thousands of years later by the American Indian, would have been used – two poles fastened to the horse, one on each side, which trailed on the ground behind, criss-crossed with rope, thongs or saplings to provide a platform. The device could be used equally to transport people as well as goods. The natural consequence was for a man to get on a horse's back: with tame animals in a herd, the act of riding could not have been long delayed.

A strong incentive for the nomad to become a horseman was that it made herding so much easier. A stray group of animals can be headed off much more quickly on four legs than on two. And a man mounted on a lead horse is immediately identified with it, and can lead rather than drive the herd, particularly if he has a couple of 'whippers-in' to bring up the rear or hold the flank.

But was there another motivation that formed the link between the nomadic herdsman and the ridden horse? Some authorities hold that cattle provided the lead-in to ridden horses. Others, I think more

The onager was available in Mesopotamia and was, therefore, used long before the horse for pulling chariots. Onager-drawn chariots are seen in Sumerian art as far back as 2500 BC. However, conformation and temperament problems with onagers meant that they were soon superseded by horses.

convincingly, believe that the first horsemen were herders, drivers and riders of reindeer. Archaeological evidence suggests that reindeer were pulling sledges in northern Europe as long ago as 5000 BC, which places the domestication of that animal at least two thousand years before that of the horse. Some authorities argue for its being very much earlier than that.

Furthermore, reindeer existed within that steppe region extending from the Great Wall of China to Outer Mongolia – the area which we believe was the cradle of the first horse cultures, and from whence successive waves of horsemen poured out to conquer the earth.

In the Ice Age, reindeer lived all over the cooler part of the Northern Temperate Zone. Numerous excavations support this view as well as the existence of reindeer depictions in the cave art of France and Spain. Thereafter the herds moved northwards as climatic changes occurred, but a sizeable pocket, a survivor of the Ice Age, remained in the Sayan Mountains of Mongolia where the 6,000ft (1,828m) high range still produces flora characteristic of the Ice Age, including reindeer moss.

Reindeer are easily tamed, easily kept and hardy. Their only disadvantage for the herdsman is their migratory cycle. They were and still are milked. They are also still ridden and used in draught, and the world still retains a strong reindeer culture. Franz Hancar, in a most exhaustive exposition of the growth of horse culture, suggests that all the signs indicate that the breeding and riding of reindeer substantially preceded that of the horse. Certainly, the saddlery of the Uryanchai people, reindeer herders, is very similar to the saddlery of early equestrian peoples.

Among people used to the management of reindeer, the change to the more versatile horse could have been effected with little difficulty. Horses, not tied into a migratory cycle, would have represented a very attractive alternative. There are scholars who find the reindeer–horse progression theory unacceptable, largely because reindeer management is said to be so dissimilar to that of the horse. But the extent of the difference would not necessarily have been so daunting to a primitive society of animal-oriented people as it might be to present-day scholars.

There are good grounds for supposing that the Scythians of the fifth century BC, like those whose elaborate deep-frozen tombs were excavated in 1929 by Dr S. I. Rudenko at Pazyryk high in the Altai Mountains of western Siberia, would originally have been tenders of reindeer in the time before they became horse people. The evidence of the tombs suggests that these people had a history of horse husbandry which extended back to somewhere around the year 3000 BC.

Before that, the theory of a reindeer culture seems more viable than any other. Quite apart from what is known about the character, habits

The Scythians of the fifth century BC are here depicted as horsemen but they had ridden reindeer for many hundreds of years before they first mounted horses.

and practices of these Scythian 'ranchers', there are close similarities between their saddlery and that employed by reindeer people. Interestingly, the horses of Pazyryk, preserved by refrigeration exactly as they were on the day of their interment, together with all their trappings, were decorated with face masks, rather like the medieval *chamfron* but extending well above the head. Some were shaped like birds or beasts of prey, but the first one to be discovered was a mask which transformed the horse's head into that of a reindeer, antlers and all. Was it a symbolic backward glance to the culture from which these horse people had sprung?

What has to be accepted is that it was from these high steppe lands that the domestic horse spread outwards into central and western Europe, into the Caucasus and onwards, into Arabia and eastwards to China. For the next four thousand years the horse remained the swiftest and most efficient form of land transport.

The argument that the prior use of cattle may have led to the adoption of the onager in Mesopotamia is a supposition more easily accepted than the reindeer theory. The onager in that part of the world

This picture of an Assyrian warrior three thousand years ago suggests that man's intervention had already produced a horse that was larger than is generally supposed.

Bitless bridles, used before 2500 BC, can still be seen in what is (wrongly) called a hackamore.

was used long in advance of the horse because of its availability. But it was temperamentally difficult to the point of being downright vicious, and was supplanted by the horse once contact was made with horse-riding and horse-herding nomads from the north east.

Onagers, the successors to the oxen, are depicted in Sumerian art of the third millenium BC (and thus well in advance of horse domestication), being driven in yokes of four abreast pulling two- and four-wheeled chariots. They were guided by reins attached to nose rings (or rings passed through the upper lip), kept in place by a strap fastened tightly under the lower jaw. Driving harness was for centuries a virtual replica of that used successfully on oxen, even though the conformation of the onager is quite different from that of the ox.

It is very reasonable to suppose, however, that the first methods of horse control were on the lines of the reindeer halter, the most basic being a piece of grass rope or a thong of leather passed round the neck just behind the ears. A more effective restraint can be exercised by passing the rope over the head, behind the ears, and then fastening it tightly in a loop round the nose just a couple of inches above the nostrils where the nasal bone ends. A pull on the nose causes a temporary interruption in the breathing which immediately makes a horse lower its head to the optimum position of control by the rider. It is the action of the 'modern' drop noseband now in almost universal use, which was certainly known and appreciated by horse people of the pre-Christian era.

Control is retained so long as the nose is lowered. To make it even

Although man had adapted the horse to his needs, these classical Greek horsemen had yet to make suitable adaptations to their clothing. But in the colder climates of the steppes, horsemen were wearing trousers.

Did the early steppe nomads, from whom this Hungarian Czikos descends, use the horse for other than strictly functional purposes?

more positive a rope can be passed through the mouth to lie on the area of gum between the molar and incisor teeth, known as the 'bars' of the mouth, and secured round the lower jaw. Wear will certainly occur but there is no danger of the horse biting through the rope. The American Indian, nearly five thousand years after the first nomad riders, employed exactly that form of control.

Early horsemen, like the American Indian and the Arab rider of today, used a single rein passing from the back of the horse's lower jaw to the hand. Obviously, if the rein passes up the left side of the horse's neck a turn in that direction presents no difficulty. It may seem to be something of a problem when one wishes to turn the horse to the right but in fact this is not so. Horses quickly learn that a rein placed against the neck (a practice known as neck-reining), combined with a shift of the rider's weight in the required direction, is a signal for them to make a turn to the side opposite and away from the pressure of the rein.

Nearly six thousand years later, using two reins, we employ exactly the same technique to effect a sharp, tight turn when coping with the twists of a showjumping course. Furthermore, horses are still ridden in what are termed (wrongly) hackamores, an updated version of the primitive thong round the nose. The modern version is used with two reins and sometimes a degree of leverage is introduced by metal cheek pieces fixed to impose a more direct pressure on the sensitive nose. Somewhere about 2500 BC, when the horse was replacing the onager, bits of bone and horn, passing across the mouth over the tongue and across the 'bars', were taking the place of the thong, allowing the rider greater control.

Clearly the first horsemen would have ridden bareback and, in climates that did not require protection against the cold, without benefit of breeches. Greek horsemen in the time of Xenophon (430–355 BC) and after rode for the most part with bare legs, Xenophon holding that bare flesh on a sweated coat gave the greatest possible purchase. But then Xenophon and his troops also rode without the benefit of saddles.

On a round-backed horse (such as Xenophon understandably advocated) bareback riding is bearable; on one of an opposite inclination it can be excruciatingly uncomfortable. What more natural then than that our early horseman should throw a skin over the horse's back, thus creating the first prototype saddle? It is possible to ride a horse with such a covering without it slipping off. The horsemen of the Hungarian plains, the Czikos (themselves descendants of nomadic herdsmen), ride in felt saddles which are not fitted with any girth, and still manage some remarkable high-speed acrobatics to the accompaniment of loud cracks from enormous herding whips.

However, the skins may well have been made more secure by being fastened with a rope tied round the barrel of the horse. It would be a logical thing to do. And if that was the case, did some ancestor push his foot through the rope to improve his security even further? The American Indian, when breaking an unridden colt, literally tied himself on by securing his lower leg between just such a rope and the horse's body. If that is how it happened, then it was the first stirrup. It is a fascinating conjecture, but a very dangerous one. As far as the evidence suggests, the stirrup was over three thousand years off and did not come into use until the early centuries of the Christian era. An unconscionable time, you may think, to produce so elementary a piece of equipment.

Those who claim that the zebra might have taken the place of the horse in domestication had he been the subject of the inventiveness of the steppe peoples, produce as evidence pictures such as this one of Lord Rothschild's carriage. However, they neglect to point out that the nearside leader is a horse!

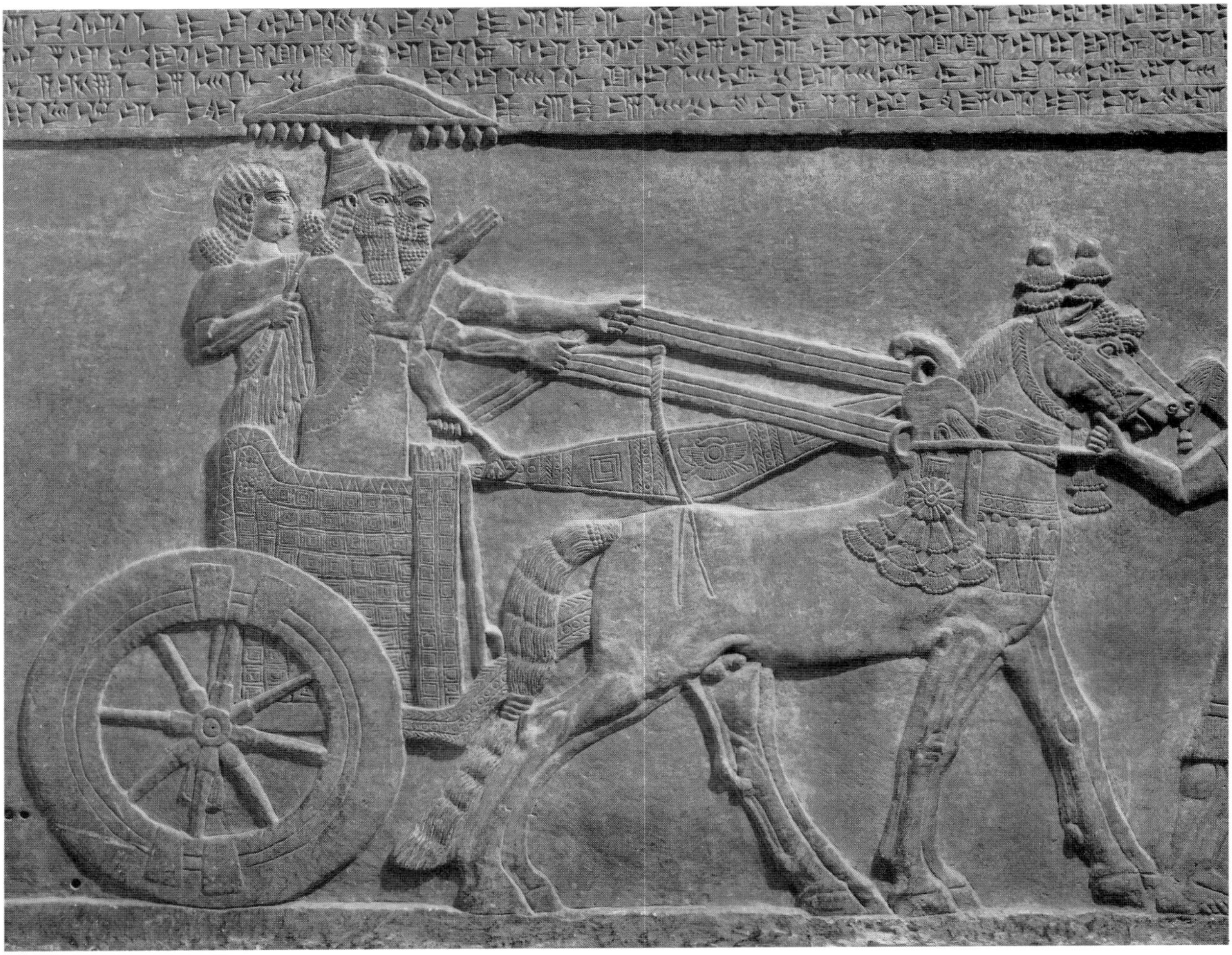

CHARIOTS AND HORSE PEOPLES

Whether riding or driving horses to wheeled vehicles came first is a subject of controversy among historians. In Syria and Egypt, and in the valley lands of the Indus, the Tigris and Euphrates, where the terrain is flat and open, the wheeled vehicle could be used to advantage. The horses in use at that time were not sufficiently big to carry a man comfortably, but, by harnessing a pair to a light chariot, transport was provided for two or even three people. By adding another two horses, to make a team of four abreast, the speed of the vehicle was increased and so was the distance which could be covered, since the effort required of each member of the team was reduced.

In mountainous country, unsuitable for wheeled vehicles, it was easier to ride, even though the horses were small. Hill ponies are notably tough and hill-men are shorter in the leg and more stockily built than plain dwellers. For them a small pony does not present the difficulty it would for taller men.

Present day ponies in northern India and the Himalayan regions are probably not so different from those used by early horsemen. They are certainly no bigger, yet they are capable of carrying heavy loads and grown men quite expeditiously over some very rough country.

Two thousand years before the birth of Christ the steppe nomads had created societies based on the horse. As their herds flourished it was necessary to secure new grazing ranges. Without permanent bases and access to commodities like iron, salt and even luxury goods, and with no ability to manufacture such items, nomads were largely dependent upon the more settled communities.

Some of their needs could be met by way of negotiated trade and, when that failed, force or the threat of force soon provided a satisfactory solution. Early in the second millenium BC the Kassites and the Elamites had conquered the north west of Persia and the Hyksos had ridden their ponies into Asia Minor, while nomadic warriors from the southern Asiatic steppes and the Ukraine were establishing a pattern of armed migrations.

After the evolution of the horse and its subsequent domestication, the next landmark in the history of man and horse was the invention of the wheel. It was in conjunction with the chariot that the first major

'The Assyrian came down like a wolf on the fold. . . .'

impact of the horse warrior was made. Aryans turned southwards out of central Asia to conquer India and Persia. Hittite-related peoples moved into and out of Asia Minor, Celts pressed into Europe – and they were all chariot people.

The wheel and the wheeled vehicle increased mobility and facilitated the movement of families and possessions. What is more, it added a new dimension to warfare, allowing military operations to be conducted over a far wider front than was possible for men fighting on foot, while it optimised the usage of animals too small to serve the purpose of mounted cavalry. The swift, co-ordinated movement of large bodies of men was simplified and, importantly, the chariot provided the means to exploit effectively the rich valley lands so suitable to warfare waged on wheels.

In comparison with those essential adjuncts of the horseman, the saddle and the stirrup, the wheel made its appearance at a remarkably early date. It was certainly in use before horse domestication. Evidence of solid wheels, possibly deriving from rollers placed under a sledge, was found in Sumerian graves excavated in the Tigris–Euphrates valley, and was dated at about 3500 BC. Spoked chariot wheels were used in Mesopotamia about a thousand years after that, war chariots in Egypt around 1600 BC, and chariots were in use in China by 1300 BC.

Using war chariots for the first time, the Hyksos broke through

Although the Egyptians were an advanced society, it was the Hittites who introduced the wheel to them and whose superior handling of a chariot arm was responsible for their victory in the greatest chariot battle of ancient times, Kadesh 1286 BC.

into the Near East out of Asia Minor, and penetrated into Egypt to create what became known as the Hittite Empire. The Hittites were a people of mixed and complex origin, speaking an Indo-European tongue. They were using chariots as early as 1600 BC, and when they defeated the Egyptian forces of Rameses I in the greatest chariot battle of antiquity, at Kadesh in 1286 BC, they had an army of 17,000 foot soldiers and 3,500 chariots – a ratio of five men to one chariot. Theirs was a sophisticated society and their management of horses and of chariot formations in the field formed the pattern for subsequent chariot-driving peoples.

The Hittite chariot was the first to employ a three-man crew – driver, shield-bearer and javelin thrower – or archer – and they were the first people, so far as we know, to produce a horse-training manual. Written for the Hittite chariot corps by Kikkuli the Mittanian in about 1360 BC, it dealt with the management of the horse as well as its training. From it we learn that Hittite chariot teams were fed on grain (barley and wheat), lucerne and chaffed straw and were conditioned by systematic exercise. The recognition of the need to relate feeding to exercise in a progressive system of conditioning is an advanced concept in horse management and it indicates both application and a pretty thorough understanding of the subject. Much of the success of the Hittite chariot corps has to be credited to their ability to bring their horses to a high state of fitness and then to maintain that condition in the field.

Chariot teams were directed and controlled by bits acting across the lower jaw, items which arrived early on the equestrian scene. Initially, bits may have been made from hardwood or as variations of the leather thong encompassing the lower jaw, but later bridles used bits made of bone and horn. By 12–1300 BC metal bits were in general use. To manoeuvre a chariot at speed in the face of the enemy (or to hunt quarry like the lion, as the Assyrian nobility did), requires an immediate response to the rein if disaster is to be averted. In a chariot the swift reaction of the horses depends certainly on their training, but also very considerably on the efficacy of the bit. And the necessity to devise efficient methods of control is, of course, intensified for a rider who lacks the security of tenure provided by saddle and stirrup.

Jointed snaffles which act in a nutcracker action across the lower jaw were stronger in their effect than a plain bar, and could be made even sharper by the mouthpiece being serrated or even fitted with 'hedgehog' spikes. Numerous variations occur in early bits, and many are remarkably modern in appearance. Their action might have been reinforced by nosebands and forms of martingales or tie-downs just as they are today, but no important alteration in bitting arrangements occurred until about the fourth century BC, when the Celts of Gaul introduced a curb bit, dependent on a leverage system.

Chariot harness was derived from the yoke used so successfully on oxen, and the practice of hitching a pair to a central pole passing between the two is of the same origin. Horses pulling sleds or a *travois* worked in 'single harness' but shafts as such, despite the prototype supplied by the *travois*, came from China and were much later.

The yoke was adapted to the conformation of the horse by being bowed and made much lighter. It was then fitted with pads which would lie on the withers, a little in advance of where the pommel of a riding saddle would rest, and was secured to the centre pole. It was kept in place by a girth and strap passing round the horse's neck, so that the horses were compelled to pull the load from that part of their anatomy and to brake it by leaning back against the yoke. In motion, the neck strap would rise up exerting pressure on the windpipe which intensified as the horses made greater efforts by stretching their necks. Probably this is the reason for the pronounced development of the underside of the horse's neck and its general ewe-necked outline depicted in art forms of the period.

The addition of another strap, fastened to the neckstrap and passing back to the girth through the forelegs, largely obviated the worst aspects of the yoke harness. This 'harness martingale' prevented the neck strap rising too far up the throat and lowered the point of traction. The system was still inefficient in terms of the ratio of effort to load, but the chariots were light and the addition of two extra horses, hitched as outriggers one on each side of the pole pair, increased the pulling power. Hittites, Babylonians, Assyrians and Egyptians all followed this practice and so, in later years, did the Romans, who used four horses in the *quadriga*, the right outrigger often being ridden by a postillion.

The Hittite Empire ceased to be a major power after about 1190 BC, but by then the chariot had conquered the civilised world and the horse had become an object of veneration and of great value. It was far too valuable to be used for menial tasks, which were left to oxen.

There is evidence from an Urartaic fortress near Eriwan, Turkey, of horses being associated with religious cults in Urartu and Chaldaea as early as the second millenium BC; certainly the use of horses in religious ritual persisted well into the Christian era. The status of the horse is reflected in a fable from Mesopotamia in which the horse, boasting to the ox, tells how *he* lives near kings and great men, eating delicately without himself being eaten – a long way from life among the steppe nomads.

Like the Hittite Empire, the martial empires of Babylon, Egypt and Assyria practised an advanced form of horse management, feeding and breeding selectively to improve the size and quality of their

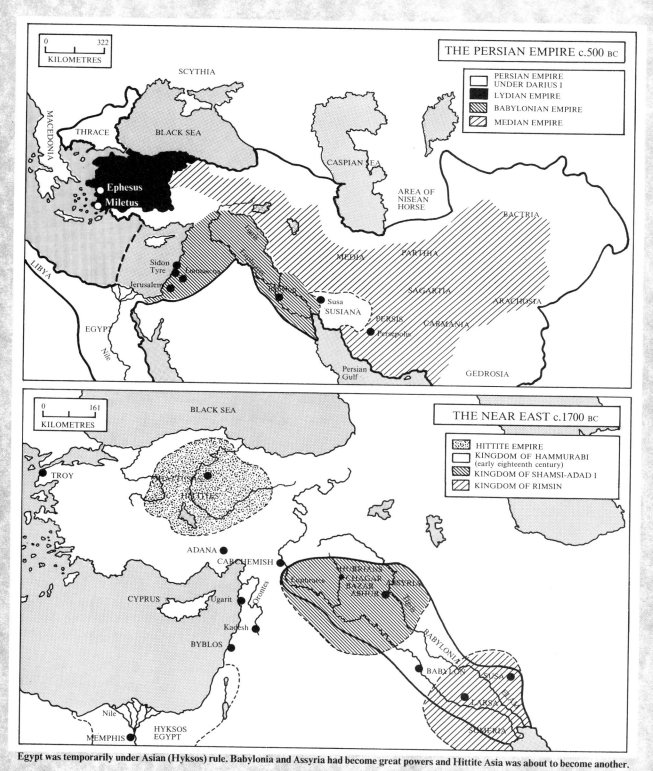

THE PERSIAN EMPIRE c.500 BC

	PERSIAN EMPIRE UNDER DARIUS I
■	LYDIAN EMPIRE
	BABYLONIAN EMPIRE
	MEDIAN EMPIRE

SCYTHIA

MACEDONIA
THRACE
BLACK SEA

CASPIAN SEA

AREA OF
NISEAN
HORSE

BACTRIA

Ephesus
Miletus

LIBYA

Sidon
Tyre
Damascus
Jerusalem

MEDIA
PARTHIA

SAGARTIA
ARACHOSIA

Susa
SUSIANA

EGYPT

Nile

PERSIS
CARMANIA

Persepolis

Persian
Gulf
GEDROSIA

THE NEAR EAST c.1700 BC

BLACK SEA

	HITTITE EMPIRE
	KINGDOM OF HAMMURABI (early eighteenth century)
	KINGDOM OF SHAMSI-ADAD I
	KINGDOM OF RIMSIN

TROY

HITTITE

ADANA
CARCHEMISH

Euphrates
ASSYRIA

CYPRUS
Ugarit
Orontes

Kadesh

BYBLOS

Tigris
BABYLONIA

BABYLON
LARSA
LARSA

SUMERIA

Nile

MEMPHIS
HYKSOS
EGYPT

Egypt was temporarily under Asian (Hyksos) rule. Babylonia and Assyria had become great powers and Hittite Asia was about to become another.

horses. As they became larger and stronger, so it became necessary to find stronger methods of control. The Egyptians of the fourteenth century BC were using a drop noseband, now an almost obligatory part of the modern horseman's equipment. The Egyptian charioteers, however, found it necessary to slit the nostrils of their horses in order to facilitate their breathing, which would have been severely restricted by the low position of the nosebands and the tightness with which they were fastened.

By the ninth century BC the formalised but often magnificently dramatic art of the Assyrians, which survives in considerable quantities, depicts well conditioned, quality horses, immaculately turned out. Manes and tails were dressed in extravagant fashion, often enclosed in a form of case and sometimes braided in meticulous style. The accoutrements were similarly splendid and very decorative.

There was, of course, a practical reason for the dressing of manes and tails in this way. Thick, loose manes might have fouled the charioteers' reins, which might also have become trapped under the tail if they were not neatly braided up. (It was for this last reason that cart and carriage horses in Europe had their tails docked – an unnecessarily cruel practice which in Britain was made illegal some thirty years ago.) When the charioteer became the horse archer, the practice of dressing the mane was continued so that it did not get in his way as he strung his bow.

Historians place the size of these Assyrian horses at about 14 hands – I would go further and estimate it in some instances as about 15 hands.

Initially, the Assyrians were chariot people, their kings and noblemen hunting from chariots, their quarry often being the lion. Later they appear as somewhat apprehensive horsemen, sitting well back on their mounts, which were led by attendants so that the rider had both hands free to draw his bow. They sit with the leg well forward, the knee bent and gripping very obviously with the calf in a proper beginner's seat. They resemble very closely what must be one of the very first records of a man mounted on an obviously spirited horse. This relief, on the tomb of Horenhab of Egypt, is dated around the year 1600 BC. It shows a rider sitting on the rump of his horse, exactly as men of his time and previously would have sat on an ass, and exactly as men in the Middle East ride a donkey today. The horse is fitted with a drop noseband which may have fastened below a bit, or may have been used alone to exert control.

By the time of Tiglath-Pileser III (747–727 BC) armoured cavalry of the day presents a different picture. Here are accomplished horsemen, archers and spearmen, sitting much further forward on cloths, or pads, secured by breastplate and girth and gripping from the thighs. Their horses, always stallions, are controlled with ornate but very

In the East the grand accompaniment to pomp and circumstance was the richly-caparisoned elephant, but for practical purposes it could not approach the swifter and more versatile horse.

In Egypt the ass was superseded by the horse once the latter became available as the result of invasions by chariot people. Horses were certainly more tractable and probably stronger. This wall-painting is from the tomb of Nebamun, Thebes and is dated at 1400 BC.

The ox preceded the horse as a means of draught by many hundreds of years and still survives in that role to the present day.

Some of the most beautiful depictions of horses are to be found in the stylised and meticulously executed Persian art-forms of the sixteenth century.

The ultimate perfection for the Ancient World was the combination in one form, the centaur, of horse and man – the two most noble products of the gods.

Chariot racing, employing teams of up to four horses, was well-established as an equestrian sport in the Greek and Roman circuses and was included in the early Olympic Games.

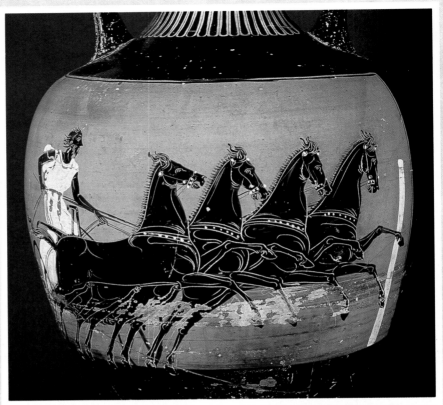

The Emperor Constantine, whose Byzantine cavalry marked a significant advance in the use of the mounted arm.

Opposite page: The pattern for equestrian statues in the heroic mould is provided by this powerful representation of the second century Roman Emperor, Marcus Aurelius.

For many this picture of jousting knights epitomises the Age of Chivalry. In reality, however, the prize was more likely to have been the favour of a high-born married lady rather than anything else.

sophisticated bridles; the bit, usually jointed, is shaped in an inverted Y, for long a general feature of the bitting arrangements of the ancient world. It has been suggested that bits of this type were originally made from antler-tine and that the later ones made of metal followed the antler design. In the seventh and eighth centuries BC they occur not only in Assyria but also on the Caucasus, in Iran and in central Asia. (The presence of bits of this sort over so wide an area adds some strength to the theory that the reindeer herders were the first horse-keepers.)

The change in emphasis from the chariot to the mounted soldier was made necessary as the Assyrian Empire, centred at the upper end of the Tigris and Euphrates basin, between the lands of the Hittites and the Persians, extended northwards into more mountainous country, a terrain unsuitable for the deployment of chariots in large numbers.

But the chariot by no means disappeared overnight. It remained an essential element for another seven hundred years or more.

By the sixth century BC military superiority was passing away from the Assyrians. The Persians became the dominant force in the struggle for power within the great Near Eastern civilisation, and chariots continued to form a large part of the Persian army.

Central to the rise of the Persian Empire was the possession of the super-horse of the ancient world, the Nisean, and, importantly, the control of the areas in which it was bred. The breeding grounds of the Nisean horse were in north western Iran, around Hamadan in what was ancient Media. In the heat of summer it was possible to drive the horses up to the cool, rich pastures of the foothills, where alfalfa, or lucerne – a nutritious, high-protein food exceptionally well suited to the rearing of young stock – was grown.

Once the breeding regions were held firmly and the Persian armies

The desire for greater horsepower was initially answered by more horses but the Assyrians recognised the need for larger horses, which they produced by improved methods of horse management.

This very romanticised version of Persian horsemen illustrates both their enthusiasm for hunting and the swiftness of the horses they used.

were straddling the Great Silk Road – the most famous trade route of antiquity which ran some six thousand miles from the Chinese Pacific coast in the east to Alexandria on the Mediterranean – they had secured an enviable cavalry supremacy and could control access to horse raising centres not only in the north west but along the Silk Road also. Control of the Silk Road, or effective control of the western sector of that part between Turkestan and Ecbatana, provided additionally a stranglehold on the merchant caravans that passed over it.

The Nisean horse had contributed largely to the ascendancy of the Babylonians and then of the powerful Assyrians. Now it underpinned the superiority of the Persian war chariots and cavalry which by the third century BC had established a Persian Empire stretching from Egypt to Asia Minor and from India to the Greek Islands. Of the armies of Cyrus the Great, Herodotus wrote: 'The armoured Persian horsemen and their death–dealing chariots were invincible, no man dared face them . . .'

This paragon among horses was a peculiar amalgam of blood. There was a relatively small indigenous horse of the region, having the characteristics of Ebhardt's Horse Type 4 and a decidedly Arabian look about it, and the steppe horse. Possibly the crossings, carried out selectively over a period of fifteen hundred years, included infusions of the Mongolian wild horse. This would certainly account for the stronger, even coarser appearance of the Persian horses, which were of a type less refined than those depicted by the Assyrians but with their own particular elegance. Out of this jigsaw came ultimately the Turkmene and that golden horse, the Akhal-Teke, both renowned for their speed and stamina.

Somewhere between them all was the Nisean, a horse generally bigger than had been used previously and an altogether stronger specimen. Its qualities made it an object of admiration in the ancient world and it filled a manifold role in Persian society, apart from its obvious usage in war.

The first people to create an empire of this magnitude, the Persians developed the first comprehensive system of communication as well. They built roads and operated a postal system of remarkable efficiency, which depended on posting stations placed one day's ride apart. A 1,500-mile (2,415km) journey was covered by royal messengers, using relays of horses, in seven to fourteen days. Some eighteen hundred years later, a strikingly similar system was operated by the Mongols of Genghis Khan, the main difference being that the Mongol rode on a saddle, well clear of his horse's back, and used stirrups, while the Persians sat on pads and had no stirrups at all.

Steppe horsemen, even when they had at last acquired the help of a stirrup, did not trot: they either walked, cantered or galloped. If the horse broke his gait, as might happen over a piece of rough ground, and fell back into a trot, the rider could either 'perch' over the movement, raising the seat out of the saddle for a few strides until the horse resumed his former gait, or he could sit for those trot strides.

'Posting' at the trot, more usually in modern times referred to as 'rising', did not enter into equitational practice until the eighteenth century, when improvements in the English roads allowed coach teams, or carriage pairs, to go over the ground at a good, spanking trot. Postillions, frequently employed in a team or a pair, found it easier and much less tiring to rise or 'post' to the trot thereby avoiding what must with some horses have been an excruciatingly uncomfortable experience. Post-boys, carrying mail on horseback, also employed the rising movement to mitigate the rough paces of the common animals with which they were supplied. Since it originated in England this postillion or post-boy trot was often known elsewhere in Europe as 'the English trot'.

With stirrups it is possible for both horse and rider to be eased at the canter or gallop if the rider puts his weight onto his knees and into his stirrup irons and raises his seat from the saddle. Without stirrups there is no alternative but to remain seated.

Probably the Persian horsemen galloped, or at any rate cantered, the stages between one post and another, but it is possible that they could have used a swift ambling horse. Very interestingly, horses employing the amble or pacing gait – where the legs are used in lateral instead of diagonal pairs – are described as early as the Hittite Kikkuli manual. In the absence of any evidence that their chariot horses paced (depictions invariably show them outstretched at the gallop), the only explanation is that pacing horses were used to ride, probably by messengers, since horse-riding was then considered unsuitable for those of noble birth. Bahdi-Lim, a nineteenth-century BC court official of Zimri-Lin, King of Mari, wrote to his master: 'My lord should not ride on a horse. Let my lord ride on a chariot or indeed on a mule, and let him honour his royal status'.

The advantage of the pacing horse is the comfort of its gait, especially when it is ridden without stirrup irons. Because the movement is a forward–backward one, instead of up and down, the horse's back remains level and the rider can sit easily and comfortably for long distances. Pacing strains occur in a variety of breeds, the gait being found in horses originating in Iran, Turkestan and neighbouring northern areas with which the Hittites were familiar. They occur, too, in the breeds of the Iberian Peninsula, the source of the 'ambling palfreys' which were so popular in England before and after the time of the Tudors.

Persian horsemen may even have employed a pace like 'the rack', which was in use throughout the equestrian world certainly from the days of the Parthians and is related to the amble. Preserved today in the USA, the rack is a pace of four distinct beats, whereas the trot and the amble are two-beat paces. The sequence of the footfalls is left hind, left fore, right hind, right fore, or vice versa – the same sequence as the conventional walk, but with far more spring about it. Performed at speed, it is as fast as a gallop and is extraordinarily comfortable.

Ownership of horses among the Persians was a status symbol, and a man's position was judged by the number of his horses. Ownership was confined, as it would be for centuries to come, to the landowning nobility, for whom appearing on foot would have been thought degrading in the extreme. This horse-owning aristocracy formed the source of the Persian cavalry and chariot formations.

Horses in this society figured often in recreational pursuits also. Hunting on horseback was general and the Persians organised regular racing on elliptical tracks of about 1,440 yards (1,317m) in length, races being run between two and nine circuits. Nine circuits would equal approximately 7 miles (11km), longer than the recorded races of either the Greeks or the Romans but, even today, not an out-of-the-way distance for the Turkmene and Akhal-Teke horses of this area.

The game of polo has its origin in sixth-century BC Persia, but it would seem that a lighter horse was developed for this purpose, if we are to judge by the elegant animals shown on hundreds of miniatures of hunting and polo scenes. Polo, as we understand the game, is connected with the central Asiatic games of *bagai* and *buzkashi* which are still played in Afghanistan and Turkestan. The name derives from the Tibetan word *pulu*, meaning ball, and in its very earliest form it could have had a religious significance. Up to a thousand men played on each side, and the ball itself was looked on as a fertility symbol.

Horses were the stuff of tribute, too – a reflection of their standing in the ancient world. The Medaean satrapy provided grazing for fifty thousand of the King's horses; the Armenians gave up twenty thousand foals each year, and the Cilicia gave one white horse for each day of the year.

White horses played a prominent part in religious ceremony, and the Persians gave particular significance to horses of this colour. Worshippers of Mithras, 'lord of the wide pastures' and a god of equally wide responsibilities, like many of the Indo-European peoples made sacrifices of horses in their religious ritual. Mithras was supposed to drive a chariot drawn by four immortal white horses, shod with gold and fed on ambrosia. On New Year's Day, horses were sacrificed to the god in recognition of these sacred white horses. Horses were also sacrificed in memory of the Persian King Cyrus the Great, on the very regular basis of one each month following his death.

The strong, high-spirited horses of the Persians, well fed and conditioned, made their army a most formidable force, but also posed problems for riders with no more than padded cloths to sit on. The chariot driver had the advantage of being able to brace himself against the front board of his vehicle and put his weight on the rein. Chenevix Trench, in *A History of Horsemanship*, suggests that the strong, thick-necked horses with their heads tucked in towards the chest, shown on Persian reliefs, had nosebands spiked on the inside, on the principle of the Spanish *careta*. This would certainly contribute to an over-bent head position, particularly as the Persian noseband appears to be attached to the bit itself. In India such a device existed in the first century, and there is no reason why it should not have existed earlier. They had continual contact with the Persians, who might well have learned the trick from them – or of course, it could have been the other way about.

The Persians seem to have been among the first people to use such a noseband. It survived into the Moorish horse culture, became part of the Iberian system, may well have inspired the restraining cavesson of the Renaissance masters of equitation and, most certainly, it went to the Americas with the *conquistadores*.

The bit employed by the Persian horsemen is also notable and is still echoed even in our twentieth-century bridles. The Persian bridle – the points of attachment made with toggles in the absence of buckles – often had straps crossing the face, and were much in the same form as the South American gaucho bridles of today. The bridle cheek divided to fasten to a phallus-shaped bit cheek, decorated at the lower end with the shape of a horse hoof. Both are symbolic of the stallion's fertility and, in a modified form, can be seen as the 'horseshoe' cheek bits used today in stallion bridles.

As the horse became bigger, stronger and better conditioned, the need to discover more effective steering and braking systems became more and more marked. This is where the division between the horseman of the so-called classic civilisations and the Asiatic rider of the steppes begins – it became the difference between Western equitation and that of the East. In the former, the riders follow the Persian style, inclining themselves a little to the rear, sitting against the horse's mouth through the rein and with a long leg position. Not so the rider from the steppes; he rides shorter, inclining the body forward and allowing his horse to move with lengthened neck and outstretched head. The melding of the two styles was not brought about until well over two thousand years after the Persian Empire declined.

For some three hundred years the Persians were masters of the greatest empire in the ancient world but, like great powers before and since, they had to endure some irritating thorns in their usually well protected sides. Principal among them were the mounted nomads from the steppes who persistently harassed their northern borders. The Persian armies, masters of the set-piece battle, were altogether out of their depth when it came to dealing with a guerilla-type opponent who never stood in convenient formations to receive a conventional attack, and whose own mode of warfare was to hit hard and swiftly and then to withdraw before the confused opposition could be manoeuvred to make any proper response.

Both Parthians and Scythians, the former probably deriving from a branch of the latter, were magnificent horsemen. Their weapon was the short, double-curved horn bow and they could loose clouds of arrows at their enemy while riding at full gallop with the reins lying on their horses' necks.

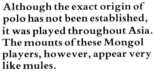

Although the exact origin of polo has not been established, it was played throughout Asia. The mounts of these Mongol players, however, appear very like mules.

The Parthians established a kingdom in Iran during the third century BC and continued to be a source of discomfiture to their neighbours for centuries to come. Even the formidable Roman legions in the first century AD had reason to respect the prowess of the Parthian horsemen. They had defeated them at Carrhae, fifty years before the birth of Christ, in the days when Rome looked down its patrician nose at mounted troops and employed only the *alae*, wings of auxiliary horses, for reconnaissance and the covering of the legions' flanks.

These are the people who gave us the term 'the Parthian shot'. A tactic of the Parthian archer was to feign flight, allowing the unwitting pursuers to come within bow range. He then swung round in his saddle and fired his arrows over the horse's tail.

The Parthian aristocracy of whom Justin wrote, 'On horses they go to war, to banquets, to public and private tasks and on them they travel, stay still, do business and chat', nonetheless followed the Persians in some respects. Their horse formations were not composed wholly of archers (*sagittari*) but also incorporated a heavy cavalry arm (*cataphracti*) similar to that of the Persians. The *cataphracti* wore plated body armour and so did their horses. Although it was relatively light in weight, it meant that bigger horses, like the Nisean or the Bactrian from the Ferghana area to the east of Iran, had to be employed.

The heavy horseman, attempting to close with infantry and thus laying himself open to being pulled off his mount (he had no stirrups), seems alien to the Parthian philosophy of swiftly moving light horsemen. He certainly did not approach the effectiveness of the horse archer on which the Parthian army greatly relied.

There does not seem to be much evidence that the Parthians made much use of heavy horsemen, but it is interesting that this is the first time that the two concepts appear alongside each other: on the one hand, the harrying light horseman, dependent upon the hit-and-run guerilla tactic and the pursuit of a retreating enemy; on the other, the strong armoured cavalryman acting in close formation to break and crush bodies of infantry.

The nomadic warriors were primarily irregular soldiers who could also harass and inconvenience the opposition to an infuriating degree. But with the exception of one or two individual encounters – like that with the legions of Crassus at Carrhae – they had not the ability to win major victories against well trained and disciplined professionals, nor to achieve and sustain conquests of a lasting nature. This was true of the Parthians and also of the Scythians, the strongest contenders for the title of the world's greatest horse people.

Scythian is a generic term applied by the Greeks to the nomadic races of southern Russia, a people who had reached Egypt in 611 BC.

The Persian god Mithras, seen here slaying the bull, is more normally associated with the title 'lord of the wide pastures'.

They moved on to the Hungarian plains and the Carpathians and were reaching outwards into Gaul in the same century. They ceased to be an effective force three hundred years later when they were absorbed by their eastern relations, the Sarmatians.

The Greeks probably relied, to some extent, on Scythian sources for their supply of cavalry mounts, which they crossed with the big Nisean horse they obtained from their Persian conquest. Possibly, these infusions of blood were from Arab-type stock.

The Scythians are something of a paradox to the historian, because they ranged over so vast an expanse and seem to have consisted of a number of tribes, bound loosely by ethnic ties but never achieving a single national cohesion. They left no written record, so what is known about them is derived largely from the neighbouring Greeks, and from the evidence obtained from the excavation of burial mounds, most notably the frozen tombs of Pazyryk, first excavated by Dr S. I. Rudenko in 1929.

In accordance with the prevailing custom of central Asia, the Scythians buried their dead with horses and saddlery and those items which would permit the deceased to carry on a life on the other side of the veil. The contents of the Pazyryk tombs, particularly those of Kurgan (barrow) Number Five, excavated in 1948, were frozen in a solid bed of ice from about the year 432 BC. Not only were leather items and textiles of all sorts preserved intact, exactly as they had been placed in the tomb, but so were the bodies of the deceased and those of the horses which were buried with them. Even articles made from ropes of vegetable fibre, such as halters and hobbles, were preserved.

The saddles were far in advance of those used by the Greeks and Romans between, say, 300 BC and the dawn of the Christian era. Made of leather and felt, they comprised two leather pads stuffed with deer hair. These lay one each side of the spine and were joined together by birchwood arches at front and rear, or more simply by a connecting piece of leather from end to end. Saddles were put on over felt saddlecloths (*numnah*) and kept in place by girths, breastbands and a form of breeching passing round the quarters well above the hocks.

The bridles were, in design, recognisably those in use in parts of Russia today, but, since this was the tomb of a great man, much more elaborate. The most common type of bit was a snaffle, very similar to the present-day 'jointed, full spoon cheek snaffle'. There were also bridles and saddles even more elaborate. All were extravagantly decorated in gold and silver, the leather tooled in swirling patterns and the felt intricately embroidered with birds, gryphons and deer.

This equipment, although so highly embellished, was nonetheless very practical. The saddlecloth saved the horse's back from being chafed and doubled as a blanket for the rider at night. Horsemen, military and otherwise, have used a saddle blanket in that fashion right up to the present day. The design of the saddle showed a clear recognition of basic principles. The first, and arguably the most important, is that the horse's spine should be free from any pressure which might cause soreness and galling or restrict freedom of movement.

The pads of the Scythian saddle, placed either side of the spine, ensured that the rider's weight was carried on the dorsal muscles and ribs. In that way a sore back was avoided, and, with the spinal complex unhampered by weight, the horse was more capable of physical exertion over long marches. The saddle resembles that used by the present-day gaucho of Argentina, particularly in respect of the pads. The gaucho, when he wishes to have a vantage point from which to see over the tall pampas grass, stands on his saddle, planting a foot on each pad. The Scythians did the same, and so did their successors on the steppes, the Huns and Mongols.

When the Plains Indians of America took to horse, they made for themselves saddles that were almost exact replicas of those used by the Scythians. Like them they delighted in decoration and like the steppe warriors they hung the scalps of their enemies from their saddle bows.

The main difference was that the Scythian did not use a stirrup. There is a suggestion, based on an illustration on the Chertomlyk Vase (fourth century BC), that the stirrup is of Scythian origin. It shows a Scythian horse with something like a loop hanging from the saddle. W. W. Arendt, the Russian archaeologist, suggested that this was a stirrup attached to the girth. On the whole, however, it seems very unlikely, if only because there is no evidence of the general use of such a device in this area at this time. Surely, if a stirrup was used in 400 BC there would be evidence of its use before, say, the fourth century AD, eight hundred years later.

The horses themselves were all caparisoned most gorgeously for their owner's funeral ceremony. They were geldings, rather than the stallions used by the grander people of the valley lands, whose pride forbade the riding of anything but an 'entire' horse, but whose practical horse knowledge did not approach the intuitive understanding of these nomad warriors. The manes were hogged, a lock or two being left to give a hand hold when the archers vaulted into their saddles. The tails were a revelation of painstaking ingenuity: plaited, braided and double-plaited in complicated knots, and encased in elaborate tail sheaths. (Both the Lippizaners of the Spanish Riding School and the horses of France's Cadre Noir wear such sheaths today, particularly those employed in the soaring 'leaps above the ground'.)

Each horse wore as a headpiece a gryphon or reindeer mask. These were royal trappings, designed to assert the standing of the deceased in

This silver-gilt dish found in the Pazyryk burial grounds of the Altai mountains is over three thousand years old. It not only shows 'The Parthian Shot' but also reflects the horse-oriented cultures of the nomadic steppe people.

This 'Laughing Cavalier', depicted on a felt wall-hanging, is another find from the Pazyryk tombs.

the next world. With him was buried his very fine, four-wheeled wagon, complete with felt top, the whole encased in a timber frame, a replica of the sort of house in which he had lived when he was not moving with the herds. Everything, from feed scoop to bucket and container bags, right up to the resplendent caravan (*vardo*) itself, was decorated by painted motif or carving. In fact, the whole tomb represented a memorial to a 'gypsy' king, which was what this well-to-do Scythian chieftain really was. The connection with modern Romany is unmistakable.

But in all the insight afforded by the ice-box of the Pazyryk burials, there is one unexplained matter. This wealthy owner of hundreds of horses, interred with all the pomp due to his station, was tattooed all over his body with designs of mythical monsters as well as with those of the wild and tame animals with which he would have been familiar in his life. But on his right arm, in what it is not unreasonable to presume would be the most honoured position, is the definitive outline of a donkey! Donkeys were held sacred in ancient Egypt and were, of course, commonplace throughout the Middle East. But they were not inhabitants of the Asian steppes. Why does the animal appear on the right arm of a Scythian king, whose contact with the species could have been no more than minimal, if, indeed, he ever saw such an animal at all?

Vestiges of the Scythian custom of symbolic horse burial were present in the funeral ceremony of the Romans, where the horse accompanied his dead master to the grave, but was not sacrificed. In Germany in the Middle Ages (as in the funeral of Johann Latomus Günther von Schwartzburg), torch bearers led horses to the altar where they were offered up symbolically and then bought by relatives, the proceeds going to church funds. Even up to recent times, a funeral could hardly justify its name without the corpse being borne to its resting place by a team of black caparisoned horses.

It is to the Scythians that we owe the convention of Western male clothing, and much else. They wore clothes suitable for 'a people born on horseback' – woollen trousers, leather boots and warm hooded tunics – whereas the Greeks and Romans wore robes of rich cloth, but not really suitable for sitting upon horses. The Scythians' principal weapon was the short bow and, though they had both sword and dagger, their tactic was not that of closing with the enemy. Swift-moving, light horsemen, they put their trust in hails of arrows fired out of reach of javelin throwers or swordsmen, and they steadfastly refused to be drawn into the conventional pattern of charge and repulse warfare. Theirs was a martial society, merciless in the ways of war. It was customary for the Scythian to behead the fallen and to decorate saddle bow and bridle with scalps or to use them as a covering for a quiver. Skulls, lined with gold, made handsome drinking cups.

They were also great hunters, pursuing anything from a hare to a wild boar or even a tiger and accounting for their quarry by singularly straight shooting. They were the prototypes for the Huns of Attila and the Mongols of Genghis Khan. Accomplished horse-dealers and breeders, they bred those 'Heavenly Horses' of China, which reached their destination through successions of middlemen down the Great Silk Road.

Unlike their neighbours, they rode geldings and practised emasculation from the beginning. Mares they used for milk and breeding, and stallions for breeding only. In battle a stallion is less reliable than a gelding: he neighs and whinneys, giving away his position to the enemy; he is distracted by the presence of mares, and he may indulge in inconvenient combat with his peers. It was also said by the Scythians that stallions stopped too frequently to stale (as a way of marking territory). The Scythian, the Hun and the Mongol, apocalyptic horsemen of the steppes, were themselves never worried by calls of nature which they accommodated without leaving the saddle. They could even sleep on horseback and, indeed, if the evidence is to be believed, they indulged in amatory acts using the same platform.

Through their descendants or through their neighbours whom they drove outwards, they raged up to the Great Wall of China, built to repel their continual incursions into the civilised pattern of Chinese life. Repulsed from there they swept westwards up to the Danube, bringing down in red ruin the calm certainty of the ancient rational world, even up to the last standings of the great Roman Empire. In blood and fire, in violence, rape and ruin they built the foundations of medieval Europe.

These nomadic horsemen remained to exert their influence over the shaping of the world, and were the prime instigators of a school of horse usage and horsemanship that exemplified the Eastern philosophy against that of the West.

The reign of the Persian kings and their great Empire itself came to an end during the period 336–323 BC at the hands of the greatest hero of antiquity and one of the finest military commanders of all time, Alexander of Macedon. There then emerged the two great classical civilisations of the ancient world: that of Greece, the very inspiration of the reasoned democratic society, and that of pragmatic Rome, whose imprint was to lie over the world into our own times. Without the partnership of man and horse, neither could have existed, let alone flourished, to hand on the torch which would, in the end, light mankind on his path to the planets.

Chapter 6

THE CLASSICAL CIVILISATIONS: GREECE & ROME

Between the establishment of the urban civilisations of ancient Greece in the eighth and seventh centuries BC, which were based soundly on regular commercial contact with Egypt and Asia, and the ultimate disintegration of the Roman Empire under the onslaught of waves of 'barbarian' (i.e. non–Hellenic and non–Roman) horsemen in the fourth century AD, there flowered the two civilisations which exerted as great an influence on the subsequent affairs of mankind as any other.

They covered a span of over a thousand years and, once they had gone, the world entered into what we call the Dark Ages. But despite the inevitable tarnish caused when great states lapse into decadence, their glories remained. The philosophies, the art forms and the cultures of Greece and Rome were so indestructible that they survived the barbarian invasions. Later men returned to them for inspiration and used them as a guide in the formation of their own societies.

Classical Greece, beginning with the defeat in 480–479 BC of the first of the Persian invasions, provided for the world the roots of the system of democracy. Its influence and that of the ordered society of Imperial Rome persist right up to our own time and are likely to extend into the forseeable future.

Neither Greeks nor Romans were horse-people in the mould of the Scythians, the Huns and the Mongols, the Romans being far less horse orientated than the Greeks. Both, however, came to rely on horses to further the boundaries of their empires, to maintain the sinews of their societies and to hold their frontiers against incursors.

Julius Caesar failed in his first attempts to conquer Britain because his cavalry did not arrive in time. When he returned with his powerful infantry supported by the mounted arm, the Roman conquest of Britain was under way. Caesar himself was reputed to be a notable horseman who, in his youth, would gallop his horse at full stretch with his arms clasped behind his back. In battle he commanded from horseback, dictating orders to his aides, in the manner adopted by generals right up to the nineteenth century. How impossible it would be to imagine Waterloo with the Iron Duke directing the battle on foot! Not for nothing was the saddle (or the horse's back) referred to in Anglo-Saxon poetry as 'the high king's seat of battle'. Napoleon, in

A perfect example of the horse being used to heighten the heroic image of his rider albeit, in this case, Napoleon's seat is less than exemplary. The horse is Napoleon's favourite charger, Marengo.

his later years, when a painful condition made riding uncomfortable for anything but short periods, used a coach as a mobile command post, and so did Marlborough, just as the Persian King Darius used his war chariot at Issus when the Greek armies under Alexander inflicted their final, decisive defeat upon the Persians, causing 110,000 casualties while they themselves suffered only 450.

It would be too much of a simplification to claim that when Rome, with its capital under the first Christian Emperor, Constantine, moved from the City of the Seven Hills to Constantinople in Byzantium, and found itself unable or unwilling to fund the maintenance and training of a cavalry arm, that the Empire went into decline as a result. There were many contributory factors leading to the fall of the Roman Empire – corruption, indulgence, internal strife and a constant state of war on its frontiers. Its decline would not have been prevented if it had channelled some of its affluence into a defence budget which supported a strong cavalry arm, but it might have been delayed.

The Greeks were certainly no better overall horsemen than their predecessors, the Assyrians and Persians, but it was they, largely through one general, Xenophon (c. 430–356 BC), who left a legacy to the world of horsemanship as an art. There is evidence of an early Greek association with the horse from about the year 2000 BC. Chariots are roughly carved on the shaft graves of Mycenae (c. 1550–1500 BC) and painted on some vases, but the earliest accounts of horses occur in Homer's *Iliad*, recorded probably around 800 BC. The Homeric heroes fought from two-horse chariots, probably because the horses were too small to ride. Frequently the noble heroes leapt from their chariots to fight with sword and spear from the ground, the chariots being driven by a man of lesser rank and withdrawn to the rear until they were required again.

> From his proud car the prince impetuous springs,
> On earth he leaps: his brazen armour rings.
> Two shining spears are brandished in his hands.
> Thus armed, he animates his drooping bands.
>
> (Homer, *Iliad*, 5)

Greece is a mountainous country, quite unsuited to the manoeuvring of large wheeled formations, but the establishment of an effective cavalry arm does not seem to have come about until Philip of Macedon, father of Alexander the Great, united the fragmented Greek states into a league against the Persians in 337 BC. He formed a cavalry force which under his son helped to secure the possession of the Near East and spearhead the victorious drive into India after the destruction of the Persian Empire of Darius.

Alexander's cavalry was a highly disciplined force, trained to act in

XENOPHON.

The first writings on the horse that have survived are those of Xenophon (430–356 BC), though they owed much to the earlier teachings of Simon of Athens.

concert with the infantry, and divided into 'heavy' cavalry, 'light horse' and what we would term 'dragoons', which for the most part rode to the battle and then dismounted to fight on foot. Before that the Greeks had fought on foot, with the nobility using chariots when this was practicable. Their first victories against the Persians were accomplished by disciplined bodies of infantry; no horses were employed, for instance, at Marathon in 490 BC, when news of the victory was carried to Athens by a runner.

Horses did, however, play a central role in Greek life well before this date and are prominent in Greek mythology. However, the first appearance of men on horseback terrified the people of Thessaly (later the foremost horse-breeding area of Greece) in the same way as the American Indians feared the Spanish *conquistadores*. The origin of the Centaur tradition is thought to lie in the herds of wild cattle that descended from Mount Pelion in the reign of King Ixion and laid waste the plain of Thessaly. A number of young blades, anxious to earn the offered reward, leapt for the first time upon chariot horses to drive off the destroying herds.

In Greek mythology Ares, the god of war, is drawn in a chariot by a team of four white horses as he precedes the rising sun. The image of the goddess Demeter was the head of a black mare and her temple priests were known as 'foals'. Poseidon, specially honoured in horse-breeding Thessaly, was 'the embodiment of all horses, their god and their lord' and later, as god of the sea, he is credited with the creation of the horse. Very occasionally, horses, which were of enormous value in ancient Greece, were offered sacrificially to Poseidon; they were not slaughtered but drowned. At Rhodes a white horse was driven into the sea drawing a flaming chariot to 'revive the sun' following the winter months.

For over fifteen hundred years chariot racing was the national sport of Greece. The goal of every Greek breeder or owner of horses was to produce a winner at the Olympic Games. Poets, such as Pindar (c. 522–440 BC), were commissioned to write poems in honour of the winners and sculptors contributed to their fame by depicting them in stone. The first chariot races, for four-horse chariots, took place at the twenty fifth Olympiad in 680 BC. Two-horse chariot racing did not come until 408 BC, but races for ridden horses were introduced in 648 BC, although they did not achieve social parity with the chariot event for at least the next three hundred years.

An early winner of the ridden race was a mare belonging to Pheidolas of Corinth. Losing her rider early on, she nonetheless continued to race and on hearing the trumpet signal for the last lap she quickened her pace to pass the winning post ahead of the field. She then of her own accord took up the place of honour before the judges. She was awarded the race and honoured by having her statue placed with those of her peers in the Sacred Grove.

The principal centres of horse-breeding in Greece were the plains of Thessaly, Argos in Peloponnesus and Elis, near to Olympia and the site of the chariot course. Of these, Thessaly was the most important, and it was from this area that the Greeks drew much of their cavalry troops.

In comparison with the horse-raising areas of western Europe, such as Britain, Ireland, and in the USA Virginia and the Kentucky Blue Grass Country, Greece has little to offer in terms of soil structure and climate suitable for equine stock. As a result, their indigenous product was small, as it is today, and they were forced to rely upon imports from their neighbours. Given fair stock they were clearly astute breeders, as their racing activities go to show. They initially improved their horses by introducing Ferghana type animals from the east, as can be seen from their horses' Arabian characteristics. Size was increased by Scythian horses (Philip of Macedon imported twenty thousand Scythian mares) and larger eastern types from the Persians (Alexander claimed a tribute of fifty thousand such horses).

The horses depicted in Greek art seem to stand about 14.2 hands high. In certain depictions they may appear smaller in comparison with standing men, but this is likely to be a convention of Greek art. The best way to assess the height is to look at the extent to which the leg of the rider hangs below the horse's girth.

Xenophon left a description of what he considered to be a good horse, and it relates very closely to those spirited horses seen on the Parthenon frieze. In his translation of Xenophon's *Art of Horsemanship*, first published in 1894 and unsurpassed to this day, Professor Morris H. Morgan quotes the equestrian writer 'Stonehenge', who referred to Xenophon's horses thus: '. . . here we have described a cobby but spirited and corky horse, with a light and somewhat peculiar carriage of the head and neck, just as we see represented on the Elgin marbles'. Morgan commented that this was 'the most exact translation of Xenophon's description which I have ever seen'.

The 'somewhat peculiar carriage of the head and neck' can be explained by the use of a relatively powerful snaffle bit (the Greeks knew of the curb bit but did not use it). It acts upwards against the corners of the lips, an action which is accentuated when the rider is sitting bareback without the support of saddle and stirrup irons. It is not difficult to see how the head as a result can be carried in the horizontal plane. The only addition which might be made to this excellent description is that the head is markedly Oriental, sufficiently so for the horse of Alexander the Great to be called Bucephalus, i.e. 'ox-head', referring to the broad forehead and slightly concave profile characteristic of Oriental blood in the equine and also of a particular Thessalian strain.

Just as it would be impossible to discuss the Greek civilisation without mentioning its most outstanding leader, Alexander, so it would be unthinkable not to relate here the story of his charger, the extraordinary Bucephalus. Described as being 'of the best Thessalian breed', he was big, by comparison with his contemporaries, black, and bore a white star on the centre of his head. Possibly, on the evidence of an unknown Greek writer, he may also have had one 'wall-eye', sometimes called a 'China eye' or, in Wales, a 'silver eye'. He was bought in 343 BC by King Philip from a Thessalian called Philoneicus for 13 talents according to Plutarch, and for 16 according to Pliny. The modern equivalent would be upwards of £10,000. When brought out before the King he was so savage and unruly that none could mount him. But young Alexander, a precocious twelve-year-old who had already seen active service, claimed that he would ride the horse. Seeing that the animal was startled by his own shadow, Alexander turned Bucephalus to face the sun then sprang lightly on his back. After 'patting and coaxing' the horse he galloped him to and fro before returning to his father. 'You must go look for a kingdom to match you, my son,' said Philip, 'Macedonia is not large enough for you.'

Thereafter Bucephalus would allow a groom to ride him bareback, but when he was caparisoned he would only be mounted by Alexander, kneeling to allow his master to get on his back more easily. He carried Alexander in all his great battles and died at the age of 30 from wounds received in the battle against the Indian King Porus at the Hydaspes in 327 BC. He was buried with all military honours and Alexander founded a city which he called Bucephalia in his honour.

There are numerous other instances of horses who became almost as

Wellington described his army as, 'The scum of society officered by the froth', but his regard for his favourite charger, Copenhagen, was encapsulated in the description that he had '. . . never got to the bottom of him!'

well known as the men they carried into battle. Napoleon had the grey, Marengo, and Wellington had the chestnut, Copenhagen, who carried him 60 miles (96 km) the day before the Battle of Waterloo and who was ridden for over fifteen hours on the day itself. Wellington was never out of the saddle throughout the day. When, finally, fatigued beyond measure, he slipped stiffly from Copenhagen, the horse expressed his relief by lashing out with both hind feet, narrowly missing the Iron Duke's head. When he died in 1836 at the age of 28 not only the Duke but the whole nation mourned. He was buried at the Duke's home, Stratfield Saye, with full military honours under a gravestone bearing this inscription:

> God's humble instrument, though meaner clay,
> Should share the glory of that glorious day.

Not the greatest couplet ever coined, but it caught the very heart of sentimental England.

My favourite story is of a less famous equine character of the seventeenth century. An ageing piebald mare, a purpose-bred (i.e. for the cavalry) Barb/Limousin cross, she was called, appropriately, La Pie, and was the charger of the Marshall General of France, the Vicomte de Turenne. One July afternoon on the Rhine, the General sat on his horse, in accordance with tradition, some dozen lengths in front of the leading ranks of his army, preparatory to moving against the Austrian enemy, whereupon an Austrian cannonball despatched him unceremoniously into the next world. The army, witnessing the demise of its General, faltered under the steady artillery fire. 'Turn the pied mare loose – she'll show us the way,' shouted a voice from the ranks. An officer released the mare, pointing her towards the distant gun flashes. She, understanding, began her well-accustomed steady march towards the enemy, and the French battalions, morale restored, followed her boldly into battle.

The Greek general Xenophon was writing his eminently practical books on agriculture, hunting, cavalry management and horsemanship some twenty three centuries ago. Not only was he technically well-qualified but, as a disciple of Socrates, his prose was remarkably lucid and reasoned. Classical Greece had a Renaissance quality about it which was epitomised by this cultured, highly articulate professional soldier. His works, particularly those on horsemanship, not only survive in their entirety today but are virtually as relevant to a present-day student of horsemanship as they would have been to a young Greek cavalry officer of his own time.

Xenophon's writings, particularly his *Hippike* and *Hipparchikos*, were the inspiration for the enquiring horsemen of the Renaissance nearly a thousand years after they were written. They were at the base of what we now term 'classical' riding. All too frequently modern dressage is described as classical, but for the most part it is not. The last remaining preserves of the classical art form are the Spanish Riding School of Vienna and, possibly, the French Cadre Noir of Saumur. Individuals in Spain and Portugal may still be exponents of classical riding, such as Maestro Nuno Oliveira of Portugal.

Xenophon came from the 'Equestrian' class of knights from a family living in Attica. As a young man he served in the Peloponnesian War and was made an officer for his part in the expedition against Artaxerxes II. After the betrayal and murder of Cyrus of Persia at Cunaxa, Xenophon took command of the Greek troops, which had been assisting Cyrus in his campaign to regain the throne from his brother, and brought the army back the hundreds of miles between the Tigris and the Black Sea.

He recounted this campaign in the *Anabasis* ('The Retreat of the Ten Thousand'). During it he would have ridden probably three thousand miles, and gained a deep understanding of cavalry management. His shrewd observations were certainly taken to heart by Alexander, and used as the basis for the handling of mounted troops in the latter's victorious campaigns.

Xenophon's book *The Cavalry Commander* remains among the most valuable of military manuals. Unfortunately, between the seventeenth and nineteenth centuries, particularly during the time when possession of 'the cavalry spirit' was considered to be more important than professional ability, the cavalry officers of Europe seem not to have been acquainted with Xenophon's treatise – had they been there might have been fewer cavalry disasters.

The Art of Horsemanship reflected the high estimation in which the horse and horsemanship were held by the Athenians. Horse-ownership in Greece was confined to a wealthy élite from which the cavalry was drawn, and horsemanship was an essential part of the education of the Greek upper classes. Breaking and backing (introducing the young horse to saddle and bridle, and accustoming him to accept a rider on his back) was carried out by grooms, and Xenophon does not concern himself in detail with it, although he acknowledges the importance of its being carried out correctly.

Thereafter, however, his instruction is detailed. Horses are trained in the paces of walk, trot, canter and gallop. (Greek horses, unlike those of the Romans, did not amble; the Greeks, obsessed with the body athletic, were no supporters of the soft life.) Emphasis is given to the horse striking off at the appropriate signal from his rider on the correct lead at canter. If a horse is cantering on a circle to the left it is necessary that he should 'lead' with his left, or nearside, foreleg if he is to retain his balance. Much use is made of the circle as a means of suppling the horse, just as it is today.

Horses were taught the demi-pirouette, a swift turn made on the pivot of the hind legs. They were schooled in an oblong 'career' having to make sharp turns at each end like a polo pony or a show jumper, and they were taught to jump and to cross rough country expeditiously, negotiating ditches and other natural hazards. Furthermore, Xenophon understood those movements which we term advanced and which are beyond the ability of 90 or more per cent of those who ride today. The parade horse, for instance, was trained to advance in a lofty, cadenced trot, the equivalent of the modern *passage* which is included only in the Grand Prix dressage test. Xenophon also was familiar with and admired the *levade* which is outside modern dressage and is practised in the High School movements of the Spanish School and the Cadre Noir. This is the movement where the horse sinks down on the haunches, the hocks flexed beneath him, while raising the forehand and tucking up the forelegs. It is in layman's terms a half-rear. 'The prettiest feat a horse can do', writes Xenophon, 'is to raise his forehand so that his belly may be seen from below and his hind legs well under the fore, and it will look to spectators as if he were doing all of his own accord.' (There is some disadvantage in teaching horses movements of this nature. Around 450 BC the luxury-loving citizens of Sybaris in southern Italy trained their horses to dance to the music of the flute. Their enemies, the people of Croton, issued their bandsmen with flutes instead of the usual trumpets. They played the dancing tune as they advanced, and the Sybarite horses promptly decanted their riders to go into their dance routine. The Crotons gained the victory.)

All this amounts to pretty highly trained horses, all the more remarkable since the Greeks had neither saddle nor stirrup. For this last reason Xenophon devotes considerable space to the business of mounting. This was normally accomplished by vaulting on to the horse, often using the javelin or spear as a vaulting pole. This is quite easily done by the young and active, and lads in modern racing stables habitually vault into the saddle on horses of far greater stature than those of the Greeks. When the rider was wearing armour the javelin might, however, have been a useful aid. Otherwise, horses were taught to kneel, or older riders used mounting blocks or employed a slave as a human block. But Greek horsemen frequently rode naked or nearly so. It is understandable that Xenophon cautioned his young men to take care when mounting lest they should appear unseemly when viewed from the rear!

Xenophon appears also to have been an excellent judge of a horse, appreciating that well made, proportionately built horses were both better balanced and better equipped to stand up to work, although, not unreasonably, he was concerned to have riding horses with round backs rather than those of an opposite conformation.

The absence of a saddle naturally imposed limitations upon the riders, however expert they were. But the Greek bitting arrangements as expounded by Xenophon are once more advanced in their understanding of the horse's mouth and of his reactions to discomfort. Bits were snaffles made 'rough' or smooth by the shape of the *icheni*, literally 'seahorses', with which they were fitted. *Icheni* were rollers encircling the mouthpiece, the spikes of which could be small and blunt or larger and sharper.

But, as Xenophon says, 'It is not the bit but its use that results in a horse showing its pleasure so that it yields to the hand; there is no need for harsh measures; he should rather be coaxed on so that he will go forward most cheerfully in his swift paces.' Soft bits were to be preferred to severe ones and continual emphasis is given to the desirability of lightness of the rider's hand. The curb bit was known but not used; use was made, however, of a metal cavesson, *psalion*, acting on the nose.

Greek cavalrymen wore armour, described in detail, and for weapons carried a spear or javelin and a sabre, the latter much shorter than the modern version. For Xenophon the best defence was a soldier's armour and his secure seat.

Alexander in his Indian campaigns used lancers, as well as javelin throwers, even though the lance was not a weapon favoured by Xenophon. To use a lance effectively the horseman has to be close to his target. In the pursuit of a retreating enemy, when horsemen will be acting either in small groups or even independently, the lack of security afforded by saddle and stirrup may not be of great significance, although such a horseman is vulnerable in close proximity to foot soldiers who can easily unhorse him. But to charge a body of steady, disciplined infantry in the knee-to-knee charge which became a near-obsession among nineteenth-century cavalry commanders would be a hazardous operation for bareback horsemen.

The tactic of the Greek cavalry was to ride along the enemy's front discharging their javelins and also to scout and to harry enemy formations. When fifty cavalrymen were sent from Sicily in 369 BC to assist the Spartans, 'These cavalrymen although few in number dispersed to different points and they would ride along the enemy line or charge towards it and throw their javelins. When the enemy moved against them they retreated and then wheeling round again threw their javelins. While pursuing these tactics they used to dismount and rest their horses and if anyone moved against them while they were dismounted, they easily vaulted on to their horses and withdrew. If on the other hand they were pursued to any great distance from the main body of the enemy, they attacked their pursuers when they retired, and hurling their javelins at them created havoc. Thus they compelled the whole army either to advance or to retire as they wished.'

Each soldier carried two javelins but once they were thrown he was left only with his personal weapon, the sword. This problem, which to a lesser extent also faced the mounted archer, could be overcome by a reserve of camels, tucked safely out of the way, which could be loaded with replacements, or by using a chariot as a mobile supply depot.

'I do not approve', wrote Xenophon, 'of a seat which is as though a man were on a chair, but rather as though he were standing upright with his legs apart.' In this way the rider got a better grip with his thighs and 'being upright, he could hurl his javelin more vigorously and strike a better blow from on horseback.' From the knee down the leg hung loosely and from the hips upward the body was kept supple. Greek horsemen are shown riding elegantly, with a fair length of leg, the only difference between their seat and that adopted today being in the position of the lower leg. The Greeks let it hang naturally and a little toward the front with the foot relaxed and pointing down. Modern horsemen tend to bring the lower leg back and raise the toe slightly. The Greek seat, with some minor adaptions, was embraced by the Western world. Indeed, it is still possible to see its influence in posed pictures of the present day. Only within living memory has there been a general inclination to draw back the lower leg.

The opposite of this classical seat was that of the barbarian horse archer, riding short with the body inclined forward and the lower leg held to form a sharp angle with the thigh. The two positions reflected distinct schools of riding. The horseman of the West rode his horse in 'collected' fashion, with the hocks engaged well beneath the body and the head held high. The barbarian rode with his horse extended: tail at one end, head and neck held low and extended at the other. The one rode by precept, the other by the light of nature; but both conformed largely to the terrain in which they operated, the type of horse ridden and the weapons they carried. So it remained until, no more than a century or so ago, European horsemen blended the two into a seat suited to the changing circumstances of their riding.

The training techniques expounded by Xenophon are remarkable in their proximity to modern equestrian theory, but even more significant is the whole approach to horses. His accent is on quiet handling and inviting the horse's cooperation: 'What is done by compulsion is done without understanding and there is no more beauty than in whipping or spurring a dancer.' Great understanding of the horse's mind is shown in the instructions about its natural tendency to be suspicious of strange objects or of sudden movements or noises. 'When the horse suspects some object and is unwilling to approach, you must make it clear that there is nothing to be afraid of . . . and if this fails you must yourself touch the object and lead him up gently. Those who compel the horse with blows make him more frightened than ever.' But this above all: 'Never lose your temper in dealing with horses; this is the one best precept and custom in horsemanship.'

Today, lip service is certainly paid to the Greek precepts and they are, one would like to think, understood and practised by the majority, but there are still areas of great ignorance when it comes to dealing with horses.

For all the humanity evident in Xenophon's works, there are continual references to the dangers associated with horses. Clearly, he followed that school which holds that equines bite at one end and kick at the other. Muzzles are advocated when horses are being groomed or led. It appears that these Greek horses may have been a pretty vicious lot, or were made so by rough treatment in the early stages of backing and breaking.

Professor Morgan thought that 'Xenophon probably came as near to loving the horse as any Greek did,' but he makes the point that nowhere does Xenophon have 'a single word of love for the horse . . . and does not even suggest that the rider should try to win his horse's affection for its own sake'. Morgan also drew attention to the fact that 'We never read of a Greek as taking a ride for pleasure'. He concluded that Greek horsemanship was essentially practical. Horses were the 'machines of battle' to the Greeks, or were esteemed for the part they played in the scarcely less warlike sports of the hippodrome. Their real business 'lay among warriors' and they played only a little part in everyday life; mules were used for journeying and in harness.

Reluctantly, one is driven to accept that love does not much enter the man–horse relationship. Respect, esteem – yes; but not love. The possible exceptions are the Anglo-Saxons: there is without doubt a very special relationship between the two in Britain. As recently as 1985 George Morris, the American Olympic rider, said: 'The British jumping team is definitely the strongest in Europe today and perhaps in the world. This is not a surprise as the English are historically great horsemen and women. They live and breathe with their horses and know their animals better than any other people in the world. They take care of their horses and really worry about their well-being.'

After the death of Alexander in 323 BC Greece reverted to a loose confederation of states. The days of Empire were over, but the Greek legacy to the world was far from being exhausted. It is not until the sixteenth century that another book on horsemanship is found. One written by Pliny was lost in the lava which overwhelmed Pompeii.

Unlike the Greeks, who became horsemen by application even if they were not natural equestrians like the riders of the steppes, the Romans were reluctant to join the hippomanic cult. It is true that Lucian (AD 125–90) made the curiously modern comment, 'The rage for horses has become a positive epidemic; many persons are infected with it whom one would have credited with more sense,' but one feels that that is about pride of possession rather than horsemanship.

Rome, like Greece, always had an effective naval force and its armies were the most formidable in the world. But on land Rome put her trust in the impenetrable shield wall of the superbly organised legions, and rarely, indeed, was it betrayed. For cavalry – to support the foot formations but to operate under the central command of the legion – Rome depended largely upon mercenary horsemen.

Chariots were the prerogative of the nobility, and chariot racing was an enormously popular spectator sport, as it was with the Greeks. Rome used racing for the very real purpose of concentrating the passions of a riotous and potentially rebellious populace on particular competitors. Originally there were four chariot groups, distinguished by colour – green, red, blue or white (for spring, summer, autumn and winter) – each supported by a political faction. In the end only the greens and blues were left, the former supported by the gentry and the

Chariot racing at the Circus Maximus diffused the political tensions in Roman society.

latter by tradesmen and artisans. Rivalry was fierce and often ended in ugly street fighting.

Many of the present equestrian circus acts have their origin in the Roman circus, although some were inherited from the Greeks. There was Roman riding, where a man galloped a pair round the arena standing with one foot on the back of each horse, and acrobatics of all kinds were performed on horseback. After the fall of the Roman Empire the Byzantine circus continued, and its carousels were a direct influence on the growth of classical riding. The circus has a strong link with advanced equitation, many of the very great innovators in equestrian thought choosing to display their art in the circus ring. Both James Fillis, Riding Master to the Tsar of Russia and architect of the Russian school of dressage, and François Baucher, one of France's greatest exponents of the classical art and a trainer of genius, had ridden in the circus. So, too, did Henri Cuyer and then, of course, there is the famous Schumann family, whose members are as talented as any horsemen riding outside the circus discipline.

The Roman circus was also a place where gladiatorial combats were staged on horseback, and mounted men fought every sort of animal from bulls to elephants. The Greeks, too, had fought bulls from horses and it is from this Graeco–Roman background that bull-fighting in Spain and Portugal is derived. Possibly, too, some of the American rodeo sports have the same origin for they, too, stem in part from the Iberian tradition.

In Spain, bull-fighting is usually carried out on foot, the wretched horses of the *picadors* playing only a supporting role. In Portugal, where the bull is not killed, the fight is between the bull and the *rejeonadore* who rides a highly schooled horse in what may be termed dressage at the gallop. This school of riding is probably closer to the classical ideal than any other, for the classicism of the Renaissance was really a simulation of the movements which a schooled charger was asked to perform on the battlefield.

The Romans were a vigorous, practical people, excellent organisers and administrators with a genius for rational thought and action. They were not great horsemen but they were good horse-breeders, organising breeding studs just as well and as systematically as they arranged their services of transport and communication. They made skilful use of the types and breeds in their vast Empire to produce a variety of horses suited to specific purposes. As well as cavalry horses and draught animals, there were parade chargers, racehorses and travelling horses. Importantly, because even the Roman road-builders could not provide a complete network of easily passable routes, there were also pack horses. Probably these were common in type but along with mules were invaluable in rough country.

Although not natural horsemen, the Romans were efficient horsebreeders and produced different types of horses for various purposes.

Many of the breeds which developed in Europe, and even much of the stock which ultimately was to create an American horse population, had their foundation in the types which had evolved in the Roman Empire by the third century.

Following the final defeat of Carthage, the Iberian Peninsula was open to infusions of hot blood from the north African Barbs. The cross with the indigenous pony produced a quality horse and in these strains ambling horses were often found. Unlike the Greeks, the Romans were enthusiastic about the ambling horse for travelling.

Crossing with the heavier types from northern Europe produced a much bigger, stronger horse, and this 'half-bred' formed the base for the parade horse, *cantherius*, which was also used as a cavalry mount. This 'parade' horse exemplifies the Roman view of the mounted Roman, which was essentially a romantic one. The horse, fiery and animated, complemented the rider of a similar outlook and increased the warlike stature of both.

Roman generals understood very well the nature of command, and it would have been inconceivable for one to have led a cavalry charge from six lengths in advance of his front rank, even had he been a horseman by inclination. Roman officers influenced the battle from its centre and between the leading and reserve formations, from which point they were in a position to command.

When they entered Rome in triumph they either did so in a 'triumphal' chariot, drawn by as many as ten horses, or they rode a snorting *cantherius*, rolling 'the collected fire under his nostrils' and picking up his feet in the lofty, animated trot which Xenophon knew and practised and which ultimately became the *passage*, the supreme movement of the dressage test. To encourage this movement – which is natural to the horse in moments of high excitement – Roman horsemasters fitted the pasterns (the area between hoof and fetlock joint) with wooden rollers, a ploy also used by the Parthians. They cause the limbs to be elevated, and are still used on American breeds such as the Saddle Horse, the Tennessee Walker and so on, to emphasise what most of us consider to be an artificial gait.

After the Punic Wars Iberia became the most important of the horse-breeding provinces, acting as a remount centre for the cavalry and supplying quality horses all through the western Empire. But for centuries before that Rome had relied upon its infantry. Early legions were made up of three thousand foot soldiers supported by three hundred, usually irregular, horsemen. By the third century a third of the army was mounted, but the accent was always on the employment of neighbouring auxiliaries for the cavalry arm. Foremost were the Numidians of north Africa, whose presence under the command of Hannibal had led to the defeat of the legions three hundred years previously, and the Mauritanians, who had served with Caesar. Also employed as cavalry *foederati* were the mysterious X Group, of unknown but Negro race. Their burial mounds and artefacts fill the Nile Valley in the area of the present-day Egyptian–Sudanese frontier. Without any doubt these people, employing saddles but no stirrups, were among the first to use the shock-tactic of the cavalry charge and to carry the lance underarm rather than using it overhand as a stabbing spear. By the third century Marcus Aurelius was using Bedouin, Syrian and Iturian cavalry, all mercenaries, against the Persians on the eastern borders of the Empire, and opposing the invasions of barbarian horsemen in the north of Italy with Goth cavalry.

However, it was not until the reforms of the Emperor Galliensis (206–68) that Roman cavalry was really organised so as to be employed with maximum effect. Armour had been copied from the Persians and improved upon; the system of remount studs provided ample cavalry horses, but the real problem was not solved until Galliensis reorganised the command structure which traditionally was centred on the legion. His solution was to form independent corps of cavalry with their own command chains. Cavalry was thus able to be used *en masse* according to the needs of the situation and could be brought swiftly into action without the delays occasioned by a more involved chain of command.

Cavalry continued to develop under Diocletian and Constantine, the Roman cavalry arm being divided into *clibanarii*, the light cavalry used to provide a swiftly moving shield for the army's flank, as well as for harassment, reconnaissance and pursuit, and the heavy cavalry, the *catafracti*, who employed the shock-tactic of the lance held underarm or with both hands. These were the forerunners of the Frankish knights who became central to the Age of Chivalry five hundred years later.

Another Roman contribution was the horseshoe, which, in fact, was borrowed from the Celts, a people experienced in working with iron. It is likely that the Celts were using shoes in the pre-Christian era, largely because the wet climate of northern Europe made a form of protection for the foot necessary. Wet conditions encourage the foot to spread and the water wears away much of the horn's protective covering, causing the hoof to break and the foot to become sore. Horses in hot, dry climates develop smaller feet, often being what is termed 'boxy' in appearance, that is, narrow and somewhat upright. The heels tend to close and the underside of the foot, including the frog, comes much higher off the ground than would be acceptable in Europe. The horn is very hard and capable of standing up to wear without the protection of an iron shoe. Wear will, of course, occur in rough terrain, when the frog will come into contact with the ground and thus fulfil what is held to be its natural function.

Northern mercenaries in the employ of Rome would certainly have used shoes, but to what extent the Romans themselves made use of them is less certain. There is considerable evidence to show that draught horses wore the iron 'hipposandal' but very little to show the general use of shoes on riding horses, at least not for a long time. The 'hipposandal' would not in any case have been a practical proposition on a riding horse, being far too clumsy for work at speed. One must conclude that the Celts were using a lighter, more refined shoe.

The Greeks did not employ shoes, although Xenophon was taught by Armenians how to protect feet with sacking-type boots. Mention is also made by Xenophon of mules shod with plaited fibre shoes and Aristotle in 346 BC described horses being equipped with the same sort of protection.

By the year 376 the Huns were pressing hard on the frontiers of the Roman Empire. Almost twenty years before the heavy, mail-clad Roman cavalry shattered the Germanic hosts at Strasbourg, Rome's supremacy was already being threatened by the Huns, who with the advantage of the stirrup, could use their galloping horses as a steady platform from which to fire a deadly rain of arrows. Initially, Roman diplomacy secured the cooperation of a sizeable number of Goth horsemen against the Huns, employing them as mercenaries. But disaffection soon set in, and the Goths, together with mercenary Huns, confronted the armies of Rome under the Emperor Valens at Adrianople in 378. The steadfast legions, closing their ranks, were first decimated by Hun archers, then died where they stood under waves of massed Goth horsemen charging with sword and lance. Valens was killed along with forty thousand Romans. These Goth charges heralded the ascendancy of heavy cavalry in Europe and ended forever the myth of Roman invincibility.

Forty years later Rome was sacked by Alaric's Goths and in 451 it fought its last battle, the biggest cavalry engagement of the ancient world, against the Hun Attila at the Catalaunian Fields. In the event the battle was not decisive, but within twenty years the Roman Empire fell. The horsemen of the steppes retreated to the plains of eastern Europe to fight among themselves, but remained, as mercenaries, a powerful force on the battlefields of Europe for the next hundred years.

Chapter 7

DEFENDERS OF THE FAITH

With the fall of Rome and the dissolution of the Hun Empire following the death of Attila in 453, the frontiers of a tiring civilisation were held by the Byzantine Empire, itself in a chronic state of warfare with Persia.

The Byzantines, largely through their greatest general, Belisarius (500–65), maintained their frontiers and their supremacy by creating a formidable cavalry based on what might be termed the all-purpose trooper. Originally Byzantium employed Hun mercenaries (horse-archers from the Caspian) as well as a heavy cavalry made up of Goths, Thracians and Lombards. They quickly adopted the stirrup (they are thought by some to have invented it) and incorporated, too, much of the mounted tactics and the weapons of the nomads into their own system.

They even used the same battle formations as the Avars (the Exiles), a Hun tribe which enjoyed a short-lived dominion in eastern Europe. The Avars, quarrelling with their neighbours and under attack from the Chinese on their border, turned their back on China and, like their nomadic predecessors, swept westwards across the steppes towards the Danube. They settled in Hungary, from whence they plagued Byzantium with continuous raiding. They stayed in Europe for nearly 250 years until Charlemagne's final mopping-up operations in 791–96, after which they and what culture they had simply disappeared. The only trace of them that remains are the stirrups found in their burial mounds – the same stirrups that they had introduced along their route from Mongolia to the Danube. The Allans took the Avar stirrup, so did a whole motley of Germanic tribes. The Persians were swift to appreciate its value and, of course, the Byzantines also. The Avar stirrup even went deep into northern Europe, carried by Viking traders and marauders. They have been excavated from graves as far north as Sweden, so perhaps those pernicious horsemen did make some useful contribution to the world's history.

Belisarius, drawing from the best aspects of the nomad practice, produced a new system of tactics, laid down clearly and comprehensively in the military manual *Strategicon*, written either by or under the direction of the Emperor Maurice Tiberius.

Byzantine troopers rode in a substantial saddle using stirrups. They

It was Attila's proud boast that, where his horse's hoof had stepped, no blade of grass would ever grow again.

Faced by Attila, the Christian world united briefly to defend their faith.

wore armour, but not of a pattern or weight which would have inhibited their movement. They had three-quarter length mail coats, rounded helmets, breeches which were not unlike those used by Scythian warriors a thousand years earlier, and long boots made of leather. Because their horses were bigger than the nomad ponies and, because it was sometimes necessary to control them without reins, they also wore prick spurs.

They were armed with a greater variety of weapons than mounted men had ever carried before. On the back of the shield they carried a selection of feathered darts for throwing or stabbing; they carried lances, broadswords, and a reinforced armour-piercing bow with its complement of arrows.

A previous weakness in the use of the mounted soldier was that once he had discharged his weapons—javelins or arrows—he was dependent on his sidearms until he could obtain replacements. To a large degree the comprehensive armoury of the Byzantine trooper overcame the difficulty.

On the other hand, such heavily armoured men, riding big horses, had to be considerable horsemen if they were to be capable in practice of the versatility which, in theory, so many weapons bestowed upon them. They were both heavy lancers, able to use the shock tactic, and light horse archers who had to string and fire their bows at the gallop, riding without reins while doing so. Since they were remarkably successful, one presumes that they were very capable horsemen indeed and highly disciplined.

Belisarius smashed the Vandals in Africa in 534–35 and in 553 the Byzantine cavalry rode down the Ostrogoths by the walls of Rome. So effective was their cavalry that ultimately, under the Emperor Heraclius, they were able to get rid of their long-time adversaries, the Persians, who had been a continual threat on their eastern frontiers.

Byzantine itself, however, fades in comparison with the Arabs who, in one of the greatest and most significant conquests in history, reached the Great Wall of China and came within an ace of enveloping Europe. There never was an occupation of so great an area which bestowed so many cultural riches upon the conquered, nor any war waged, ostensibly, for higher motives. Its purpose was evangelical, an expansion not of possessions but of the Islamic faith. And it was made possible by the possession of horses which were of superior quality to any other. It was said of them that 'from Malaysia to Morocco the Muslim faith was "founded in the hoofprints of the Arabian horse." '

Initially, the Arabs were by no means horsemen. They had ridden camels and dromedaries with Alexander and had sometimes been employed in the same transport role by the Romans. But by the fourth century their use of the horse had increased considerably and an

The Bruce before Bannockburn,
where the fallibility of heavily
armoured cavalry was
demonstrated by the defeat of the
English by the more mobile,
swiftly-moving light horsemen of
the Scots.

Opposite page: Symbolic of the
militaristic Japanese state was the
warrior horseman of noble birth,
the Samurai. The traditional and
necessary accomplishments of this
highly professional military caste
included skill at ju-jitsu, fencing,
archery and horsemanship.

Charge of the Samurai. The élite of
Japanese chivalry in action at the
Battle of the Shizugatake Pass
during the Japanese Civil War of
1583.

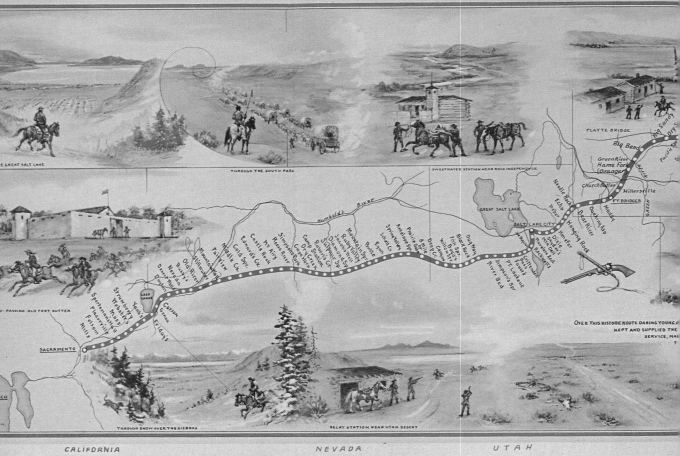

FLATTE BRIDGE

Big Bend

Big Sandy

Dry S

Pacific Sp

Green River
Hams Fork
(Granger)

Millersville

Churchbutter

FT. BRIDGER

Needle Rock

Hanging Rock

Echo

Weber

Duckling Sp

Muddy

Bear River

Dixie

Hunter

SALT LAKE CITY

GREAT SALT LAKE

Humboldt   River

Simpson's Sp
Reese River
Mt. Airy
Castle Ck.
Edwards Ck.
Cold Spr.
Middle Ck.
Fairview
Simpson Park
Dry Creek
Camp Station
Roberts Ck.
Sulphur Sp
Jacobs Well
Ruby Valley
Mountain Spr.
Antelope Spr.
Spring Valley
Schell Ck.
Egan
Deep Ck.
Willow Spr.
Fish Spr.
Black Rock
Dug Way

Pt. Lookout
Simpson's Sp
Fort
Crittenden
Rush Valley
Faust
Pt. Lookout
Camp
Floyd
ROCKWELL'S
River Bed

Mormon
Station

Stillwater
Old River
Bucky's
Nevada
Desert
Dayton

Yank's
Strawberry
Webster's
Moore's
Sportsman's
Placerville
Folsom
Mills

Carson
Genoa
Friday's

LAKE
TAHOE

SACRAMENTO

Passing Old Fort Sutter

OVER THIS HISTORIC ROUTE DARING YOUNG
KEPT AND SUPPLIED THE
SERVICE, MAI
T

THROUGH SNOW OVER THE SIERRAS   RELAY STATION NEAR UTAH DESERT

CALIFORNIA   NEVADA   UTAH

ISSUED BY THE AMERICAN PIONEER TRAILS ASSOCIATION IN COMMEMO

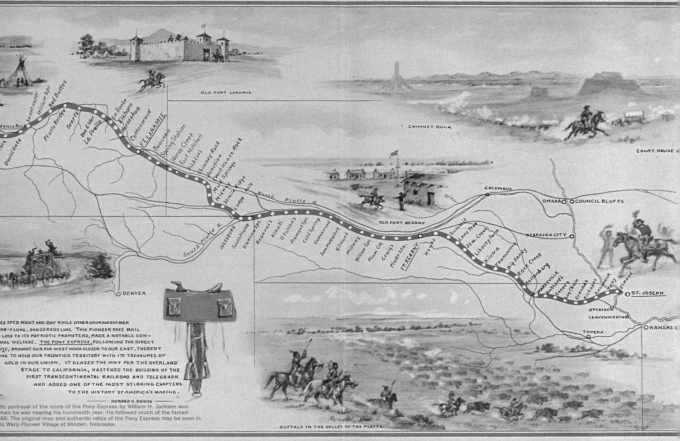

Although short-lived, the Pony Express quickly became central to the legend of the American West. This map shows the 1966-mile (3164-km) mail route from St Joseph, Missouri to Sacramento, California.

By the late nineteenth century, the carriages and turn-outs of the well-to-do New Yorkers were just as important as a lady's silk finery or the fashionable cut of a gentleman's coat.

BUFFALO BILL'S WILD WEST
AND CONGRESS OF ROUGH RIDERS OF THE WORLD.

ON THE STAGE COACH · THE ORIGINAL DEADWOOD COACH, MOST FAMOUS VEHICLE IN HISTORY.

Without the horse what form would American folk history have taken, and what substitute could there have been for the Western film?

REGISTERED AT THE G. P. O. AS A NEWSPAPER.

THE MILLION

· EDITED · = BY = GEO. NEWNES.

No. 39, Vol. 2.]   FOR THE WEEK ENDING SATURDAY, DECEMBER 17, 1892.   [Price One Penny.

enormous impetus was given to breeding and ownership when Mohammed gave the Arabian horse an important place in the Islamic religion.

Mohammed died in 632 but within a decade his successor Abubekr had led his fanatical desert warriors to conquer the most valued possessions of the Byzantine Empire: Syria, Palestine, Mesopotamia, Armenia and then, between 639 and 643, North Africa itself. When they had taken the Mediterranean islands they were poised to attack Constantinople itself.

With their swiftly moving horsemen on steeds of great speed and stamina, they destroyed the Persian army, whose cavalry was much heavier, in 642. They reached the Indus valley twenty years later. In the following century, between 706 and 716, Islam controlled the whole cockpit of central Asia encompassed by Khorasan, Bokhara, Samarkand and Ferghana. But they could not get beyond the Great Wall into China.

In 711, the Moorish followers of Mohammed crossed the Strait of Gibraltar into Spain, where they met and defeated the last of the Visigoth Kings, Roderic. With the whole of the Iberian Peninsula secured they advanced over the Pyrenees and thrust into Gaul.

For a time it appeared that Christendom was in danger of total eclipse and that Europe would be overrun by the Muslims. The Frankish kingdom of Gaul was ill equipped to oppose them. After the fall of Rome, Gaul had declined. Equestrian civilisations were in a state of decay; their powerful mounted arms had gone. The last of the Merovingian Kings of Gaul had been reduced to travelling in an ox-cart, and when the Franks had fought against the Goths in Italy in 539 and 552 they had done so as infantry, with only their King and his bodyguard mounted. Without cavalry support it was impossible for the Franks even to have brought the Moors to battle, let alone have any hope of defeating them.

But now the scene was set for yet another of those momentous historical landmarks. Under repeated attacks from the Moors and conscious of their growing strength, Charles Martel, the first minister to the Frankish King, set about the re-organisation of the Frankish army. The new emphasis was to be on a strong mounted arm of heavily armoured knights, the forerunners of the 'steel wall' of Western chivalry.

One hundred years after the death of Mohammed, in 732, Charles Martel and his armoured cavalry met the Moorish invaders at Poitiers. Just as the epic battle of the Catalaunian Fields represented a turning point for both Rome and the Hun Empire of Attila, this battle signalled the ultimate defeat of the Moors, even though they continued to occupy the Iberian Peninsula for almost another seven

Opposite page: **The circus tradition is essentially equestrian–based and has its roots in the circuses of Ancient Greece, Rome and Byzantium, in which the horse was the central factor.**

Charles Martel, the 'Hammer of Christendom', began life in service to the last of the Frankish Kings. He may have even entered Paris, as this picture suggests, but probably using stirrups.

The Battles of Tours and Poitiers, which turned back the Saracen advance into Europe, were in fact one and the same thing. Less easily explained is the presence of the lady.

hundred years, and it marked the resurgence of Christian Europe.

The Muslim horsemen rode short with a bent knee – light men on small, agile horses that were not more than 14 hands high. Their seat was, in fact, not very different from our modern one although they used a shorter stirrup. The lower leg was drawn back and the body weight was positioned over the stirrup, giving them the advantage of mobility: such a seat places the rider's centre of gravity in line with that of the horse and his weight is the least possible encumbrance to the horse's balance and movement. The archer can use his weapon more effectively if he adopts this position and stands in his stirrups like a polo player when he strikes the ball, and it is easier to get the weight behind the sword when it is used in a downward slash.

But this seat, ideal for swiftly moving light cavalry, is no good at all when it meets a charge of heavy, armoured men on heavier horses. The terrific impact of the armoured Frank, braced in his saddle by a long, forward-thrust leg, simply knocked the Muslim cavalry off its feet. The Franks steadily repulsed the repeated attacks of the Moors and then, when the moment was right, went in to counter-attack. The victory was a decisive one, although the Frankish horses were not fast enough to pursue the broken enemy.

Although it may not have seemed so to the Christians at the time, the effects of the Arab conquests were more constructive than otherwise. These were not barbarians, advancing across the world in a welter of blood and leaving behind them nothing but scorched earth. The Arabic invaders brought with them the cultural heritage of the Middle East and Asia, the source of the classicism of antiquity. Europe's cultural riches lay in ruins. Now, as north Africa became an extension of Asia rather than of Europe, the Arabic culture acted as a reinvigorating force that had a profound effect, stretching upwards through Spain and producing ripples which touched the heart of Europe.

In Spain itself the Moorish influence was pervasive and stimulating. The Caliphate of Cordova became a seat of learning and excellence. The Moors introduced their graceful architecture, and brought improvements in agriculture and horticulture, and an appreciation of literature, poetry, philosophy and theology. They delighted in the study of mathematics, medicine and the natural sciences.

But there were other developments, too. Martel had raised his force of mounted knights by making grants of land in return for their services. In doing so he instituted a system which became the dominant factor in the political and social systems of the Middle Ages.

Martel's recognition of the need to establish and maintain a cavalry arm of strength encouraged the breeding of suitable horses, large enough to carry the weight of a knight but also with stamina and courage. What he needed was a cross between Europe's cold-blooded horses, descended from the primitive Forest type, and the hot-blooded Oriental horse which the Arabic invasion had supplied.

It is a popular misconception that early medieval knights rode on horses resembling the modern Shire or Suffolk Punch. Breeds as big as these were not developed until very much later and then only in response to agricultural needs. The Bayeux Tapestry shows clearly the sort of horse employed by the Normans at Hastings in 1066. It is really no more than a light or middleweight hunter type, though smaller than its modern equivalent. The greatest weight those horses would have carried would have been around 16 stone (102kg), for this was some three hundred years before the introduction of plate armour. As a point of comparison, a British cavalry horse of 1914 carried 17–18 stone (108–114kg).

The 'great horse' used between the thirteenth and fifteenth centuries was certainly larger and more ponderous, particularly towards the end of the period when armour for both horse and man was employed to counter the longbowmen's merciless hail of arrows. The fifteenth century charger, at the height of the armoured period, probably carried 30 stone (190kg), which was a very great weight indeed. Furthermore, it was smaller than the present-day Shire, probably resembling the present-day Jutland horse or the now extinct Welsh

GIS·A ICCECI ADERVN A·V SIMVL· ANGLI ET FRA NCI· INPRELIO·· HIC

Although Oriental-type horses were in use at this time, the ones depicted in the Bayeux Tapestry appear to be unusually small.

Charlemagne, the founding father of the romantic image of the knight.

cart horse which was based on the Welsh Cob. To raise a lumbering trot the firm application of long sharp spurs was required. From these horses, which derived from the cold-bloods of northern Europe, came the farm and heavy draught horses of Renaissance times. Until the improvement in roads these were the sort of horses that pulled the early coaches.

Charlemagne, grandson of Charles Martel, making use again of heavily armoured cavalry, was responsible for driving the Moors from northern Spain and for the unification of central Europe. Under him the concept of Christian chivalry, embodied in the knight who became the symbol of order and decency, took firm root. The knight represented the highest ideals of the age; he became the image of right over wrong.

Now it became the turn of mounted Christendom from the west to take the offensive. Ruy Diaz, El Cid, the national hero of Spain, led the era of Reconquista, taking Valencia in 1094. He was, like the *conquistadores* who conquered the Americas, not much more than a 'hired gun'. His philosophy is encapsulated in a reply he made to the query of an admirer: 'Lady, you see the horse sweating and the sword bloody, *that* is how one vanquishes Moors in the field'.

The war horse of El Cid, his renowned Babieca, is worthy of a place in history alongside Alexander's Bucephalus. A horse of the celebrated Andalusian breed, the luxury horse of Europe up to the end of the eighteenth century, he was the ideal of the war horse. Up to weight, handy to ride, quite fast enough for what was required, he was full of the *brio escondido*, the hidden metal, which gave him fire and spirit while he retained his gentle and amenable nature. As befitted the mount of a great General, Babieca was grey, becoming naturally whiter as he grew older. The companion of El Cid for over twenty years of hard campaigning, he is immortalised with his master in the twelfth-century epic, *Poema del Cid*.

Ruy (or Rodrigo) Diaz was born at Vivar near Burgos in Castile around the year 1040. A ruthless freelance (in the original meaning of the word) he became a national hero known by the Arabs as *Al Sid* (the

Lord), which in Spanish became El Cid. He was also known simply as The Warrior (El Campeador).

His godfather, a priest, promised the young Ruy a horse. The Church was much concerned with the breeding of horses throughout Spain's history, some of the best Spanish horses being bred by the Carthusian monks at Jerez de la Frontera (who, charmingly, called their horses' retirement ranch *Galto al Cielo*, 'The Springboard to Heaven'). Horses are still bred there today.

The boy chose a particularly plain colt, at which his godfather cried, '*Babieca*!' (Stupid!) Ruy called the horse that from the day he owned him, and by that name he became famous throughout Spain. Once, when El Cid offered his horse to King Alfonso of Leon and Castile, the king declined, saying 'God forbid that I should take him! A horse like Babieca deserves no other rider than you, my Cid, so that both together you may drive the Moors from the field and go in their pursuit. May God hide his favour from any who would take Babieca from you; for you and this horse have brought us great honour.'

El Cid died in 1099 at Valencia when the Moors were once again besieging the city. Knowing that news of his death would lower the morale of his men, he gave his last macabre order. His body was ingeniously secured upright in Babieca's saddle, his shield was fastened in place, and, wearing his armour and with his sword in his lifeless hand, El Cid led his silent horsemen out of the gates and towards the Moorish encampment exactly at midnight. The knights were dressed all in white and carried white banners. The visor of El Cid's helmet was open and it was said that his bearded face shone with an 'unearthly luminence'.

This ghostly horseman, upright on his white horse with sword held high, was too much for the Moors. Raising the cry that *Al Sid* was risen from the dead, they fled in panic, to be pursued and cut down by the Spanish knights.

El Cid was buried at the monastery of San Pedro de Cardena, near Burgos; his body was later moved to Burgos Cathedral. Babieca went into retirement and no one ever rode him again. He died some two

A perfect example of the seat adopted by the Christian knights.

years later at the advanced age of forty, and was buried outside the gates of the monastery under two elm trees. The exact position of his grave is not now known, but as recently as 1948 a memorial to him was erected on the site of the monastery.

El Cid founded a Christian order of chivalry intent upon the protection of the faith and the liberation of the Iberian Peninsula from the Moors. That liberation began in 1212 with the victories at Las Navas de Tolosa by the combined forces of the kings of Castile and Aragon. After that the Moorish rule in Spain went into decline.

In 1095 Pope Urban II at the Synod of Clermont called on the Christian powers to join in a Crusade to rid the Holy Land of the infidel, in this instance the Seljik Turks who had conquered Palestine a quarter of a century before.

Godfrey de Bouillon led the first Crusade into Asia Minor in 1097 and Jerusalem fell to the power of the knights in 1101. The orders of the Templars, the Knights Hospitallers and the Teutonic Knights thereafter held Jerusalem, if somewhat precariously, against repeated attacks from the Turks.

The Crusades were a knightly duty undertaken in the service of God and one's liege lord. Hundreds of thousands of Christian knights journeyed eastwards to suffer the hardships of the Outremer and did so almost in the way of a pilgrimage. In a sense the Crusades were an aristocratic game, and when they were over or one had had enough of the hardships, there was an attractive alternative in the tournament.

Tournaments developed from nasty little battles fought between gangs of knights roughly equal in number, but they were soon formalised into single combats run under very strict rules. They provided some hope of profit as well as honour, and without too much risk or discomfort. Central to them was the idea of 'courtly love', knights fighting in honour of the married ladies they loved, and usually wearing their tokens. This was not the case in England, where tournaments were regarded rather as serious training for war or occasions for fresh air and exercise!

As well as the ordinary knights, there were also the highly skilled professionals, who toured the tournament circuit rather like modern showjumpers, and made a fair living from the sale of the horses and armour of the knights they defeated, those items being forfeited.

Although the effective use of light cavalry had been amply demonstrated by the Moors and Saracens in the Crusades and earlier by successive hordes of nomad horsemen, western horsemen, having made successful use of heavy, armoured horses, obstinately refused to contemplate change. This unfortunate characteristic plagued the cavalry arm almost up to the time it relinquished the horse.

By the late thirteenth and early fourteenth centuries, armour and weaponry were becoming more and more heavy as western Europe became increasingly concerned with the shattering effect of the shock tactic. That was all very well on suitable ground and so long as it did not limit the manoeuvrability of the horse and inhibit the freedom of the rider. But the increase in weight made it essential to use heavier, less responsive, and therefore less mobile, horses.

The fallibility of heavy armour in medieval warfare was made abundantly clear at Bannockburn in 1314. There, Robert the Bruce, placing the forces of Edward II at a disadvantage by his choice of ground, defeated an English army of four thousand mounted knights and ten thousand foot. The English cavalry were literally bogged down in the marshy, broken ground because of the weight of their armour. The Bruce, using light cavalry mounted on rough Highland ponies, was able to destroy the English foot soldiers while their supporting cavalry lay helpless among the bogs and ditches and were dealt with by the Scottish foot soldiers.

Edward was unable to employ his longbowmen effectively against

At Bannockburn, the intelligent use of cavalry by the Scots outmanoeuvred and crushed the numerically far superior English knights. Robert the Bruce, however, had learned his tactics from the English.

the Scottish spearmen, his archers being charged and broken by the Scottish light horse before they could be properly deployed. Previously, English longbowmen had operated with devastating effect against the Scots, a fact which was neither realised nor appreciated by the cavalry of Europe.

Bannockburn caused the English to change to 'hobilars', light horsemen who wore leather jerkins, carried swords and spears, and rode quick-moving, sure-footed ponies. The French, meanwhile, clung to their gloriously arrayed knights and put their trust in the ability to deliver the *coup de grâce* in an earth-shattering charge.

They knew better after Crécy in 1346. Here the longbow fulfilled every bit of its potential as the most deadly weapon of the Middle Ages. Stationed on the English flanks, the longbowmen reduced the French cavalry to a chaos made even more terrible by the plunging of panic-stricken wounded horses.

Inevitably, to counter the longbow, plate armour replaced mail, but that was no good unless the horse was armoured similarly. By 1415 French armour was of grotesque proportions. Like the early tanks of the First World War in the mud of the Somme, the French cavalry at Agincourt floundered to a halt like some prehistoric mastodons and Henry V's light horsemen finished them off at will.

When gunpowder came to be increasingly used there was no longer room for the knight on the battlefield. The tournament, as a training for war, was similarly irrelevant, and had in any case lost its appeal, along with the idea of chivalry. But the horse itself lost none of its social cachet, and the ability to ride and be seen to ride well remained a highly esteemed attribute of any gentleman. The tournament gave way to the stately carousel, in which gentlemen demonstrated their skill in horsemanship in musical rides.

By the time the Renaissance dawned on Europe it was time for the horse to play a new role as a partner in the art form which became known as 'classical equitation'.

The Battle of Crécy should have pointed the way to a change of tactics in the use of the Heavy Cavalry. After his defeat of the French, the Black Prince went to the aid of Pedro the Great, the Moorish King of Seville. As a reward for his help the Black Prince received the large ruby which is now the centrepiece of the Imperial State Crown.

Chapter 8

BEYOND THE GREAT WALL

Nowhere in history has the distinction between the nomadic herds-man and the settled agriculturalist been so clearly drawn as it was between the cultured Chinese civilisation, east and north east of the Great Wall, and the restless, Asiatic nomad on the other.

> According to the system established . . . those to the north of the Great Wall, the nations which draw the bow, shall live under the rule of Shan-yu. Within the Great Wall . . . I have mastery. I command my people to till and weave; you command your people to hunt wild beasts for food and clothing.

This was how Emperor Wen wrote to the nomad leader Shan-yu in 162 BC when an uneasy armed truce, frequently broken by the nomad raiding parties, was in operation.

Sections of the Wall had been built by individual states following the decline of the Chou power in the fourth century BC; which had resulted in the break-up of the Empire. Almost two hundred years later the reunification of China was effected by the kingdom of Ch'in. In the north west of China, it was in constant contact with its nomadic, horse-riding neighbours, many of whom it absorbed into its own society. Under the Ch'in dynasty, largely in the time of the Emperor Ch'in Shih Huang Ti, the Wall was completed to an unbroken length of some 1,400 miles (2,253km). It is acknowledged as one of the eight wonders of the world and is one of the few objects on earth easily identifiable from outer space.

The purpose of the Wall was a simple one: it was built to keep out the Asiatic Huns. It was, in a sense, the line of demarcation between settled order and a violent fluidity – in the pre-Christian world it was almost the division between darkness and light. Importantly, it represented the limit of nomadic expansion eastwards and contri-buted, in the end, to the recoil of the Asiatic horsemen towards the west and the resultant descent of Europe into the Dark Ages.

The threat of the nomadic horse tribes of the north dominated Chinese military thinking for two thousand years, the obsession often resulting in a neglect of their defences elsewhere. To some degree, it explains China's inability to defend its eastern seaboard in the nineteenth century against European invaders. Even today, the feeling

The Great Wall of China, which was the symbolic division between the sedentary farmer and the pastoral nomad, a diversification of interests that was to continue until modern times.

of vulnerability is not entirely dispelled, for modern China maintains cavalry divisions in the north west to keep the frontier and to keep an eye on the neighbours.

In China people took to riding horses late in the day, some four centuries after cavalry had replaced the chariot in the Near East, for instance. The Ch'in, like the Romans, were practical people and excellent organisers. They were able not only to plan and to instigate, but also to implement effectively – the mark of people with the ability to govern. Under the Ch'in there was a standardisation of the writing system, of weights and measures and of axle widths so that the roads could be used more effectively (roads were classified for narrow-gauge vehicles, broad-gauge vehicles, and those that were wide enough for wagons to pass one another or to take three wagons abreast). Advances were made in harnessing horses to wheeled vehicles which culminated in the invention of the breeching and collar.

The Ch'in laid the foundations for an Empire which was to last upwards of two thousand years, and in which aspirations in art, literature and the sciences were encouraged and flourished. They became horsemen, or rather they created bodies of professional horsemen by design rather than by natural inclination, appreciating that if their Empire was to be free of its troublesome neighbours it would be necessary to adopt some of their strategy.

The enemy on the frontier caused the Ch'in to concentrate more on the use of mounted troops after first obtaining and then breeding a superior type of horse for their use. Up to the third century BC the Chinese had relied principally on infantry borne in carts, an altogether too cumbersome arrangement to stand up to the hard-riding, swiftly moving nomads. The change came with the Emperor Wu Ti, whose martial spirit would not countenance a policy of appeasement. The nomadic people of the north, under the leadership of the tribe called Hsiung-hu (hence the name Huns) had formed a great confederation.

They were a highly organised society with allegiance to one leader, the Shan-yu. To hold the federation together it was necessary for the numerous chieftains to acknowledge the sovereignty of the Shan-yu, and that would be achieved only by the provision of sufficient booty. The greater the amount which could be obtained, the greater was the standing of the chieftain within his tribe and the more secure was the federation and the position of the Shan-yu at its head.

Wu Ti, resolving upon direct action against the nomadic people, challenged the leadership of the Shan-yu by refusing to pay what was frequently a humiliating tribute – at one period the Hsiung-hu were demanding numbers of well-born virgins. In retaliation the Huns broke through the Wall and attempted to overrun China. Initially, because of their highly developed techniques in the use of mounted forces, they penetrated deep into Chinese territory, easily disposing of the Chinese cavalry and out-manoeuvring the slow-moving infantry trains. A Chinese official recorded that 'the Chinese horses cannot vie with their horses in climbing rocky heights or fording mountain torrents, nor our horsemen with theirs, in galloping over steep paths or shooting arrows while in rapid motion.'

To remedy the position, Emperor Wu Ti sent envoys to Bactria to buy breeding stock of the Golden Horses of Samarkand, descendants of Alexander's Nisean horses. These horses are called by several names – the Heavenly Horses, the Celestial Horses, the 'blood-

More than two thousand years ago, the Chinese, as great innovators of equestrian equipment, introduced this breast harness which was used with vehicles of surprisingly modern design.

The Chinese believed that the horse would be as important in the next world as it was in this. These terracotta figures date from the Qin Dynasty and were found near the junctures of the Ba, Wei and Qing Rivers.

sweating' breed, later the Ili. They were obtainable around the area of Tayuan on the upper Syr Darya river (Jaxartes) in Turkestan and on the other side of the Tien Shan mountains in Ferghana – the very areas which from antiquity had been concerned with the breeding of the best type of horses. From the Ili and the Ferghana horses, which were probably not too different, descend the Akhal-Teke, a golden horse if ever there was one, whose coat has a unique metallic sheen, and the Turkmene, a horse that combines enormous powers of endurance with considerable speed.

There can be little doubt that many of these horses exhibited the spotted coat pattern and characteristics of what is now called the Appaloosa, a breed raised by the Nez Perce Indians of Idaho along the valley of the Palouse river. Numerous Chinese artefacts depict this coat colouring. 'Blood sweating', which occurs in horses of this colouring more frequently than it does in others, is caused by a subcutaneous parasite which brings about minimal bleeding when the horse is active in warm weather. Sweat mixes with the blood to form a pink-coloured paste. The parasite is common in Central Asia but isolated instances of 'blood sweating' also occur in Europe, and there is evidence of Arabian horses displaying the phenomenon, particularly when there is a patch of different pigmentation on the shoulder or when the horse is flecked, as in the case of roans.

The Emperor's envoy Chang Ch'ien visited these areas between 138 and 126 BC. On his second mission he was in contact with the Wu-sun, who lived in the Ili valley south of Lake Balkhash. Twice the Wu-sun presented large studs of horses to the Chinese Imperial Court and thereafter Wu Ti sent up to ten trade missions every year to the western states of Aorsi, Tayuan, the Yueh-chi and Parthia. Horses were obtained in exchange for Chinese silk, jade and coral.

All went well until the ruler of Ferghana refused to trade any more and had the Chinese envoys put to death. As a result, in 104 BC, Wu Ti sent an invading army over the three thousand miles separating him from the source of the Heavenly Horses in order to seize them by force. But the expedition, under the command of the brother of Wu Ti's favourite concubine, was an unmitigated disaster and costly in terms of men and precious horses.

Two years later a second expedition was despatched with more success. It returned with thirty pure-bred horses and three thousand half-bred mares and stallions. The cost of these incursions was very high. It was estimated at several hundred thousand troops, as well as the accompanying equipment commensurate with such numbers, and in one year the Chinese may have lost as many as a hundred thousand horses.

There seems to be no doubt that the object of these large-scale operations was to obtain a supply of quality cavalry horses, faster and stronger than the steppe ponies, which would allow the Chinese armies to inflict punishing defeats on the nomad peoples. Having acquired them, the Chinese lost little time in creating breeding studs. In the Tang dynasty of the seventh century, stud farms for over three quarters of a million horses were established in the limestone steppes of the north which supported hard grasses rich in protein. Alfalfa was imported into China to be grown for fodder as early as 111 BC.

Wu Ti formed armies in which the cavalry was a major component. The bow was retained for light formations but the heavy cavalry, riding in wood framed saddles, wore flexible link-type armour and had as their weapons the two-edged broadsword and a lance. The establishment of cavalry of this calibre had far-reaching results. Through Wu Ti's expeditions Chinese influence spread into central Asia, opening up trade routes for commerce of all sorts both in and out of China. The effect on Chinese civilisation was profound.

As a further and lasting by-product there was a change in Chinese clothes as a result of the long conflict with the nomads. To ride effectively, the Chinese discarded their flowing robes for more practical tunics, trousers and boots similar to those worn by Asian horsemen. Since then, little has altered, modern Chinese clothes being virtually the same as those worn by the first Chinese cavalrymen.

Although China never bred horses specifically for draught, the peaceful uses in which horses were employed were not exceeded elsewhere in the pre-Christian era other than in Rome. For centuries, however, China maintained a powerful cavalry arm. When the Sung rulers lost control of the horse-breeding areas in the north their decline and ultimate defeat by opponents combining administrative ability with the effective use of the horse became inevitable.

This combination was possible only along China's northern frontiers, from whence came the great conquerors of China, the Mongols and the Manchus. The Manchus ruled for nearly three hundred years and when they fell in 1912 it was not to the nomadic horsemen from the north but to the onslaught of the modern world.

Following the example of their nomadic neighbours, the Chinese rode with the shortened stirrup and bent knee, which is reminiscent of the modern seat.

御渾故位武 ᠪᠣᡤᡩᠠ

太祖輕之遂與金絕及病革謂左右曰金精
難以驟破若假道於宋宋金世仇必能許我

直擣大梁金
闋然千里赴
破之必矣言
二十二年號
壽六十六

THE DEADLY HORSEMEN

Chapter 9

In the course of civilisation there have been many times when people could have been forgiven for imagining that the Four Deadly Horsemen had been loosed to do their work in preparation for the end of the world. Both Huns and Moors struck fear and awful dread in the hearts of men, but they could not compare with the Mongol hordes of Genghis Khan, who inspired absolute terror.

In 1206 Genghis Khan moved into northern China and in the space of twenty years his hordes had stormed through Cathay, roared like a whirlwind of destruction across Asia into eastern Europe and had reached the banks of the Danube. The destruction of life and property they caused is incomprehensible, even when judged beside the two world wars of the twentieth century. They did not so much destroy what lay in their path as obliterate it entirely.

Prayers were offered continually in the churches in the thirteenth century for deliverance from the Mongols. Muslims as well as Christians were convinced that the end of the world was at hand in a holocaust of fire and blood, and that the Mongols represented a supernatural power.

Frederick II of Germany, writing to Henry III of England, concluded that these terrible horsemen were the punishment of God, visited upon Christendom for its sins. Roger Bacon was more explicit. To him the Mongols were the soldiers of Antichrist come to reap the last dreadful harvest, as prophesied by St Jerome, who had spoken of the race of 'Turks' that would come from the land of Gog and Magog, behind the mountains of Asia: 'A race polluted and unwashed using neither wine nor salt nor wheat'.

Mongol babies were toughened up by daily dips in ice-cold water. Thereafter, not surprisingly, they forsook water as a cleansing agent. Clothes, repositories for food and the rancid mares' butter which was used in all sorts of delicacies, were never washed, only eventually replaced. One can understand how it was that with the wind in the right direction, the approach of a Mongol army could be smelled up to twenty miles away.

Genghis Khan was a King at the age of 13 and he succeeded like no other nomadic leader, not even Attila, in uniting the Mongol tribes while commanding an awe-inspiring personal loyalty. This illiterate

Genghis Khan, an illiterate nomad but the world's greatest cavalry general.

Kublai Khan, whose armies
were the first victims of attack
by *Kamikaze*.

but enormously charismatic son of the Gobi Desert (next to the polar regions perhaps the ultimate wasteland of the earth) was recognised as the Kha Khan, the Power of God on Earth, the Scourge of God, the Emperor of Mankind, the Mighty Manslayer, the Perfect Warrior and the Master of Thrones and Crowns. Genghis Khan contented himself by having his seal engraved thus: 'God in Heaven. The Kha Khan, the Power of God, on Earth'.

But for all this, the Mongol contribution to the advancement of man, horse, or anything else, is minimal. The Empire of Genghis Khan lasted for less than a hundred years and though its influence persisted for a limited time it was never a major factor in world events. It was, if anything, a transitory interruption, violent and destructive – a sort of earthquake in the overall affairs of mankind. It bore out, indisputably, the remark of a contemporary Chinese general, Yeh-lu T'su T'su, who said of the Mongol dominion: 'the Empire was won on horseback, but you cannot govern on horseback'.

The positive effects of the 'Pax Mongolica' were to open up once more the Silk Road to trade and to cultural exchange between Europe and China. Muslim dominance of the Near East had been ended, and the reunification of China in 1279 by Genghis's grandson Kublai Khan created a base for new and more culturally active empires in the future.

Kublai Khan attempted the invasion of Japan using South Korea as his base. The Japanese had been introduced to the horse via Korea some time during the third century. In 682 a Japanese decree stated that 'in a government, military matters are an essential thing. All Civil and Military Officials should therefore sedulously practise the use of arms and riding on horseback'. By the eleventh century the Japanese noble, the warrior horseman, was the armoured knight and was involved in a feudal system not unlike that of Europe. Japan became a militaristic state symbolised by the mounted warrior, the romantic view of the Japanese Middle Ages being the 'Trinity of the Horse, the Warrior and the Flower'. The obligatory accomplishments of the Samurai warrior knight were 'skill in horsemanship, archery, fencing and ju-jitsu'.

These two widely differing societies, the Mongol and the Japanese, were now destined to meet in a confrontation whose outcome depended not on their skill at arms but upon a whim of nature. Kublai Khan landed at Hakata in 1274 and his superior forces seemed likely to overwhelm the Japanese, but a sudden storm forced their withdrawal. They returned seven years later with a strength of a hundred and fifty thousand but could make no impression on the improved Japanese defences. Nor did they take note of another impending storm: the typhoon known as the *Kamikaze* (the Wind of Heaven) sank nearly the whole of Kublai Khan's armada and drowned most of his army.

The last of the Mongol nomads, the Tartars, were on the move less than a hundred years later under another of Genghis Khan's descendants, Tamurlane, who sought to resurrect the Empire of his ancestors. Tamurlane became the ruler of Samarkand in 1369 and from there he set off to conquer the world. In rapid campaigns he conquered Asia and the Near East, threatening to destroy the Turkish Empire and to drive on into eastern Europe. But he died in 1405 and his Empire broke up, leaving behind a memory of death and destruction accomplished brilliantly on the backs of horses.

Along with Genghis Khan and his principal Orkhons (divisional commanders), Tamurlane was among the greatest cavalry commanders in history, and was possibly the most capable. Notable European Generals, such as Gustavus Adolphus of Sweden, King John of Poland and even Napoleon, made serious studies of Tamurlane's campaigns. All, in one form or another, adopted his *tulughma*, the 'standard sweep' that turns the enemy's flank to take him in the rear.

Tamurlane was also responsible for making substantial improvements in the quality of his horses by continual introductions of Arab blood. It is as the last great horse society that the Mongol hordes are deserving of attention and respect. No cavalry arm in the history of the world was so brilliantly effective.

Mongol armies were composed solely of horsemen, although they had a siege division, a *tuman*, (i.e. ten thousand men) under a Cathayan officer, the *Ko pau yu*, or Master of Artillery. The connotation of 'hordes' (the term used by the Mongols themselves) is somewhat misleading. It implies a huge rabble of mounted men, each acting individually, but nothing could be further from the truth. The armies of the Kha Khan were tightly organised and very strictly disciplined.

All the people of the Khan lived under the *Yassa*, the Mongol code of laws which was as comprehensive as the Napoleonic Code established nearly six hundred years later. The *Yassa*, in this military society, was in reality the standing orders for the armies. Every man was compelled to do military service; no warrior was ever to forsake any one of his comrades in the section of ten, the smallest unit in the *tuman*, nor was he ever to leave a wounded man. There were strict rules on looting, which was not permitted while battle was in progress. In action no man was to give or ask quarter; all prisoners were to be killed. Discipline and adherence to the *Yassa* were enforced mercilessly. Here is an extract from an order of the day issued by the Kha Khan during a campaign:

Take care of the led Horses in your troop, before they lose condition. For once they have lost it you may spare them as much as

More ruthless even than Genghis Khan, Tamurlane's Tartars left a pyramid made up of seventy thousand human skulls to mark their visit to Isphan, Persia.

you will, they will never recover it on Campaign . . . You will encounter much game on the march. Do not let the men go after it . . . Do not let the men tie anything to the back of the saddle. Bridles will not be worn on the march – the horses are to have their mouths free. If this is done the men cannot march at the gallop. If an order has been given, then those who disobey it must be beaten and put under arrest. But as for those who have disobeyed my personal orders, send those who are worth serious consideration to me. The rest, the unimportant ones, are to be beheaded on the spot . . .

The essence of the Mongol hordes was that they needed no cumbersome supply train to keep them in the field. They lived off the land and could, when occasion demanded, subsist on their iron rations, dried meat laid under the saddles and dehydrated mares' curds carried in leather bags across the saddle bow. These bags served a dual purpose, being inflated to form a sort of water wing when it was necessary to cross rivers.

The nomad custom of carrying meat under the saddle, or even in the seat of the breeches, was neatly summarised by Samuel Butler:

> . . . his countrymen the Huns
> Did stew their meat between their bums
> And the horses' backs whereon they straddle,
> And every man eats up his saddle.

(*Hudibras*)

Each man had at least three horses, changing from one to another as the *tumans* galloped over the Persian sands or the Russian steppes. Behind the main body came a large herd of horses. These spares followed a bell mare or a man on a lead horse, as was the nomadic custom. The herd served many purposes, and was the supply organisation of the *tumans*, allowing large bodies to cover as much as 80 miles (124km) a day. Two of their greatest commanders, Subutai Bahadur ('The Valiant') and Chepe Noyan ('The Arrow Prince'), pursued the Emperor Mohammed Shah from Samarkand to Afghanistan, followed him to the Caspian Sea and, after his death, drove into the Caucasus and northwards to the Volga before they were recalled to the Gobi Desert, 2,000 miles (3,220km) away. All that took less than two years.

The herd supplied replacement mounts too. The mares gave milk and there was always plenty of fresh meat. On the march blood could be taken from a horse's neck, thickened over heat and then eaten like a black pudding.

But the supporting herd served another more sinister purpose. It helped to create the impression of a vast host. Sometimes the Mongols tied dummies on to the spare horses so that the enemy should think

Even Napoleon studied the classical cavalry tactics of Tamurlane's Tartars. Tamurlane originated the pincer movement, which has been so widely favoured in armoured warfare right up to the present time.

that their force was much bigger than it was. This ploy, carried out by armies down the centuries, may account for the large numbers attributed to the hordes. In fact, the largest army Genghis Khan ever put in the field was about 230,000.

The horses, really ponies, were predominantly of Mongolian type and showed pronounced Przewalskii features. But the Mongols would, of course, in all their journeyings have acquired horses of other breeds. They would hardly have ignored good horses, even if they were only used for food. Ogotai, the son of Genghis Khan, when he forced the surrender of Baghdad, demanded a ransom which included 'tall horses, with long necks of Western breed'.

In battle, they made much use of the swift encircling tactic to take the enemy in the rear and were masters of the feigned withdrawal. They might retreat for perhaps two days then, mounting fresh horses, turn about and recover the distance in less than a day to deliver ferocious assaults on their enemy's extended lines. Invariably the Mongol attacks were preceded by careful reconnaissance, a lesson which frequently took European cavalry a long time to learn.

The Khan trained his troops and occupied them when they were not campaigning by means of the 'Great Hunt', the strict rules of which were incorporated in the *Yassa*. The hunt advanced over perhaps a 100-mile (161-km) front, over all sorts of ground, mountains, rivers and chasms, in a wide semi-circle, driving the game before and allowing nothing to escape. Gradually the circle was closed and then, after the Khan and his nobles had entered the ring and killed their share, the horde was loosed for the slaughter, which might last for a whole day. The hunt involved hard riding and placed premiums on control, command and communication.

To operate effectively over such huge areas the Mongols devised the Yam, a sort of pony express. Relays of messengers galloped along the caravan tracks; they rode 150 miles (242km) a day and it was possible to obtain the return of a divisional commander from a distance of 2,000 miles (3,220km) within only a month. No courier carrying the seal of the Khan would ever be stopped on these journeys; it was said that, with the seal, 'a virgin carrying a pot of gold' could cross the Khan's territories without coming to harm.

Europe was nearly lost on account of the horses with which Genghis Khan built his empire. But perhaps it was also saved by a horse too: in 1227 Genghis Khan died when his horse, startled by a herd of wild horses, reared and came down on him while hunting.

Chapter 10

AMERICA AND THE LAST HORSE PEOPLE

The spirit of exploration was strong in Europe from the thirteenth century onwards. Marco Polo travelled overland to China in the late thirteenth century, served Kublai Khan for many years and returned home to Venice eventually by sea. The fifteenth and sixteenth centuries were the great period of exploration by the Portuguese and Spanish. Inspired by Prince Henry 'the Navigator' of Portugal, a Portuguese fleet explored the coast of Africa, the Azores, Madeira, the Canaries and the Cape Verde Islands, seeking trade routes to the east. In 1488, nearly thirty years after Henry's death, Bartholomew Diaz rounded the Cape of Good Hope and in 1497–98 Vasco de Gama reached India.

The continent of America, on which the horse had been extinct for some eight thousand years and which, even with its mighty empires of the Inca and Aztec, had remained isolated, was ripe for discovery, exploration and, naturally, exploitation.

Columbus, also with the object of pioneering trade routes, made landfall in the Bahamas and the West Indies in 1493 and on subsequent voyages visited South America and the Gulf of Mexico. The new continent was named after a Florentine explorer, Amerigo Vespucci (1451–1512).

Additional impetus was given to the spirit of exploration in Spain when the seven hundred-year-old Moorish occupation of the Iberian Peninsula was brought to an end. The nucleus of skilful professional soldiers, who knew no other trade and were without employment, were spurred on by tales of fabulous wealth and rich pickings to be had for the asking in the New World. It was largely these mercenary adventurers who were the hard core of the Spanish conquests of Mexico and South America.

On the whole they were a pretty unsavoury lot, and the atrocities they committed, often in the name of God but usually in the spirit of unbounded avarice, were marked by a callous disregard for human values that was probably not exceeded until the Nazis rampaged through Europe four centuries later.

Francisco Pizarro (1478?–1541), the prototype thug, and a man of energy and ability, conquered the Incas of Peru in South America,

The power of the horseman was never better demonstrated than in the victories achieved by the *conquistadores'* cavalry over the Aztecs.

while Hernan Cortes (1485–1547), just as able a leader but embodying the better virtues of his age, crushed the Aztecs in Mexico, where he landed in 1519, with a force of only six hundred Spaniards, two hundred and fifty Indians and sixteen horses. 'Next to God, we owed the victory to the horses', he claimed, for they were objects of terror to the natives, who fled panic-stricken before these armoured beasts the like of which they had never seen before.

The psychological effect of an armoured horse and rider, the sixteenth-century equivalent of a tank, must have been considerable. The disciplined Spanish infantry probably did most of the damage, cutting and thrusting with terrible short, sharp swords, but the effect of even a dozen mounted men charging at the gallop into the Indian flank was clearly enormous.

Cortes's sixteen horses reinstated the equine species in the American continent. (Four hundred years later, when America had become the most powerful nation in the world, the horse population was estimated as being upwards of twenty five million – one horse to every three people.) They were documented in considerable detail. There were eleven stallions, two of which were pintos (literally 'spotted', meaning horses with parti-coloured coat patterns), and five mares, and they came principally from the Cordoba breed. Among them was Cortes's own charger, El Morzillo ('The Black One'). Cortes rode this horse on the Honduras expedition of 1524, when his cavalry force had been increased to ninety.

Much of the way was through tropical forest. The expedition had, also, to cope with severe mountain terrain, to cross rivers and to cope with swampland. It was certainly the worst sort of country for cavalry. Eventually the expedition reached the plains surrounding the lake of Peten-Itza. There, very unwisely, the horsemen pursued the abundant game, exhausting their already fatigued horses. They were forced to rest as a result, but when later they advanced over the rough hill country of La Sierra de los Pedernales El Morzillo damaged a foot and was unable to continue. Cortes left the horse in the care of an Indian chief promising to return for him. This was in 1525 and Cortes wrote in his diary: 'The chief promised to take care of him, but I do not know that he will succeed or what he will do with him'.

The superstitious Indians, full of fear and awe for this strange animal, who was associated so closely with the power and strength of the white men, did their best. They housed the horse in a temple, and garlanded maidens served him choice fruits and dishes of chicken. El Morzillo appreciated neither his deification nor his diet, and died. This was a catastrophe for the Indians, who feared reprisals. To propitiate the fury of Cortes they created, with naive inspiration, a statue of El Morzillo. It was a curious thing, depicting the stallion

Like all conquerors, the victorious Cortes is seen mounted on a mettlesome horse for his entry into Mexico.

sitting on his hindquarters with his forelegs outstretched in front of him, in a posture which could have been indicative of his last weak condition.

They placed the statue on one of the many islands in the lake where it became symbolic of the power of the white invaders. In time, awe turned to adoration and the Indians worshipped the statue as Tziunchan, the God of Thunder and Lightning, to whom they prayed and made sacrifice.

Cortes never returned. In 1697, 172 years later, Spanish armies journeyed into Yucatan seeking more wealth to plunder, and behind them came the priests, as acquisitive of spiritual treasure as the *conquistadores* were of gold and silver. Two Franciscans, Fathers Orbieta and Fuensalida, came to the lake. They spoke the Maya language but made no converts, although the people received them well enough. They did, however, destroy numerous idols and images and eventually, on a high platform on one of the last lake islands they visited, they came upon the abomination of the great god Tziunchan. Father Orbieta, 'filled with the Spirit of the Lord and carried off with furious zeal for the honour of God', tore down the effigy, breaking it up with a rock while the onlooking Indians lamented loudly in rage and fear. And that was the end of El Morzillo.

Columbus had taken thirty horses to Hispaniola (Haiti) and by his death in 1506 the Spanish had established breeding studs on the larger islands of the West Indies. By the early years of the seventeenth century they had developed horse-raising settlements in the American south-west, centred particularly around Santa Fe.

It was largely from these concentrations that horses spread north and east and into the possession of the Plains Indians who acquired them through trade or by theft. Some would have been obtained from feral groups, for as early as 1579 there were herds of wild horses in north central Mexico.

There now occurred a new era of equestrian nomadism, almost as though the nomad horse tribes of Asia were being recreated in the New World. There are, indeed, great similarities between the Asian horse peoples and the nomadic society of the American Indian. Shamanism, for example, was a characteristic of both societies. Shamanism, the recognition of the spirits of good and evil which can be influenced only by Shamans (the priest of Asia or the medicine man of American Indian culture), was the religion of the Ural-Altaic peoples of Siberia and, in much the same form, was embraced by the American Indian.

Both peoples made use of the dog long before they had horses; the American Indian of the Plains used dogs for pack transport and for pulling *travois*. Since they had no word for 'horse', they called horses 'big dogs'.

But there were differences. The wealth of the Plains Indians came to lie in horses not, as in Eurasia, in herds of cattle, sheep and goats. Horses were the means of their livelihood because they made the hunting of the buffalo easier. The Indians were hunters on horseback not herdsmen, and they never achieved the advanced social structures of the Eurasian nomad. Nor, of course, did they ever approach their number. It would never have been possible for the Indians to have carried out large-scale offensive operations, far less to create empires like those of the Hun and the Mongol.

The possession of the horse conferred on the Indian a new mobility; it shortened the time taken to move camp and it liberated the Indian woman from the labour involved in transporting possessions, even when there were dogs in plenty, to pull the *travois* and to carry the smaller loads. The horse altered the whole concept of Indian life and created a unique life-style. This all happened within the space of barely two hundred years, during which time the Plains Indians became the last of the world's 'Horse people'. No sooner, however, had that way of life been established than it was destroyed by the incursions of the white settlers.

Like the steppe nomads, the Plains Indian revealed a natural aptitude for horsemanship and used a similar riding style to his Asian counterparts.

The horse culture period of the Indian tribes of the Great Plains has been placed between 1540 and 1880, but for the majority it began considerably later, in some cases as late as the early 1600s. The Pueblo Indians of Mexico, living in an area where horses were easily available, were mounted by 1582, but some of the powerful northern tribes like the Blackfoot did not become horse Indians until around 1730, and the Dakota tribe was still using canoes in 1766.

The early Spaniards did not encourage the Indians to own horses. They preferred to keep the native population in fear and awe of the animals, and encouraged them to think of the horse as a fierce, dangerous creature. They had no objection to the Indian looking upon the horse as a god. After all, 'the native fear of horses was the most effective weapon the Spaniards possessed'.

Inevitably, however, Indians began to be employed as grooms and *vaqueros* to tend the growing herds of cattle. They formed a nucleus of men familiar with the handling of horses and they passed their knowledge on. They would have learnt to ride from watching the Spaniards. 'Once mounted,' wrote Denhardt, 'the Indian with his quiver of arrows was superior to the Spaniard with his single-shot arquebus.'

Towards the end of the horse culture period, when statistics became available, the number of horses owned by some Indian tribes was very large. In total it is estimated that in 1874 some hundred and twenty thousand Plains Indians owned a hundred and sixty thousand horses. Tribes like the Nez Perce, renowned as breeders of the spotted Appaloosa horse, had as many as twelve thousand, while the Cayuse and Umatilla had a ratio of 11.7 horses to one person.

A wealthy Blackfoot owned probably forty horses, but poorer men in the tribe might have had only five or six. A really poor man had fewer than five horses and would often be lent mounts to ride in the hunts for buffalo. The Blackfoot recognised ten types of horse. An average family, to be comfortable, required twelve horses to fulfil the primary requirements of hunting, warfare and moving camp. There was the buffalo and war horse; a winter hunting horse; a riding horse; a *travois* horse; a pack horse; a horse to drag the tepi poles; a racehorse; the stallion; the brood mare and, finally, a lead mare for the grazing herds.

Before the Indian took to horse, buffalo hunting was carried out on foot employing what has become known as 'the surround', which involved the encirclement of a group of buffalo by swift runners who then drove the animals into a semi-circular fence built from up-ended *travois* roped together. The braves then moved in from behind and from each side, killing the buffalo with lance and bow and arrow.

On horseback, the surround method was used again but without

Indian children learned their art from the cradle.

the need of a *travois* fence. The riders encircled the herd and closed in for the kill in much the same way as the Asian horsemen and they carried out the same practice in warfare, where it was possible.

The buffalo horse was of enormous importance to the Indian. Its training and selection were matters on which much time and consideration was spent. Training began at four years, and the horses were carefully looked after, well fed and kept in top condition. Like the medieval knight with his *destrier* (war horse), the Indian led his buffalo horse to the hunting grounds, riding it only during the hunt itself.

The Indian horseman rode with a simple bridle formed of a single length of rope 16–30ft (5–9m) long. Fitted with a loop at one end, the rope was passed round the head and secured round the lower jaw to make a two-rein bridle. The spare end was coiled and placed under the rider's belt. If the rider fell this long rope saved him from losing his horse.

A pad saddle, with girth and stirrups, almost identical to that used by the early Scythians, was used for war and hunting and its use was virtually universal among the Plains Indians.

Women, who made the saddles and all the other items of horse equipment, rode on wood-framed saddles, copied from those of the Europeans and ingeniously constructed. Such saddles were also used for the older members of the tribe and for the children. Covered in deer or elk hide, the wood-framed saddles were high-piqued fore and aft, but one popular pattern, the 'prairie chicken snare', was built lower at cantle and pommel, a design which made mounting more easily accomplished. Both saddles doubled as pack saddles.

Simple equipment seems to have been the hallmark of the 'natural' horseman from the beginnings of history. It is only the 'civilised' horsemen who need to employ severe methods of restraint and who concern themselves with systems based on mechanics. In the nineteenth and twentieth centuries the proliferation of bits, even though no more than variations on the basic forms, was remarkable. It resulted, I think, in riders becoming unduly concerned with the front end of the horse and failing to appreciate that impulsion comes about because of the engagement of the quarters in response to the action of the rider's legs. Happy is the natural horseman who achieves everything he wants with minimum effort and the most elementary equipment.

Whether the American Indian as a rider was in the same class as a Hun or a Mongol might be arguable, but at his best he could not have been far short. Indian children, both boys and girls, learnt to ride at a very early age; for them riding was a fundamental skill.

Mounted bareback, the Indian at the slower paces sat upright with his legs held very much in the fashion of Xenophon's Greeks. At the gallop, he pulled up his knees to adopt the crouch of nomad horsemen the world over. Using stirrups, he rode again with bent knee and short leathers, *a la gineta*, Plains style. This is the classic position for the horse-archer and the lancer. Enormously supple, the Indian could leap on and off his horse at the gallop and was adept at lying along the side of the horse so that the only target offered to the opposition was an inch or two of heel projecting above the horse's back. Plains Indians practised the castration of colts, believing that the operation made the horse more fleet of foot. They always rode geldings to hunt and for raiding parties.

Just as valuable as the buffalo horse were the horses used for racing and they, too, received special attention. The Indians were much addicted to horse-racing and to the opportunities it gave them to gamble. Furthermore, it seems that the Indian pony was more than a match for the often bigger horse of the white man. There are numerous tales of races between Indian ponies and the horses of army officers, and always it is the shaggy Indian pony, discounted by the white officers because of its rough appearance, that in the end wins the big race, on which the Indians have betted heavily, and leaves the field spread out behind him.

The horse made moving from one camping site to another easier and faster, but meant that the Indians for the first time had to consider pasturage. They quickly discovered which grasses were best suited to maintain condition in their horses, and chose their sites accordingly. Indian ponies seem to have managed very well on range feed, wiry grasses being quite sufficient for their needs. Corn was not fed, but the clay around alkali sinks, which would have contained salt and other minerals, was given to horses. In winter the feed of the racers and buffalo hunters was supplemented by quantities of the inner bark of the cottonwood tree.

Shoeing was not practised, but a sore foot was treated by packing it with manure and encasing it in a rawhide boot, a remedy which is by no means unknown today. Medicine men, who might act both as vets and doctors, used a variety of herbs in their medicine.

Selective breeding was certainly in force and the end product, the hardy Indian pony, was a very useful animal – tough, enduring, sure-footed and very fast. By the mid-eighteenth century it was described by Anthony Hendry as being a recognisable type standing about 14 hands high, fine and tractable, lively and clean made. They were by no means beautiful, for their heads were usually common, but they were faster and tougher than the bigger horses used by the US cavalry.

Their origins were the early horses imported by the Spaniards, which had a considerable element of Barb blood crossed with native Spanish stock. These Andalusian horses, as they became generally known, were one of the greatest influences in the development of the world's equine population, along with the Arab and, much later, the Thoroughbred. Because of in-breeding, climatic changes and plain hard work, the Indian pony became reduced in both size and quality, but it did not lose its hereditary constitution. Colonel de Trobriand of the US cavalry wrote in 1867: 'The Indian pony without stopping can cover a distance of from 60 to 80 miles [96–129km] between sunrise and sunset, while most of our horses are tired out at the end of 30 or 40 miles [48–64km]'.

The most gifted breeders of horses were the Nez Perce, who lived in the area around the north-east corner of Oregon, the south-east corner of Washington and the bordering Idaho country. They enforced a strict breeding policy which produced a distinctive type, apart from the colouring. Winter keep for the horses was in the sheltered canyons of the Snake, Clearwater and Palouse rivers, the latter being known loosely as Palouse country. The horses took that name, Palouse horses, which finally became Apalousie and Appaloosa.

By 1877 the US Government was committed to a policy of confining the Plains Indians in reservations and depriving them of their traditional lands. Rather than submit, the Nez Perce fought the US army and, under Chief Joseph, attempted to cross the border into Canada, 1,800 miles (2,897km) away over some of the most mountainous terrain in the West. They mistook the Missouri for the border, and were brought to bay in the Bear Paw Mountains of Montana. Now numbering just 87 warriors, 40 of them wounded, they were finally forced to surrender. Instead of treating them honourably, the army systematically slaughtered their herds. The Appaloosa became virtually extinct.

But sixty years later, in 1937, Claude Thompson of Moro, Oregon, formed an association to save what was left of this famous breed. Today the Appaloosa is one of the most popular of the American breeds (there are some seventy thousand registered in America) and it is also increasingly prominent in Britain.

The name Appaloosa may be of recent origin, but the breed itself goes back into antiquity. There are depictions of horses bearing the unmistakable spotted markings on the walls of Ice Age caves in Europe which may be twenty thousand years old. Chinese art from about 500 BC is full of them and they are to be seen again in Persian art of the fourteenth century. They appear once more in the paintings of the seventeenth and eighteenth centuries. Those were the proud Spanish horses, the Andalusians much favoured by royalty; while the early Lippizaners of the Spanish Riding School often had the spotted coat pattern. The American spotted horse derived from the early Spanish imports, possibly from those two pintos which came to Mexico with Cortes.

In the end the horse culture period left no notable legacy to the brash, get-up-and-go society which was to become America, and with which it was so impossibly incompatible. But possibly the presence of the mounted Plains Indians blocked the northward expansion of the Spanish Empire. Otherwise there was just a legend (desperately misrepresented, for the most part, in those Western movies) and a fruitful subject for study by social historians.

A nearly parallel horse culture development took place in South America, where Spanish colonists introduced the horse into the Pampas and Patagonia. The South American tribes were affected in much the same way as the Plains Indians, giving up the life of small cultivators to become nomadic horsemen. On the South American plains, possession of the horse improved the efficiency with which game could be hunted. Once more it increased mobility and allowed a tribe to own a wider range of possessions, which they could more easily transport.

South American Indians were not, however, so advanced as horse people as their cousins in the north. They were never horse-breeders. Instead they relied for their supply of horses on the Spanish settlements, which they raided continually, driving off cattle as well as horses. It was said that in a single raid a man might return with four hundred horses.

Like the horse culture of the north, the South American version did not last very long. Today it survives, in part, in the Spanish-style ranching enterprises which still employ the gaucho. In modern times he has become the world's best producer of polo ponies, while Argentina has been the world's leading polo nation since the 1930s, the game being introduced there by English sportsmen in 1877.

The American cattle industry was inspired by the Spanish settlers who brought with them to the New World a tradition of cattle ranching. The earliest ranching was carried on in Mexico and Argentina. To start with cattle were raised to supply leather, but by the nineteenth century the pressures of population and industrialisation in both America and Europe had created a demand for beef. As a result cattle ranching spread rapidly into the western United States and Argentina became the principal supplier of beef to Britain and other parts of Europe.

Cattle ranching involved the use of horses in large numbers. It was integral to the myth of the Wild West, created first by the novelists and then turned into an entertainment industry by the Hollywood movies. It made the cowboy, in a much romanticised version, a national folk hero, the central figure in·a morality play where the values were straightforward and the hero symbolised the victory of good over evil. The Western movie, followed and often imitated in countries as far apart as Japan and Finland, became one of the great phenomena of the twentieth century, and it has hardly lost its appeal today. The reality, of course, was less romantic and not at all heroic.

The horse was essential not only to cattle raising. The railroads, for instance, were largely dependent on horse-power. Goods and materials had to be carried hundreds of miles to railheads, and around the railway a vast system of communication and transport was maintained by thousands of horses.

Communication was the theme of the legendary Pony Express, formed to carry the mails between Missouri and San Francisco. The exploits of the Pony Express riders thrilled contemporary Americans and were ultimately incorporated in the very heart of the American legend, epitomising the 'frontier spirit'.

'The Greatest Enterprise of Modern Times' was the brainchild of William H. Russell, 'the Napoleon of the Plains'. His service was inaugurated in April 1860, before the coming of the telegraph. A series of riders took the mails in relays through what was often hostile Indian territory, each man riding 60 miles (96km) as fast as his pony's legs would carry him. The route was from St Joseph, Missouri, through Kansas, Nebraska, Colorado, Wyoming, Utah and Nevada to Sacramento, California, a distance of 1,966 miles (3,164km) which was covered, using four hundred ponies, in ten days.

Russell inserted this advertisement in the frontier papers: 'WANTED — young, skinny, wiry fellows, not over 18. Must be expert riders willing to risk death daily. Orphans preferred'.

There were plenty willing to take it on, and those chosen – after swearing solemnly never to use bad language, get drunk, gamble, be cruel to horses or interfere with the rights of others, Indian or white – were given a Bible, a pair of revolvers and a rifle.

At one time there were a hundred riders, four hundred horses, 190 relay stations and four hundred station staff. The fastest run was made in March 1861 by 'Pony Bob' Haslam who carried the mail 120 miles (193km) from Smith's Creek to Fort Churchill, Nevada, in eight hours and ten minutes. This was a remarkable feat of endurance, for Haslam, whose relief had been killed, covered 380 miles (612km) with his jaw broken by an Indian arrow and with a bullet wound in his arm.

The Pony Express lasted a bare two years before the company, Russell, Majors & Wadell, had to call a halt because of the losses they incurred. Nonetheless, it had pioneered the most practical route across the continent – one which, in part, was followed by the famous Wells Fargo Overland Stage. Russell himself died in California at an advanced age in 1934.

Wells Fargo was the San Francisco agent for the Pony Express, and grew to be the biggest and most reliable transport agency in the West and a legend in its own right. Founded in 1852, it carried vast amounts of gold bullion as well as mail and passengers. It was big enough to have its own detective force and its guards were often the only upholders of the law in the isolated western territories.

These were the pioneer days but, hard on their heels and in some areas preceding them, came the growth of American agriculture and of the whole economy. The employment of horses was crucial to both. In the 1860s the American horse population was around seven million. It rose to twenty five million by 1914, and in 1900 American wheat acreage was half as large again as the whole of the cultivated area of Britain.

These millions of acres were cultivated and harvested by horses drawing huge machines, developed in America as early as the 1840s. By 1890 horse-drawn combine harvesters weighing 15 tonnes and up to 40ft (12m) wide were being used in the west. They were drawn by teams of up to 42 horses and needed a crew of six men. One man would often drive a 36-horse team to a set of harrows or drills. On the prairies there were the four to five bottom ploughs known as 'horse-killers', pulled by teams of up to eight. The horse had created a bread basket for the world. In the southern states of America the mule was used for a variety of purposes both in the countryside and the town. The mule population of the United States was 559,000 in 1850 but by 1920 had increased to 5,432,000, which was far in excess of the numbers used by any other nation in the world. Mules were and are employed largely on account of their hardiness and longevity. They

The South American gaucho is the natural descendant of the Spanish *peon*.

The Pony Express created its own heroic images.

The legendary Pony Express, though it lasted a mere two years, pioneered the most practical route across the United States from Missouri to San Francisco.

are, moreover, cheap to keep and withstand heat better than horses.

By 1940 horses had largely been supplanted by tractors, and something like twenty million horses became redundant. This released nearly eighty million acres (32.4 million ha) of land which, up to then, had been used to grow feed for horses. However, there was a counter-balancing factor. Horses may consume feed, but tractors consume fuel oil, which is just as delicate an economic consideration. Farming remains today the USA's greatest single user of oil. So far no one has conducted a study to establish which is the more economically viable – the horse or the tractor. There is probably less in it than one would imagine. Tractors do the job more quickly, but they pollute the atmosphere and they do not reproduce themselves. Horses produce more horses; their waste enriches the land that feeds them, without recourse to artificial fertilisers.

Horses, however, did create their own problems of pollution. At the end of the century the horse population of New York produced enough manure to make a pile 175ft (53m) high, covering an acre (0.4ha) of ground and breeding sixteen *billion* flies. Streets were fouled with dung and urine, there was the problem of stabling and, also, of the disposal of animals no longer fit for work.

In Europe, the situation was the same. Up to 1939 there were 650,000 horses working on British farms, supplying something like 70 per cent of the total draught power. And at the turn of the century there were more horses working in towns in Britain than on the land. In the 1890s there were 150,000 horses on the streets of London alone.

The concentration of numbers had caused a virtual crisis. Complaints were made about the congestion and chaos on the streets, the breaking-up of roadways under all those thousands of iron-shod feet, and, of course, the waste disposal problem. Some five to six hundred million tonnes of horse excrement had to be removed each year. British agriculture managed to feed this army of horses, but only with the help of hay imported from Argentina and oats and barley from Canada and the USA. In the end it was the internal combustion engine which solved the problem for good.

If the initial influence on the American horse was Spanish, the other, coming from the north, was predominantly English. These two factors are responsible for the wide variety of horse to be found in America today. The early colonists fairly soon divided themselves into the property-owning south, seeking to perpetuate the horse-riding aristocracy of the country gentry, and the more egalitarian north, with its Puritan overtones. The two philosophies clashed finally in the American Civil War but between them, with some help in the heavy horse sector from colonists who formed Dutch, German and even Swedish and Finnish enclaves, they produced a horse population as varied and as large as almost any in the world.

The English, with their love of racing and hunting, were bringing horses into the Massachusetts Bay Colony in 1629 and some years before Irish horses had been exported to Virginia. The first race-course, near the site of the present Belmont Park, was laid at Long Island in 1666 by Richard Nicolls, who captured New Amsterdam, now New York, from the Dutch and became its first Governor. His object was 'the bettering of the breed of horses', and the pattern sought after was that of the English racer, which at that time had yet to achieve the title and status of Thoroughbred. Within a century, however, the English Thoroughbred was a major influence in American breeding.

The Spanish influence in the USA is manifest in the colour breeds, like the golden-bodied Palomino and the spotted Appaloosa, but also, most particularly, in the American 'gaited' horses. Foremost among them was the now extinct Narragansett Pacer which took its name from Narragansett Bay, Rhode Island, from where it was exported to the planters of the West Indies in great numbers.

The old ambling or pacing breeds of England had declined once the popularity of racing was re-established under Charles II. Many of the best amblers, often with some Spanish background in their pedigrees, found their way to north America, particularly to New England. When crossed with Spanish stock, brought up from the south, they founded the Narragansett Pacer breed which became popular with property owners in the area.

The Narragansett disappeared, but not before it had played its part in the emergence of America's superlative harness racer, the Standard-bred, and one or two other breeds as well. The Standardbred evolved

The employment of horses was a vital factor in the growth of American agriculture in the second half of the nineteenth century.

The fastest harness racing horse today is the Standardbred derived from the Norfolk Trotter.

from a mixture of Narragansett and Morgan blood, strongly infused with its principal ingredient, the Thoroughbred. Standardbreds, or at any rate 90 per cent of them, stem from Hambletonian 10 (Rysdyk's Hambletonian), who was foaled in 1840 and gave the breed its outstanding pacing and trotting performance. He was a great-grandson of Messenger (1780) and sired 1,335 offspring between 1851 and 1875. Messenger's sire was Mambrino, a notable trotting horse in direct descent from the Darley Arabian.

Harness racing still attracts as large an audience as flat racing in the USA, where there are over eight hundred racetracks. In Britain the sport enjoys only a minimal popularity, but it is carried on enthusiastically in other European countries, where the Standardbred figures very prominently.

America's supreme gaited horse is the American Saddlebred, formerly called the Kentucky Saddler. Originally it was a pure utility horse, used by Kentucky planters for its comfort and its unique appearance. In the show ring the Saddlebred performs in three or five gaits and is also shown in harness. The three-gaited horse is shown at the distinctive walk, trot and canter, while the five-gaited shows also the slow-gait (an elevated four-beat pace), and the 'rack', (the slow-gait speeded up).

The other American gaited horses, both evolved for the practical purposes of farm inspection, are the Tennessee Walker, called the 'Turn-Row' for its ability to go up and down rows of plants without damaging them, and the Missouri Fox Trotter, originating in Missouri's Ozark Hills in about 1820. The former has a comfortable half-walk, half-run gliding pace, while the latter walks swiftly in front and trots behind. Both owe their existence to an amalgam of bloods, with the Narragansett prominent in the early breeding of the Walker and the Saddlebred. The Missouri Fox Trotter's foundation sire was the Thoroughbred Denmark (1839) and his son Denmark 61, out of a pacing mare.

The most numerous of the American breeds is the Quarter Horse. Over eight hundred thousand are registered in the USA alone, by a registry which employs two hundred people and is the largest in the world. The Quarter Horse is the supreme cow-pony, although it originated in the colonial seaboard settlements of the Carolinas and Virginia. Derived from crosses between imported Thoroughbreds and Spanish stock, it got its name from the extraordinary speed with which it covers a quarter-mile distance. Early settlers raced these powerful horses over rough tracks or even down the length of village streets which rarely exceeded a quarter of a mile (402m). Moved to the west, the Quarter Horse developed an uncanny 'cow-sense', handling cattle in the same instinctive way as a sheepdog controls a bunch of ewes. Today it is the all-American pleasure mount, a rodeo star and a racehorse. The All-American Futurity Stakes for Quarter Horses is among the most valuable races in the world, worth over $600,000.

Less well known but just as much a part of the American legend is the Morgan Horse, which goes under harness or in saddle. Unusually, it descends from one exceptional foundation sire, first called Figure but later known by the name of his second owner, the Vermont schoolmaster Justin Morgan. Its breeding is obscure, the most likely theory being that it was of Welsh extraction, essentially a Welsh Cob with a percentage of Thoroughbred or Arab blood. Certainly it came from a Welsh community in an area to which Welsh Cobs had been exported.

Morgan got the horse around 1795 and although it stood only about 14 hands high it was never beaten in a race under saddle or in harness, nor in any of the severe weight-pulling contests in which it competed. Furthermore, this gallant little horse worked unremittingly, clearing timber, dragging heavy loads and at the plough as well as carrying out its numerous stud duties. It is commemorated by a statue at the University of Vermont.

The heavy draught breeds in the USA came principally from the massive Belgian horses, but there are also many Percherons. Modern America also has a large imported horse population, and the biggest number of Arab horses of any country in the world.

South America has two notable breeds based on the Spanish imports of the sixteenth century and after. There is the laterally gaited Peruvian Paso and the tough little Criollo of Argentina, descended from Spanish horses carrying a good percentage of Barb blood. Using the Criollo as the base stock and continually introducing Thorough-bred blood, the Argentinians have produced what is acknowledged to be the finest polo pony in the world.

Ponies were never used in coalmines in the USA, as they were in Britain, where thousands spent their lives underground until as late as 1971, but throughout the United States and in Canada horse farms are maintained for medicinal and cosmetic purposes. Many of these are pregnant mares' urine farms. Their purpose is to produce oestrogen for the manufacture of the contraceptive pill.

Could there be a moral here, albeit an obscure one?

The Quarter in the title 'Quarter' Horse is often thought to refer to its breeding but, in fact, it refers only to the racing distance for which it was originally bred.

Chapter 11

AGES OF DISCOVERY AND ENLIGHTENMENT

We left Europe on the brink of the Renaissance. By the sixteenth century the advent of the longbow, and then of gunpowder and firearms had made the medieval heavily armoured knight and his ponderous, similarly protected Great Horse anachronisms on the battlefields of Europe. But it was the knight and his movements in battle, real or imagined, that formed part of the inspiration for the growth of school riding in the Renaissance period, a practice which later came to be termed 'classical' riding.

The huge resurgence of classical learning in the Renaissance, a new age of hope and boundless curiosity, has no more perfect symbol than those restless horses on the façade of St Mark's Cathedral in Venice. The group, which has an extraordinary lightness and elegance combined with strength and mobility, is said to be by the Greek sculptor Lysippos and to have been brought from Chios to Constantinople in the fifth century. Thence it was taken to Venice in 1204. Some researchers, however, think that the work might not be by Lysippos, but a Roman copy of a Greek sculpture executed between the third and fourth centuries. It is cast not in bronze but from a copper, silver and gold mixture which allows the skin texture on the horses' bodies to be varied. Its rare fusion of truth and beauty embodies the spirit of Renaissance Europe, and seems to represent the link between Byzantine Greece, Roman art and the new realism.

The revival of interest in the Classics led to the rediscovery of Xenophon, who was seized upon with enthusiasm, studied avidly and used as a basis for discussion and training.

It should not be thought, however, that no systematic method of equitation was known until the Renaissance improved and extended upon Xenophon's practice. The Renaissance horsemen, while drawing on Xenophon's work, were improving and extending a system of horsemanship which already existed, although little was put on record.

The medieval knights may not have been great hands with the pen, but they were competent horsemen and some were accomplished ones. They rode with one hand and for that reason alone must have understood the use of the legs, not only to urge the horse forward but

In Renaissance Europe, horsemanship was an essential accomplishment for a gentleman. Now, the horse entered into a new role as a partner in an art form on a par with dancing and music.

The Spanish Riding School, together with the Cadre Noir, remain as the last repositories of the classical art.

also to keep the animal straight and to position his quarters correctly to make changes of direction.

The horse had to be obedient and handy when he and his rider were in actual physical contact with foot soldiers intent upon unhorsing the rider, or when engaged in close combat with other cavalry, and that would have demanded a high standard of horsemanship.

Many of the movements expected of the warhorse were designed to discourage the proximity of foot soldiers. These movements form the basis for what are called the 'airs, or schools, above the ground', – the rears, leaps and kicks which are still practised at the Spanish Riding School at Vienna and the Cadre Noir at Fontainebleau.

To what extent and with what precision the medieval knight did in fact practise or teach these 'airs' is not easy to tell. Certainly, those performed at the four hundred-year-old Spanish School today cannot be looked upon as accurate representations of medieval movements. They are supreme refinements of a medieval ideal which may not have had much basis in reality. As the English writer Thomas Blundeville asked, who wants a horse who in the press of battle 'falls a' hopping and dancing up and down in one place'? (There are still English hunting men who ask the same question about competitive dressage.)

Xenophon, we know, was concerned to produce two types of horse: a serviceable campaign horse, and a parade-horse on which great men could show themselves glamorously and heroically. We know that Xenophon was familiar with the parade paces of *piaffe* and *passage* and that they were employed in the Panathenaea, the great processions held in honour of the goddess Athena. Indeed, those movements were known to horsemen before his day. Xenophon also describes the *levade*, and we see it enacted on all sorts of Greek artefacts. He knew too about the *pirouette*, the turn on the base of the haunches, and about the *volte*, the circle which could be reduced to what was virtually a near-full pirouette.

Although, with some exceptions of varying merit, there is little written information about medieval horsemanship, most remaining manuscripts being concerned almost exclusively with management, disease, bitting etc., there is evidence that horses in the Roman (Byzantine) circus performed the *piaffe* (*tripudium*). Byzantine practices certainly survived in European travelling circuses, and there is pictorial evidence of medieval horses performing some recognisable 'airs above the ground'.

It is entirely possible that medieval warhorses were trained to kick out behind if threatened by infantry approaching from the rear. They might also have used something like the *levade* as a deterrent and, if the horse could be persuaded to leap forward from the half-rear position (the basis for the modern *capriole*) that would have had a salutary and

The pace of the 'parade' horse from pre-Christian times was the lofty, cadenced movement of the *passage* enhancing the heroic stature of the rider.

In a state of high collection the horse, through the imperceptible 'aids' given by his rider, moves from *passage* into *piaffe*, executing the same movement energetically but without moving to his front.

51

The 'leap of the goat' – the ultimate 'air above the ground' – is the soaring *capriole*, to be executed as it is here with the rider displaying an admirable nonchalance.

scattering effect on any opposition unwise enough to be in the way. A pirouette, or a half-pirouette, would also have been a useful accomplishment, allowing all-round use of the sword. Whether in the final period of mounted armour those overweighted mastodons ever raised much more than a trot, let alone a leap or a nimble pirouette, is very unlikely; but by then it was a different game.

Unlike the tournament and joust, Renaissance riding in the *manège* (ultimately refined to those splendidly baroque riding halls built everywhere by the European nobility) was not a training exercise for the battlefield. Armoured cavalry and 'walls of steel' were irrelevant to the warfare of the day and so riding in the *manège* was performed for its own sake and for the sake of art. To ride well in the advanced figures was difficult and required a degree of dedication that discouraged the dilettante, although there were doubtless a number of those. It was nonetheless deeply satisfying, as is the pursuit of any art form, and it was a wonderful opportunity to appear in a glamorous light. Riding, I was once told by a very great teacher, was about showing off, both your horse and yourself. 'Don't be afraid to swank,' he used to say, 'but always swank with restraint – a horseman is never vulgar.'

The centre of the Renaissance revival in educated riding was Naples, which Belisarius had reconquered for Byzantium in 536. A riding academy was founded here by a Byzantine group in 1134. Their training methods and movements were concerned naturally enough with the circus and there is no doubt that the tradition of Byzantine horsemanship was maintained in Naples between the twelfth and sixteenth centuries to become the inheritance of the Renaissance riding masters. It received additional impetus in the fifteenth century when refugees from the Ottoman advance left Constantinople to settle in Naples.

A chain of equestrian authors, inspired by the Byzantine school, were being published before the sixteenth century. The majority are obscure and not of much value but they are there. Giordano Ruffo di Calabria wrote *Hippiatria* in Sicilian in 1240–50; Pier de Crescenzi, the Bolognese senator who settled in Naples, produced sometime between 1300 and 1309 *Opus Ruralum Commodorum*; Lorenzio Rusio, a master farrier, was writing perhaps thirty years later and Leone Battista Alberti, precursor of Leonardo da Vinci, wrote *De Equo Animante* in 1440, though it seems not to have entered general publication for another hundred years.

The foundations for a centre of classical riding had therefore been well and truly laid when, in 1532, a Neapolitan nobleman, Federico Grisone, opened what was to become the most famous riding school in the world. It had a fundamental influence on the evolution of academic horsemanship all over Europe.

His academy derived its teaching from Xenophon, but also from the existing Byzantine tradition. Grisone is now accounted as the first of the classical masters.

He had at his disposal a selection of very severe bits, some of which were of his own invention. They were sufficiently strong to elicit a response from the most insensitive of warhorses, yet he was insistent on the horse having a light, responsive mouth and sought 'the gentle, good contact at the mouth, foundation of the entire doctrine'. He obtained a light mouth by schooling the horse first in a cavesson (a noseband) which could be fitted with studs or even spikes to make its effect more immediate. As the horse became more obedient and balanced so the contact and the control passed to the bit which, though it was potentially very severe, did not need to be handled other than with the lightest of hands.

In 1550 Grisone's book *Gli Ordini di Cavalcare* ('The Rules of Riding') was published in Naples by his friend Giovan Paulo Suganappo. It became the equestrian best-seller of all time and it heralded a positive spate of equestrian books which continues up to the present day. The book was printed on the recently invented printing press and it carried the blessing of Pope Julius III. With the increasing use of presses and greater knowledge of printing techniques, it was translated and published in no less than five European languages, including English at the command of Elizabeth I. It ran to eight new editions between 1550 and 1600, which constituted a record of considerable proportions.

Admittedly the book contains some horrific 'cures' for the recalcitrant equine. 'In breaking young horses, put them in a circular pit; be very severe with those that are sensitive and of high courage: beat them between the ears with a stick.' There are instructions, too, on the remedies to be employed with 'nappy' horses (those that resist by refusing to go forward, often running backwards or even declining to move at all). A bundle of flaming straw, a cat or a lively hedgehog secured to the underside of the tail are all mentioned. Or a footman or two could be employed to come up behind the horse with all sorts of inquisitorial instruments, sharp spikes, infuriated cats tied to long poles and such like. (One Neapolitan instructor, Vincentio Respini, consulted about a nappy horse ridden by the king, advised the use of a hedgehog between the thighs. It worked, but 'in such sort that he had much ado to prevent the contrary vice of running away'.)

For all that, and for all those fierce bits, fitted with spikes and burrs and with the cruellest sorts of mouthpieces, Grisone continued to insist upon the importance of a light mouth and he did impress upon his readers that the true horseman should have no need of extreme measures.

A near-contemporary of Grisone was Cesare Fiaschi, who opened his school at Ferrara two years later. Fiaschi published his book in 1556 under the title *Trattato dell'Imbrigliare, Maneggiare e Ferrare Cavalli* ('A Treatise on the Bridling, Managing and Shoeing of Horses'). Fiaschi was the greatest authority of his time on the shoeing of the horse, and was not exceeded until the second half of the eighteenth century. His particular distinction was the way in which he used music in the training and riding of horses. Nothing, he maintained, could be achieved 'without beat and measure'. The theory is arguable, but, though it could not be described as a training aid, it is true that the contemporary Portuguese master, Nuno Oliveira, rides his horses to a background of grand opera!

The methods of the sixteenth century were often brutal in the extreme, but it must be remembered that the horses available to Grisone were the left-overs of a previous era – heavy, common horses bred to carry the knight and his armour. For this elephantine creature to be able to execute the balanced, highly collected paces of the *manège* it was necessary to put his weight over his quarters and engaged hind legs so that his forehand could be lightened and raised. This was accomplished by the mechanical forces of the bit which caused him to tuck his head into his chest and which *pulled* him back on his haunches. The latter were meanwhile being encouraged to play their part by the application of sharp spurs and some timely assistance from the ground.

Before the horse could hope to perform the 'airs above the ground' it was essential that he was put into this collected position, hocks well under the body, head and neck held high with the nose retracted. The more he was almost sitting over his hocks and the less the weight carried on the forehand, the more easily would he be able to carry out the leaps which were the ultimate achievement of the *manège*. To assist in the attainment of these leaps and in particular the most difficult of them, the *capriole*, in which the horse is required to bound in the air while simultaneously kicking out with the hind legs, the animal, by energetic application of spur and whip, was encouraged to 'yerk', to kick out behind, and he was taught the 'advance', a series of half-rears.

In this coercive school of riding resort was frequently made to fierce bits and understanding of the horse's mentality, so assiduously encouraged by Xenophon, received little more than lip-service, if it was not overlooked altogether. In a curious way these early masters, who did obtain remarkable results, regarded the horse as a brute while at the same time giving him credit for an intelligence which he could not possibly possess. They took an inability to perform a movement or to understand what was required as evidence of a contrary nature to be exorcised accordingly. The emphasis lay in breaking resistance by 'correction'. The horse was rewarded by cherishing or a cessation of punishment.

The desire to advance academic riding resulted, however, in the breeding and use of better, lighter, more responsive horses. Naples was under Spanish rule from 1504 to 1713. From the middle of the sixteenth century the far superior Spanish, or Andalusian, horse was used in increasing numbers; it was this noble horse that became the very cornerstone of classical riding.

Wonderfully proportioned, with enormous presence, the Andalusian is possessed of great agility and fire, but yet has a friendly, docile temperament. The carriage of its powerful head and neck is naturally high and, just as naturally, the Andalusian carries his weight over his quarters in perfect balance. He was the luxury school horse *par excellence* and it can only be the whims of changing fashion that, for the moment, deny him his place in competitive dressage – that and perhaps the extraordinarily extravagant and high action of his forelegs. The Andalusian does, in fact, 'dish', – that is, he throws his forelegs in an outward arc before putting his feet to the ground. In Spain the action is highly esteemed but in countries like England it is not appreciated at all.

The Andalusian horse went with the *conquistadores* to the Americas, where he contributed to the foundation of numerous American breeds. In Europe he was at the base of the Frederiksborg, the royal horse of Denmark, the Neapolitan horse and the Austrian Kladruber. The Andalusian was also a background influence in some of the British breeds, notably the Cleveland Bay, the Hackney, the Connemara pony of Ireland and probably the Welsh Cob.

Direct descendants of the Andalusian horse are the Lippizaners of the Spanish Riding School. The stud at Lippiza, near Trieste, then part of the Austrian Empire, from which they take their name, was founded by the Archduke Charles II in 1580, when his emissary, the Freiherr von Khevenhiller, brought nine stallions and twenty four mares there from Spain.

Outside blood was introduced from time to time and in the eighteenth and nineteenth centuries six principal lines were established, deriving from the white Pluto, a Spanish pure-bred born in 1765 who came from the Royal Danish Court Stud at Frederiksborg; the black Conversano, a Neapolitan (a breed of direct Spanish descent), born in 1767; the dun Favory, born in 1779, who came from the stud at Kladrub; the bay Neapolitano born in 1790, who came from Polesina, Italy; the white Siglavy, an Arabian, born in 1810, and the white Maestoso, born in 1819 at Mezohegyes, Hungary, out of a Spanish mare by a Neapolitan sire.

These lines are continued today. With occasional exceptions (it is traditional for the Spanish School to have one bay horse, for instance), the Lippizaner is a white horse, but the early ones, right up to the mid-eighteenth century, were a mixture of bays, browns, duns, creams and even spotted coat patterns.

Lippiza supplied the horses for the school in Vienna and also for the court stables, for Lippizaners are very well suited to carriage work. During the First World War the stud was transferred to Laxenburg and Kladrub and then to Piber, where it remains and from where the dancing white stallions are still sent to Vienna.

The Spanish Riding School was founded in 1572 as the Spanische Reitschule in a wooden building in Vienna. The present school, the Winter Riding Hall, was built near the site of the old one to the design of Josef Emanuel Fischer von Erlach between 1729 and 1735 when the Austrian Empire was at its peak. The school was founded as an adjunct to the court for the education of the nobility in the equitational arts. It was called the Spanish School because right from its formation only Spanish stallions were used there.

Initially its doctrine was that of the early Neapolitan school. Its final influence, however, was that of the most articulate and literate of the French masters, François Robichon de La Guérinière (1688–1751). His book, *École de Cavalerie*, published in 1733, was adopted as holy writ by Vienna and its author virtually canonised. Thereafter the school devoted itself zealously to the preservation of his clearly expressed principles in all their purity, even perpetuating throughout the centuries the breed of horse from which it took its name.

For over four hundred years the school has preserved and demons-

Great riding masters became a mandatory requirement in the leading courts of Europe. Antoine de Pluvinel was tutor to Louis XIII.

trated the classical principles of riding. Riders, who give regular public displays, dress in the traditional uniform of brown tailcoat, white breeches, high black boots and black bicorne hat. When they enter the glittering white pillared hall, either in training sessions or for performances, they doff their hats in salute to the portrait of Charles VI, their first patron.

The most famous pupil of the Neapolitan Grisone, and he may also have learnt from Fiaschi, was Giovanni Baptista Pignatelli, who developed the theories of his masters while moderating their more extreme physical methods. He was strongly influenced by the Byzantine circus practice and incorporated much of that system into his work, which was characterised by a lightness which did not depend so much on the strength of the bit and which was absent from the teaching of his masters. For the most part, however, he was dealing with better-class horses.

He is known as 'the third man' of the Neapolitan School and he marked the division between the schools of Italy and the enlightenment in equestrian training represented by the later masters of France. His contribution was to hand to his pupils, La Broue, de Pluvinel, Saint-Antoine (equerry to both James I and Charles I of England), the German Fayser and the Spaniards Vargas and Paolo d'Aquino, a basic training formula for *manège* riding. They built on the basis he provided.

Salomon La Broue published his first book *La Cavalerie Francoys* in 1593–94 and from then on leadership in equitation passed from Italy to France, culminating by the end of the century in the École de Versailles and the École de Saumur.

La Broue certainly initiated the change from the harsh methods of Naples to the more enlightened systems of France, but the first of the French masters was the gifted, supremely intelligent Antoine de Pluvinel (1555–1620), a member of the gentry, a diplomat and a soldier. He became tutor to King Louis XIII and was the author, in 1623, of *Manège du Roy*, which appeared five years later as *L'Instruction du Roy en l'exercise de monter à cheval*.

The book is presented in the form of a dialogue between de Pluvinel and his pupil and shows the continual emphasis of Pluvinel's humanitarian approach, based on an understanding of the horse's physical and mental capabilities. The frontispiece is exemplary as an indication of the author's attitudes. On one side is a hugely-muscled male figure having obvious difficulty in controlling a rearing horse in a relatively simple bridle. On the other side is a nymph-like creature, *Scientia*. The provocatively clothed young lady is leading a docile stallion from a curb bit which she holds lightly in one hand while the other holds the book she is studying.

The British, despite their natural affinity with the horse, produced only one of the great masters, the unsuccessful cavalry commander, William Cavendish, Duke of Newcastle.

WILLIAM CAVENDISH
Duke of Newcastle.

Pluvinel introduced gymnastic exercises to supple the horse and invented the 'pillars', between which the horse is taught the principles of collection and the first of the 'airs above the ground', the *levade*.

Fifty years after de Pluvinel, the sole British master, William Cavendish, Duke of Newcastle, was operating on much the same lines, counselling patience and gentle handling. As a soldier, Newcastle ranks among the cavalry incompetents: he was the Royalist commander largely responsible for the defeat of the Battle of Marston Moor. But he ranks also, despite an ineffable conceit, as one of the masters of equitation.

But standing head and shoulders above them all is the aristocratic François Robichon de La Guérinière. La Guérinière, royal riding master and director of the royal *manège* of the Tuileries as equerry to Louis XIV from 1730 to 1751, formulated, refined and expanded the principles of equitation as a rational science (rather than an instinctive accomplishment). It is largely on his account that the French influence became the decisive and lasting factor in world equitation.

He taught riders to adopt the classical position, which is accepted for school riding today and which with no more than small adaptations is the basis of a modern cross-country seat (although that was not to be appreciated until some hundred and fifty years after his death). La Guérinière had his riders sitting upright, with braced back and fairly long stirrups, but he asked for the lower leg to be held behind the vertical.

On the training of the horse, he wrote that systematic work involving suppling and balancing exercises made the horse calm, light and obedient, so that it was pleasant to ride and comfortable in all its paces. This definition corresponds very closely to that issued on dressage by the twentieth-century *Fédération Équèstre Internationale*.

La Guérinière invented the supreme suppling and balancing exercise of the shoulder-in (*l'épaule en dedans*). In this the horse moves on 'two tracks', the forelegs following one course and the hind legs a separate one, so that the horse is moving sideways. He was also responsible for the flying change at canter, when the leading leg is changed in the air, rather than after some strides at trot. He initiated the exercise of counter-canter, a balancing and obedience exercise in which the horse canters on a 'false' lead, i.e. he canters with the right fore as the leading leg on a left circle. Very importantly, he defined as never before the use of hand and leg in inconspicuous combination.

Largely as the result of La Guérinière's work two great streams of classical equitation sprang up in Europe, the one in France, first at Versailles and then at Saumur, where the famous Cadre Noir preserved the French tradition, and the other at Vienna with the Spanish Riding School.

The French school differed from Vienna on account of its role as a cavalry school. Unlike the Spanish school, it was in a state of more or less constant development and never lacked innovators or original thinkers. Classicism remained the base, but it was combined with other forms of competitive equitation. The philosophy was broader because it was largely the Thoroughbred or Anglo–Arab type which was favoured at Saumur.

The school at Saumur (*'la ville du cheval'*) was founded in 1593 when a riding wing was added to the Protestant college by the Comte Duplessis-Mornay. The first troops stationed there were the King's Gentlemen of the Arquebuse. It was not until 1763 that Saumur became France's leading school of equitation, when the Duc de Choiseul recommended to Louis XV that his brother's regiment, the *Carabiniers de Monsieur*, should for its own good be stationed in the provinces and away from the fleshpots of Paris. (It is only by chance that they went to Saumur. The first suggestion, Angers-sur-Loire, was strongly opposed by the town's bishop who feared for the immortal souls of his flock. In Saumur the females were Protestant and so presumably had no souls to bother about.)

Following the Revolution, Napoleon and the restoration of the monarchy, Saumur became the *École Royal de Cavalerie*, replacing the royal school of Versailles. Founded in 1680, Versailles had been accepted as the model for all Europe and had become a forum for a succession of horsemen whose collective talent has never been exceeded. The Cadre Noir, with its black uniform, became the instructors' corps for the Saumur school, taking the place of the old *Carabiniers de Monsieur*.

Although French horsemanship was by far the most innovative in Europe, European cavalry by the end of the nineteenth century was dominated largely by the German schools. Their training, carried out in the *manège*, was based on the classical principles of high collection. Jumping and cross-country riding formed only a minimal part of the trooper's training. Indeed, early photographs illustrating military jumping are not far short of horrific. The riders leant well back, ungiving hands held at chest height, while the horses jumped with hollow backs and mouths wide open in an agonised attempt to avoid the punishing action of the bit.

In Britain, where no tradition of indoor riding existed, cavalry officers and country gentlemen rode across country in pursuit of the fox, jumping what obstacles were met. Their approach may not have been exactly scientific, but though they leant back over their fences they did not interfere with their horses' mouths and the very nature of the sport encouraged a degree of self-balance and initiative in the horse. In continental Europe, the enclosure of fields had come much later and hunting was not carried out in the English manner. Jumping, as a result, was neither much practised nor understood.

Yet the role of cavalry in warfare had undoubtedly changed, even if the thinking of many cavalry officers had not. Faced with the machine-gun and improvements to the rifle, cavalry had henceforth to become again light horsemen, able to cross country swiftly to probe and reconnoitre, negotiating whatever obstacles they met. Precise wheeling and advances in perfectly dressed ranks were simply irrelevant to modern conditions. A classical education at slow collected paces was no preparation, and was actually restrictive to cross-country riding.

Just as Xenophon and the later advent of the stirrup were landmarks in equestrian history, so was the formulation of a system of natural riding designed to equip horse and rider to go across country and over obstacles. The man responsible for the new thinking was an Italian cavalry officer, Captain Federico Caprilli (1868–1907). In his short life this supreme innovator accomplished an equestrian revolution which quite simply changed the concept of active, outdoor riding forever. His only equal in five thousand years of equestrian history was Xenophon.

In brief, he discarded the system of school riding with its accent on the slow, collected paces and evolved a 'forward system', training horses to acquire a natural balance by schooling them over the sort of country in which they would have to operate. The curb bit was replaced by the snaffle and the horse was allowed free extension of the head and neck, especially over fences.

Instead of the completely dominated, collected school horse he asked for unfettered extension. Instead of the rider insisting upon the horse conforming to his hand and to a form which was in itself unnatural, he asked his riders to conform to the horse's natural movement and outline. They rode with a much shortened stirrup, perching forward so that their weight was carried as nearly as possible over the horse's centre of balance, where it would be the least possible encumbrance to a free and even movement. They sat forward over every type of fence and even when riding up or down the most fearsome inclines. It was, in essence, the very same sort of seat that generations of steppe nomads and eastern horsemen had used for centuries.

As a result of Caprilli's teachings at Tor di Quinto and Pinerolo, the Italian cavalry school, Italian horsemen became pre-eminent in jumping competitions. The Italian army adopted the system officially in 1907, the year of Caprilli's death, and it was introduced at many other cavalry schools throughout the world by officers trained at Pinerolo.

These photographs perfectly illustrate the influence of Caprilli Before . . .

Today, the world sits forward over its fences in the Caprilli manner. The theory has not perhaps survived in its entirety, since there has been a blending of the classical with the Caprilli system. But competitive riding at the level of the present day would be unthinkable without Caprilli's '*sistema*'.

By the time of Caprilli's death there were far more uses for the horse than as an instrument of war or for the purpose of 'a' hopping and dancing' in riding *manèges*. By far the greatest number of horses in Europe were those working on farms or in some aspect of transport. They shunted railway stock, hauled timber or pulled barges on canals, while thousands of ponies in Britain were harnessed to coal trucks in the mines. They represent man's association with horses in a largely peaceful, constructive context.

. . . **and After.**

AT THE FRONT!

Every fit Briton should join our brave men at the Front.

ENLIST NOW.

HORSES AND POWER AND WAR

Chapter 12

> Four things greater than all things are –
> Women and Horses and Power and War.
>
> (Rudyard Kipling, *The Ballad of the King's Jest*)

The turning point in the use of horses in war came in the sixteenth century with the invention of firearms and artillery, the 'villainous saltpetre'. Initially, however, both cannon and hand-gun were unreliable and largely ineffectual. Both had a habit of blowing up in the faces of their operators; cannon were so unwieldy and cumbersome that once positioned they were virtually immobile and could only with great difficulty be redirected to bring fire on another part of the field. The hand gun, the primitive arquebus (or harquebus) of the fifteenth century, took up to a minute to load, was inaccurate in the extreme and had a very limited range – at a distance of 80 yards (73m), for instance, it would have stopped nothing. It was, in fact, a weapon better suited to firing through the loopholes cut in a castle wall, for it was clumsy and so heavy that it had to be fired from a rest.

Far more effective was the longbow with its range of 250 yards (229m). An archer band, with each man able to fire ten arrows to the minute, was capable of such a concentration of fire as to create a 'beaten zone' in which neither man nor horse could hope to survive. The Battle of Crécy, at which longbows were used so effectively, was fought in 1346, yet it took almost four hundred years before the preponderance of fire-power was sufficient and efficient enough to demote the cavalry arm to the inevitable supportive role. In too many instances the cavalry hierarchy – the natural breeding ground of the general officer – found it impossible to contemplate abdicating its position as 'the arm of the gods', and it refused to recognise an increasingly apparent fact of war.

Writing in the *Art of War* as early as 1520, the prescient Machiavelli gave a definition of cavalry duty that was brusque to the point of being brutal, but was indisputably accurate:

> It is right to have some cavalry to support and assist infantry, but not to look upon them as the main force of the army, for they are highly necessary to reconnoitre, to scour roads . . . and to lay waste an enemy's country and to cut off their convoys; but in the field, in

The role of the horse in the First World War was a far cry from the romantic image of the hussars.

battles which commonly decide the fate of nations, they are fitter to pursue an enemy that is routed and flying than anything else.

Clearly the compilers of the 1907 edition of the British *Cavalry Training* were not conversant with Machiavelli, asserting with a frightening assurance: 'It must be accepted in principle that the rifle, effective as it is, cannot replace the effect produced by the speed of the horse, the magnetism of the charge, and the terror of cold steel'.

Even in 1916, when the opposing armies of the First World War were literally bogged down in the miseries of protracted trench warfare – dominated by machine guns, the artillery barrage, the barbed wire entanglements and sometimes the horribly lethal gas canister – Generals, mostly cavalrymen, were still basing their strategies (as far as any strategy could be possible under such conditions) on the ultimate 'cavalry breakthrough' which would allegedly provide a decisive end to the conflict. In support of that impossible dream, more than a million cavalry horses were held behind the fronts, the biggest concentration of cavalry in the history of the world. There were occasions, however, when great victories and campaigns were won by cavalry, when they were handled effectively by outstanding commanders.

For a period, however, cavalry was in danger of losing the prime advantages of the mounted soldier: mobility and the momentum which could break an enemy line.

After the wheel-lock musket of the sixteenth century came the much improved flint-lock in about 1650. The production of a spark by the cock striking a flint against a piece of steel directly over the pan was far more reliable than the old wheel-lock method, in which a shell struck sparks from a piece of pyrites in the cock – and, very importantly, it was much quicker. In time the flint-lock method produced the musket which became the weapon of British infantry up to Waterloo and afterwards, the famous Brown Bess.

Muskets in the hands of steady troops drawn up in squares effectively discouraged cavalry from getting close enough to use either lance or sword. So the cavalry reverted to the practice of antiquity. Greek cavalry, without saddles or stirrups, had ridden across the enemy's front to hurl their javelins. Sixteenth-century cavalry did much the same thing, only instead of throwing javelins they discharged pistols.

All through the seventeenth century and some way into the eighteenth too, cavalry forsook the traditional cold steel for the pistol. But it was far from effective or efficient. To use firearms from the back of a horse with any degree of accuracy is not easy; moreover, it can be attended by all sorts of dangers. Horses can easily take fright and take off, or they may rear and put their riders on the ground. Or, indeed, the pistoleer might in the heat of the moment shoot his own horse through the head.

It is possible to train horses to accept a weapon being fired from their backs, but they will only learn if the practice is habitual and only then if they are naturally steady. The American Indian sometimes used a rifle from the saddle but more often relied on the bow as being more accurate and less disturbing to the horse. The only people who may be said to have mastered the art were the Boer farmers who presented such a problem to Britain's Imperial forces between 1900 and 1902.

Led by the French, the western European nations introduced the 'dragoon', so called after the *dragon*, the short carbine, with which he was equipped. He rode to the battlefield, usually on a nondescript mount, and then fought on foot as an infantryman. Dr Johnson, in his famous dictionary, defined a dragoon as 'a kind of soldier that serves indifferently either on foot or on horseback'.

Meanwhile, the new ideal of the mounted arm was gathering force in the Hungarian plains. The hussars were the natural successors to the Hun and the Mongol. Mobile in the extreme and not reliant on slow-moving supply trains, the hussar was the first exponent of the *Blitzkrieg* attack. Without warning or any of the softening-up processes which had become a necessary formality in the west, they hit swiftly with devastating force made even more effective by the element of surprise. Their method of attack became known as the *coup d'hussard* (the name 'hussar' itself is derived from *hazar*, meaning 'twentieth', which refers to the corps of soldiers raised by Matthias Corvinus, King of Hungary, in the fifteenth century when one man in twenty from each village was required to serve under arms).

The hussars rode as their forebears with bent knee, short stirrup and trunk inclined forward, for all the world as in *il sistema* formulated by Caprilli. They never did have anything to do with the restricting form of collection inherent in the classical method (*à la bride*) of the Renaissance and after.

When Ferdinand of Naples sent King Matthias a 'Spanish' expert to instruct the 'barbarians', he was sent packing:

> With the horses which we trained ourselves we defeated the Turks, subjected Siberia, and vanquished all before us, honourably by means of our horses. We have no desire for horses that hop about with bent hocks in the Spanish fashion; we do not want them even as a pastime still less for serious business.

Subsequent Hungarian horsemen went so far as to describe the Spanish School in Vienna as 'a purgatory for horses'.

Western Europe did not follow the Hungarian example exactly – its horses were not always fitted to the role – but in the end all Europe had hussars as the élite of the mounted arm. The Hungarian example contributed largely to the revival of the shock tactic which Prince Rupert used with such effect in 1642 at Edge Hill in the English Civil War. Although King Gustavus Adolphus of Sweden, one of the most intuitively brilliant of cavalry commanders, is often credited with the reintroduction of the cavalry shock tactic during the Thirty Years War (1618–48), it was really Rupert who set the example. Gustavus Adolphus had his cavalry trot to the enemy, discharge their pistols, and then 'fall on' with the sword. Rupert's troops charged in line at the gallop with swords alone, epitomising the highest aspiration of cavalrymen.

The trouble with Rupert's cavalry, however, as with subsequent horse formations, was that while they never lacked courage almost to the degree of imbecility, they lacked control. They never could re-form after their wild gallop through the enemy lines, and by the time they could again be persuaded to act as a cohesive force the battle had either passed them by or their horses were exhausted. Cromwell, a cavalry leader of greater intelligence than the dashing Rupert, imposed a rigid discipline on his troopers and drilled them precisely. He charged at a 'good, round trot' and created horsed regiments that 'stood in advance of all Europe'.

In 1683 the great Polish King John III Sobieski, 'the Savour of Vienna', defeated the Turks with twenty thousand light horsemen, a victory to be repeated by Allenby with the same number over the same people two centuries later. Under commanders of the calibre of Charles XII, Marlborough and Frederick II of Prussia, cavalry reached heights which were never again surpassed. Here was the real birth of the 'cavalry spirit', which was so disastrously misunderstood by the playboy British officers of the nineteenth century, whose bravery was often exceeded only by their lack of expertise and intelligence.

Under these commanders the physical and moral superiority of massed cavalry was displayed to the full. Marlborough, using cavalry mounted on good half-bred English horses, up to weight but not without quality, relied, like Rupert, on the sword. But unlike Rupert his troops charged at the trot, regrouped immediately, turned under perfect discipline and charged again.

Out of twenty-two major battles fought by Frederick the Great, fifteen were certainly won by cavalry action. He too was a strict, ruthless disciplinarian. His squadrons under Seydlitz and von Ziethen were supreme in their day: 'Every horse and trooper', he wrote, 'has been finished with the same care a watchmaker bestows upon each wheel of the mechanism.'

The Prussian cavalry, which practised high standards of horse

Oliver Cromwell fully understood the importance of caring for the horse off the field of battle.

mastership, rode Trakehner horses from East Prussia, a breed carefully produced by crossing the native Schweiken, a solid pony sort, with carefully chosen introductions of Arab and Thoroughbred blood, the mixture being leavened with an occasional outcross to Danish or other European half-breds. Frederick introduced to the battlefield the first mobile artillery, six-pounders drawn by horse teams at the gallop and used in support of the cavalry. The limbers, just as those of the British Royal Horse Artillery, the King's Troop, which derived from Frederick's horse-gunners, were drawn by a six-horse team with the drivers riding the near-side horses and the gunners mounted on their own horses and not on the limbers.

Napoleon, a gunner of genius, also employed massed cavalry brilliantly, although he was prodigal in the way he used them. French cavalry was never other than supremely courageous, but French troopers were not the best of horsemen nor were they good horsemasters. Murat, a very good cavalry commander, manoeuvred his troops at the trot and was content to do so, rather than expose their lack of horsemanship, but he lost eighteen thousand horses through wastage within two months in Russia and on the retreat from Moscow thirty thousand died. As General Nansouty, Commandant of the Cavalry of the Guard observed, 'The horses of the Cuirassiers not, unfortunately, being able to sustain themselves on patriotism, fell down by the roadside and died.' Napoleon maintained his cavalry strength by remounts from the national studs which had been formed

Below left: **King John III Sobieski was able to discipline the volatile Polish cavalrymen thus winning, to the consternation of the Turks, a throne.**

Below right: **By introducing horse artillery, Frederick the Great redressed the balance in favour of the cavalry.**

for the purpose and which made much use of Barb and Arab crosses to produce hardy, enduring cavalry mounts.

Wellington was less fortunate and in the Peninsular War, which he described as 'the grave of horses', was always short of remounts. Probably the British trooper was not much better a horsemaster than his French counterpart, but because he was led by officers bred as fox-hunting thrusters, he rode with more dash and invariably charged at the gallop. Wellington, by upbringing and instinct an infantryman, was frequently let down by his cavalry on this very account – the enthusiasm of his officers allowing the squadrons to get out of hand.

At Waterloo, the last major engagement of cavalry in European history, Napoleon had sixteen thousand cavalry at his command and Wellington thirteen thousand. Once more the impetuosity of Wellington's cavalry prevented his making a pursuit after the victory, and placed more responsibility on the stubborn, enduring British infantry – to whom, with the Horse Gunners, the day rightly belonged. The British heavy brigades charged magnificently, routing an infantry corps, field batteries and a whole cavalry brigade, but they failed once

An unusual incident in the American Civil War. Normally the mounted troops on both sides fought dismounted.

more to re-form. Elsewhere, they performed miracles of valour and dash but suffered heavy casualties.

The French under Ney, 'the bravest of the brave', launched repeated attacks on the British squares and were as repeatedly repulsed, leaving walls of dead piled up in front of the resolute infantry. They, too, suffered terrible losses.

Cavalry remained integral to warfare for some time after 1815. In the American Civil War cavalry was used by the North as mounted infantry. The war involved thousands of horses, and it was lack of cavalry that contributed to the Confederate defeat.

In the reign of Queen Victoria the British army was involved in over eighty campaigns, in all of which cavalry featured prominently and sometimes tragically. There was the charge of the Light Brigade at Balaclava in 1854 which, in fairness, was not the fault of the grossly incompetent commanders concerned, the indecisive Lucan, nick-named Lord Look-On, and the vain, arrogant, and near unbalanced Cardigan, the Noble Yachtsman, who quartered himself in his own, amply provisioned yacht while his soldiers (and, in fairness again, Lord Lucan), endured the miseries of a Crimean winter under canvas, supported by a commissariat that had neither the means nor the ability to carry out its task.

During the abortive charge, 470 out of the original 673 horses were killed, 42 were wounded and another 43 were later destroyed. Many more horses died of starvation. Within two months of Balaclava the cavalry division had lost 1,800 of its 2,000 horses and the 13th Light Dragoons mustered only 12 out of 250 horses brought out from England. The only redeeming feature of the campaign was the successful, controlled charge of Scarlett and his Heavy Brigade which sent the Russians reeling back. Tennyson commemorated this event in 'The Charge of the Three Hundred', but it was the action of the Light Brigade and Cardigan's subsequent heroic appearances on his charger Ronald when he returned to England that caught the public fancy and were remembered.

The Boer War was possibly the most salutary lesson ever administered to the British cavalry. The Boer farmers on their tough ponies ran rings round them – in the end, they had to follow the American example and operate with the tough, more flexible Colonial horsemen as mounted infantry. Most of the horse losses incurred by the British were the result of poor management. One regular regiment calculated that it lost one horse for every 3½ miles (5.6km) it marched. A total of 326,000 horses out of 494,000 were lost between 1899 and 1902, and only a few as the result of enemy action. At the subsequent enquiry Major-General Brabazon, a forthright man, condemned the 'shameful abuse of horseflesh', declaring himself both 'shocked' and 'horrified'.

The Captor of Jerusalem: General Sir Edmund Allenby.

General Allenby's use of the horse in the First World War was every bit as inventive as Rommel's use of armour in the Second.

The final cavalry encounter which went a long way towards redressing the balance was the classic and victorious campaign waged by General Allenby against the Turks in Palestine in 1917–18. Allenby was arguably the most gifted commander of the First World War on either side. He was made Inspector-General of Cavalry in 1910 and was responsible for the high level of horse-management, in appalling conditions, which was practised by the British in France and also for the exemplary conduct shown by the British cavalry, when, for instance, they fought as infantry in the first battle of Ypres in 1914.

Of all the cavalry forces in the opening stages of the Great War only the British, by superior management and handling of a high professional order, remained operational. The German cavalry failed in its advance to the Aisne because of the high rate of casualties suffered by the horses – casualties which occurred not because of enemy action but from disease, lameness, debility and so on; incompetent horse-management, in fact. The French were almost as bad. Unlike the British, who dismounted to rest their horses or to lead them when there was no immediate necessity to ride, the French division sat on their horses the day through, and never removed the saddles. The horses suffered from such sore backs that it was said that their suppurating galls could be smelled a mile away if the wind was in the right direction. In Palestine, for much the same reasons, the French cavalry contingent had to withdraw from Allenby's force. British cavalry, which had produced shameful performances in the Boer War a dozen years previously and which before that had suffered frequently from unprofessional leadership, had at last learnt its lesson. Officers now observed the golden rule, 'Look after the horses first, then the men, and then yourself'.

Field Marshall Lord Wavell wrote of Allenby that his . . .

training of the cavalry was on sound and practical lines. He held a middle course between the hotheads who would have it that the 'cavalry spirit' demanded the solution of all problems by shock action and those who would have discarded sword and lance altogether and treated the cavalry merely as mounted riflemen. He supported the introduction of machine-guns and stressed the value of fire-power but taught that many opportunities for intervention by mounted action and the sword would still occur on the modern battlefield.

He proved all of this in 1918 at Beersheba and Meggido when the shock tactic was used with devastating effect.

Allenby's Desert Mounted Corps was made up of twenty thousand horsemen from Australian, New Zealand, Indian and British regiments, the latter yeomanry regiments mounted on English hunter types. Long marches in arid desert conditions with temperatures rising to 100°F (38°C) became commonplace, the columns covering 60 miles (96km) a day and more. In November 1917 the whole army marched 170 miles (273km) in four days. Chenevix Trench wrote of his own experience:

In the Indian Cavalry Division's final pursuit to Damascus my own regiment, Hodson's Horse, having led the breakthrough to the coast and outpaced messengers sent to slow down its advance, rode 56 miles [90km] in the first 26 hours, in great heat, fighting several stiff actions. Thirteen exhausting days later the regiment reached Damascus after a final day's march of 63 miles [101km] with negligible horse-wastage.

It was during this advance that the Berkshire Yeomanry's horse artillery battery accomplished, with the guns, a march of 78 miles (125km) in 36 hours.

The campaign ended with the occupation in October 1918 of Aleppo, a city founded by one of the earliest of the horse peoples, the Hittites. Sixty miles (96km) from Aleppo, at Alexandretta, Alexander the Great had won his first victory over the Persian King Darius. The twilight of the cavalry could not have been preceded by a more glorious sunset.

Lloyd George, the 'cottage-bred man' and the antithesis of the cavalryman who represented the social orders which he disliked so heartily, had frequently been at loggerheads with Haig and had just as frequently openly criticised the Generals for their 'ridiculous cavalry obsession'. Now he was just as fulsome in his praise of Allenby's horsemen: 'Their contribution to the rout of the Turkish army will always be quoted as a conspicuous example of the services which cavalry can render in war.' Of the horses he said: 'they were as unbeatable as the riders.'

But then the politicians, as is their way, having produced something like the right words at the right moment, turned their backs in an act of betrayal which did little credit to Britain. Some twenty thousand horses were sold in Egypt to lives of brutal neglect and callous cruelty, being worked to death in the streets of Cairo. It was left to an individual to right this wrong, or at least to attempt to alleviate the sufferings of the survivors. Dorothy Brooke, wife of Major-General Sir Geoffrey Brooke who commanded the Cavalry Brigade in Egypt in 1930, campaigned vigorously to save the old horses from further privation. Some she bought herself, others with money raised by appeals. She got enough to build stables in Cairo, and to provide proper veterinary attention for the inmates. Today the Brooke Hospital for Animals in Cairo opens its doors to all sick animals, without charge. It remains the memorial to a lady who 'hated to remember, but could not forget' – and a reminder, perhaps, of a country's shame.

On the Western Front thousands of draught horses serviced the opposing armies, hauling supplies through the deep, holding morass; bringing up the guns and drawing the ambulances. The British alone lost nearly half a million horses, mostly due to exposure which made them vulnerable to lung and digestive disorders. Only a quarter of that number died as the result of enemy action.

Nonetheless, cavalry survived into the Second World War. In 1930 there was still a strong cavalry lobby in Britain. A year or two later Guderian, appointed in 1935 to command Hitler's 2nd Panzer Division, had transferred the cavalry and its unquenchable spirit into

steel tanks and was planning his *Blitzkrieg* of Europe. The Polish cavalry went down before the German armour. Poland, almost the last of the horse nations, had gone to war with no less than eighty six thousand horses. In 1939 the Pomeranian Cavalry Brigade lost two thousand horses out of three thousand in the space of half an hour when attacked by dive-bombers.

The German Army, armoured *Blitzkrieg* or no, employed vast numbers of horses, particularly on the Eastern Front, but nowhere near the size of the Russian cavalry formations. They had thirty cavalry divisions supported by horse artillery, as well as eight hundred thousand draught horses – a total of some 1.2 million horses. In November 1941, as the Germans were striking towards Moscow, the German 106th Infantry Division and the supporting 107th Artillery were attacked near the village of Musino by the 44th Mongolian Cavalry Division. They charged 'stirrup touching stirrup, riders low on the horses' necks, drawn sabres over their shoulders'. The astonished Germans opened fire. In minutes 2,000 horses and riders were lying dead or dying. There was not one German casualty.

Nearly every cavalry action was magnificent. But too many, we may think, had little to do with war.

Care in place of despair. The Brooke Hospital for Animals in Cairo was founded to save the old Cavalry Brigade horses that had been abandoned by the British Government.

SINEWS OF PEACE | *Chapter 13*

For upwards of four thousand years the primary use of the horse was for the purpose of war. There were, of course, peaceful uses to which the horse could be put. He could draw loads in harness, pull a travelling chariot, take men hunting or carry herdsmen round their flocks, but it was a very long time before horses were used in the cultivation of land. It is true that in northern Europe there are Bronze Age rock drawings which show horses working at the plough, but these should not be taken as an indication of established practice for horses also figured in religious ritual, and it is that with which these horses were concerned. They were harnessed to the plough for a symbolic cutting of the first furrow. After that the job was taken over by oxen.

In the Middle East and Asia, where so much of our history began, horses were for long held in such esteem that their employment in lowly tasks could not have been contemplated. Oxen and donkeys did the work perfectly well, as indeed they do today throughout the Mediterranean area and eastwards. Mules and donkeys are also far better suited to narrow vineyard tracks and in Europe it was not really until the eighteenth century that horses finally supplanted oxen in the plough. Even then there were the diehards who clung stubbornly to the ox as being more economically viable. In Britain the ox was championed by no less a person than Arthur Young, a leading agriculturalist of the eighteenth century and the first Secretary of the newly formed Board of Agriculture. Opposition to horses came also from farm workers who saw their jobs threatened by the increasing use of horse-powered machines.

Oxen were cheaper to keep, as Britain's oldest agricultural authority, Walter of Henley, was at pains to show when he wrote on the subject in 1286. At that time an ox could be kept for a full year for a quarter the cost of a horse. Furthermore, when the ox was at the end of its working life it could be fattened and sold profitably, whereas an old, worn-out horse was worth nothing more than his hide in a country in which the eating of horse-flesh was taboo.

Nonetheless, the ox is much slower than the horse. It needs pasturage close to the work, for its slow pace prohibits its being kept anywhere but on site. Being a ruminant, it must also be given time for cud-chewing.

The demise of the heavy horse in agriculture was caused by the introduction of motorised transport in the city rather than by the tractor on the farm.

Above and opposite page:
**Man's dependence on the
horse is amply demonstrated
by these twentieth-century
records.**

Eventually, so far as north western Europe was concerned, the horse won the battle of agricultural motive-power, but the golden age of horse-power farming was, like the golden age of coaching, a short-lived affair. The tractor took over from the farm horse and the railways from the coach, though neither did away with the need for horses. In fact, the railways provided more opportunities for their employment.

In Europe it was not until the eighth century that harness and horseshoes had been sufficiently developed for horses to be able to carry out agricultural work, and at that time they were really not big enough to undertake more than a limited range of tasks. By the eleventh century bigger horses, based on the heavy cold-bloods of Europe, deriving from the ancient Forest horse, were being bred for warfare. It was this that was partially responsible for the eventual production of the powerful heavy draught breeds like the present-day Shire, Suffolk, Ardennes, Clydesdale and Percheron.

Other very relevant factors in the development of the heavy agricultural horse were the introduction, after the eleventh century, of the three crop rotational system (cereals and roots followed by the return to grass), and the later invention of more sophisticated farm machinery better adapted to the quick, even action of the horse than to the slower-moving oxen.

In the eighteenth and nineteenth centuries, as agricultural practice became more efficient to correspond with burgeoning populations and a greater demand for foodstuffs, an increased variety of cereals and roots was grown in greater quantity, as well, of course, as grasses and clovers suitable for stock feeding. By then the horse was firmly established in agriculture, a process accompanied and assisted by continual innovations in the design of implements.

The eighteenth century produced no great quantity of horse machinery but there were some notable inventions. In 1731 Jethro Tull's horse-drawn seed drill made its debut, to be followed by a horse hoe. The year before had seen the introduction of the Rotherham swing plough, an improvement on a Dutch design and much lighter in draught. After that came the Arbuthnot swing plough, which turned the spit (the furrow slice) cleaner and more easily than anything else. A test proved that the Arbuthnot plough, drawn by two horses, could till more land in a day than a team of six oxen using an older pattern plough.

By the middle of the nineteenth century the machinery was becoming increasingly sophisticated. There were threshing machines, corn grinders, elevators, multi-furrowed ploughs, special sub-soiling ploughs, reaping machines, cutters, binders and even, in the USA, the forty-horse team combined harvesters.

This all represented heavy work for the horses, sometimes brutally heavy, and it required the heaviest and most powerful animals. In France, the Low Countries, Germany and Scandinavia a great number of heavy breeds existed and were developed. Notable were the Belgian Heavy Draughts, exported in large numbers to the USA and Canada in the nineteenth century, and descendants of the Flanders or Flemish horses which are concerned time and time again with the European breeds. These Flanders horses derived virtually directly from the Forest type of cold-blooded horse and were the foundation for much of Europe's armoured chivalry.

Best known of all, perhaps, and more effectively developed, are the massive Shire horse, the Suffolk of East Anglia and the Scottish Clydesdale. The Percheron, almost the single most popular of the heavy breeds, belongs to France but is also bred in Britain and elsewhere. These provided the most effective agricultural horses throughout the horse-farming period of the eighteenth and nineteenth centuries and, indeed, well into the first half of the twentieth century. This was especially so in Britain, with its high standard of agriculture.

The Shire is the descendant of the English Great Horse of the Middle Ages, which in turn derived from the heavy horses brought into England soon after the Norman conquest. Henry VIII passed laws to encourage the breeding of larger horses; in 1540, for instance, no stallion under 15 hands high was allowed to run out at pasture. The Great Horse of the period, on the evidence of the horse armour which can be seen on display today in the Tower of London, could not at this point have stood much over 15.2 hands and it was very far from resembling the massive modern Shire.

Henry's daughter, Elizabeth I, acquired a coach in 1564. In 1572 she made the journey to Warwick from London in this conveyance pulled by 'six of the biggest and strongest horses available, and as a result was unable to sit down for days'. The horses would have been the Great Horses, by then outmoded as warhorses. The reason for Her Majesty's discomfort, apart from the lack of springs, was the condition of the roadways, insofar as any existed. So rough were these tracks, being heavily rutted in summer and deep in mud during winter that coaches and wagons were not so much drawn as hauled across the countryside. Nonetheless, the use of the Great Horse in this capacity marked the appearance of a heavy draught horse in Britain and a notable change in the role of the warhorse that had been bred to carry body armour and an armoured horseman.

Thomas Blundeville (the one who objected to horses which fell to 'a' hopping and dancing up and down in one place'), writing about the importation of heavy horses from Europe during this period, makes specific mention of three breeds: the German draught horse, which he terms the Almaine; the Frisian, and the Flemish (or Flanders horse), both from the Low Countries. This last, which like the Frisian was predominantly black, appears continually in the evolution of the Shire and has to be regarded as the ancestor of the breed, although the lighter, very active Frisian, now a trotting horse of some note, also played a part. Both were crossed with the indigenous horse, the Flemish on account of its size having the greater influence. The Frisian cross provided refinement and a better, freer movement.

A factor in the development of the Shire was the draining of the Fens in the mid-seventeenth century, work which was not completed until the nineteenth. It encouraged the breeding of big, powerful horses, for it was work demanding of both weight and strength. The best were bred on the Fens and the adjoining areas of Leicestershire and Staffordshire and parts of Derbyshire, but there was a great variation in type. It was in the early part of this period that Cromwell, a

Huntingdon man himself and an agriculturalist, gave the name Blacks to the English draught horses and from that point we hear no more of England's Great Horse.

The first stallion which may be said to have had the status of a foundation horse was the curiously named Packington Blind Horse who stood at or near the village of Packington, near Ashby de la Zouche, between 1755 and 1770. He appears in the first Shire stud book largely on account of his descendants.

The Shire Horse Society was formed in 1884, eight years after the appearance of the first stud book and after it had discarded its original title of 'English Cart Horse Society'. Between 1901 and 1914 over five thousand animals were registered each year and the big export market to the USA was a strong incentive to breeders.

But by 1947, after the Second World War, there was little place for the Shire either in industry or agriculture. Remarkably, however, the breed survived. Today the Society holds an annual show which attracts large numbers of spectators. The breed has, indeed, staged a revival. At the 1986 show, for instance, three hundred horses competed and were watched by over fifteen thousand enthusiasts.

The present-day Shire has more quality than his forbears, inclining more towards the horse that was bred in the Midlands rather than the coarser Fen type. The average Shire weighs 20–22cwt (1016–1118kg) and stands upwards of 17 hands. The legs carry a considerable amount of hair (called 'feather'), a characteristic which at one time lost the Shire breeders an important market: the Americans did not like excessive feather which under working conditions produces an irritative skin condition called 'grease'. Modern Shires, however, are not expected to carry the heavy feather which was commonplace half a century ago.

The strength of the Shire can be judged from some of the weight-pulling demonstrations which were popular in the breed's heyday. At the Wembley Exhibition in 1924 a pair pulling against a dynometer (a device for measuring mechanical power) exceeded the maximum possible reading. It was estimated that they exerted a pull equal to a starting load of 50 tonnes. The same pair, driven in tandem (i.e. one behind the other) moved an actual load of 18.5 tonnes on slippery granite setts, with no difficulty at all. Indeed, the shaft horse had started the load alone before his companion in the trace had got into his collar and begun to pull.

Midland breeders for many years used mares to within two months of their foaling for farm work, perpetuating the medieval system in which the stallions were used solely for war. Foals often ran by their dams as the latter were working.

Oldest of these heavy English breeds is the Suffolk of East Anglia,

The Suffolk Punch.

The Clydesdale.

The Percheron of French origin.

most often known as the Suffolk Punch. A Punch is defined as 'a variety of English horse, short-legged and barrel-bodied, a short, fat fellow'. The early origins of the breed are obscure. William Youatt, writing in 1831, considered the Suffolk to be a cross between imported Norman horses, by which he might have meant Percherons, and the local Suffolk cart mares. Since the Norman conquest there had been plenty of those about. William Fitzstephen mentions 'mares suitable for the plough, the sleigh and the cart' in his account of Smithfield Market, which was written in 1170. William Camden, writing in *Brittania* in 1586, refers to the Suffolk breed and says that they were in existence eighty years earlier.

What is certain is that every Suffolk alive today traces back on the male side to a single stallion, Crisp's Horse of Ufford (probably in fact Orford, where a Crisp family is known to have owned land). This horse was foaled in 1760.

A pure breed, the Suffolk is ideally suited to working on the heavy clay soils of East Anglia and has the advantage of being 'clean-legged', that is, without the feather of the Shire. It weighs about the same as a Shire, but stands at about 16–16.3 hands. Its action is longer and lower than the high, more wasteful, movement of the Shire and East Anglian farmers held that no other horse exceeds it in working their heavy soils. It is very long–lived, with enormous tractive power and the ability to work long hours on smaller rations than other breeds. In other words it is an effective convertor of food.

On an East Anglian farm a team of Suffolks would be fed and groomed at 4.30 am. At 6.30, after two hours for digestion, they were led to work. Halfway through the morning, other heavy working breeds stopped for the agricultural equivalent of 'elevenses' from a nosebag, after which time had to be given for the digestive process to be completed. But the Suffolk, with only short rests, worked through without a break until 2.30 pm.

The colour of the Suffolk is always 'chesnut', and is spelt that way. Seven shades are recognised officially by the Suffolk Horse Society, formed in 1877. They range from a pale, mealy tone to a dark colour, nearly brown. The most common is a bright, reddish shade. Suffolk horses have been exported to the USSR, Australia, Africa and to Pakistan, where they are still used in the breeding of army remounts.

Of the three British breeds, the one with the most influence is the Clydesdale. It may not possess the massive presence of the Shire nor the roly-poly solidity of the Suffolk, but it has the best action. What is more, it has been bred consistently for good feet and hereditary soundness. This policy paid dividends for Clydesdales have been exported in larger numbers all over the world than any other English breed. It was teams of Clydesdales that cultivated the prairies of

America and Canada. There was a thriving trade with South Africa, New Zealand and Europe, while in Australia they have been called 'the breed that built Australia'.

The breed as we know it is not much more than a hundred and fifty years old, but at the beginning of the eighteenth century Flemish stallions were certainly imported to the area round the Clyde valley in Lanarkshire to be crossed with the much smaller native draught horse. Between 1715 and 1720 the sixth Duke of Hamilton and particularly John Paterson of Lochlyoch imported Flemish stallions, and a little later there were undoubtedly infusions of Shire blood made into the breed. It is also possible that the traffic was two-way and that the Shire benefited from some exchange with the Clydesdale. Lawrence Drew, steward to the eleventh Duke of Hamilton at Merryton in the late nineteenth century, believed firmly that Shires and Clydesdales were two wings of one breed.

The emphasis on excellence, particularly in respect of legs and feet and free, swift movement at walk and trot, established the Clydesdale as a superlative working horse. It was the Scottish genius for promoting a good product, however, that made the Clydesdale one of the world's most influential working breeds.

The last of this notable quartet is the Percheron, the most stylish and handsome of all the heavy breeds and the one with the most romantic history. In its time the Percheron has been used for all sorts of purposes: as warhorse, coach horse, farm horse, gun horse, and even riding horse. It originates in the limestone country of Le Perche in Normandy and it is claimed that its forbears carried the knights of Charles Martel to their victory over the Moors at Poitiers in 732. Following that battle Oriental blood was made available and used extensively. More Arab blood was introduced by Robert, Count of Rotrou, after the First Crusade in 1096–99, and in 1760 the royal stud at Le Pin made Arab sires available to Percheron breeders.

A nineteenth-century authority, indulging possibly in a little Gallic expansiveness, was moved to claim that the Percheron is 'an Arab influenced by climate and the agricultural work for which it has been used for centuries'. That may be an over-emphasis of the Arabian influence but the greatest of the Percheron stallions and the most influential lines are without doubt dominated by the Arab. Two very great Arab stallions used as further outcrosses were Godolphin and Gallipoly, the latter being the sire of Jean le Blanc, foaled in 1830 at Mauvres-sur-Huisne, the most famous of all Percheron stallions.

The significance of Arabian blood, the purest in the world, is that it allows the breeder, if he crosses judiciously, to produce a required type and to do so consistently and within a relatively short period of time. Percheron breeders made the most of their advantages and bred, very successfully, to market requirements, switching from coach horse to heavy draught towards the end of the nineteenth century.

The breed was at its zenith between 1880 and 1920 when Percherons were in great demand in the USA, Australia, South Africa and South America. Britain founded its own enthusiastic society in 1918. In the USA $5000 was the going rate for a good Percheron just before the turn of the century. In 1880 over five thousand stallions and somewhere between two and three thousand mares were imported. Twenty years later there were over five thousand breeders and stock registrations between 1900 and 1910 reached a massive thirty-one thousand nine hundred. Top horses were then making upwards of $40,000. America, of course, had to produce the world's biggest horse. The Percheron Dr Le Gear, foaled in 1902, weighed 27cwt (1,372kg) and stood 21 hands high.

To replace the enormous loss of horses in the First World War, Britain imported Percherons and part-bred Percherons from the USA and Canada. Thousands of them went to France after 1915 and formed a large percentage of Britain's total horse casualties – an appalling half a million between 1914 and 1918.

Western Europe concentrated on the heavy breeds which suited the land and the improved methods of agriculture. Eastern Europe, however, where farming was not so advanced, acreages smaller, and the ground often much lighter, never adopted the heavy horse. It did not suit the conditions and would also have been more expensive to feed than lighter types. Eastern Europeans wanted an all-round horse which could pull a cart, be ridden and also be put to heavier work. Horse ownership was traditional in a way that it was not in western Europe; in a peasant society of smallholders, ownership was not only widespread but a sign of social standing and prosperity. Under those circumstances there was no place for slow, heavy horses which were expensive to keep and limited in their use.

These light horses did, however, provide the basis for the breeding of the famous eastern European coach horses between the seventeenth and nineteenth centuries. These, in turn, became foundation stock for the modern continental warm-blood competition horses.

With the demise of the feudal system came the growth of a rural middle class, either owning property or holding it on lease. These yeoman farmers – some of whom, in Britain, became sufficiently wealthy to take their place among the gentry – owned and bred horses for farming. As they became more prosperous they kept a trap horse for market days. Some even aspired to a carriage horse and there would most likely have been a riding cob or a hunter or both.

In the Low Countries, Germany and France agrarian capitalist societies evolved in a slightly different way as peasants bought their own land. Most of them were not much more than smallholders but they, too, needed to keep a horse for farm work. The spread of horse ownership was increased immeasurably as it became open to social classes other than the aristocracy.

From the beginning of the horse–man relationship, the horse has been the symbol of power and authority. The mounted man was always superior to the man who got about on his feet. The horseman was compelled to look down on the pedestrian, just as the latter was forced to look up to a man whose knee was above the level of his eyes. That aspect of the horse did not change. Gentlemen were still expected to ride or to cut a dash in a carriage, and those that would be gentlemen followed suit. The middle-class yeoman rode a horse for practical reasons perhaps, but also to signify this standing. Such was the prestige of the horse that a hierarchy quickly formed among the workers who cared for him, particularly within the farming community. Among farmworkers the head horseman took priority, and none would question his right to be the first to lead out his horse in the morning. In *Life in a Welsh Countryside*, A. D. Rees makes the point that it was the eldest brother who cared for the horses, the second being assigned the cattle and the third the sheep. This attitude he considers to derive from an English 'horse culture', associated with a higher social standing. Cattle, for example, were always given Welsh names, but the prestigious horse was called by an English name which acknowledged an aristocratic standing: Prince, Captain, Duke or King.

In the nineteenth century many waggoners or horsemen belonged to a sort of freemasonry, the Horseman's Society, which had its own secret ritual and initiation ceremonies. Members pooled their knowledge and helped each other with difficult horses. At the centre of it all was the 'Horseman's Word' which acted not just as a password but as a means of obtaining dominance over any horse. The employment of charms was known in East Anglia and there were numerous recipes and oils which were thought to control a horse's behaviour.

Although the farm horse was essential to any agricultural enterprise, a far greater number of working horses were employed in transport and industry. Without a system of horse transport to move raw materials to work sites and then collect and deliver finished goods, no industrial activity would have been possible.

With the opening up of the New World the balance of trade shifted from the Mediterranean countries to northern Europe. From there trade with America and the West Indies developed. As early as the late sixteenth century there was a huge flow of goods in and out of the north European ports. In Antwerp alone over two hundred heavy loads of merchandise and general goods were moved in and out of the port and to and from France and Germany each week, while local traffic amounted to over ten thousand wagon loads.

In Britain, the country which spearheaded the Industrial Revolution, systems of transport had already evolved prior to the age of the railway, and horses were used in the mines before James Watt invented the steam engine in 1769. The power the new machine produced, namely that required to raise 550lb one foot in one second (equivalent to 745.7 watts), was measured as one horsepower.

Horses worked at the pitheads turning the windlass of the hoist, as well as drawing coal wagons, and were the source of power for many other pieces of heavy machinery. There were horse mills, worked often by blind or lame horses, where windmills and water mills were impracticable; and a whole variety of machinery used on farms, like grist mills, root choppers and so on were of necessity horse-powered.

Ponies were used regularly underground in British coalmines from the nineteenth century onwards, once the vertical shaft had been replaced by horizontal 'drifts' which allowed the ponies to walk to the coal faces, and 'cages' had been introduced in which they could be lowered down the shaft.

The ponies lived underground, where for the most part they were very well cared for. A substantial trade existed for breeders and dealers to supply ponies suitable for the pits. In Scotland, Shetland ponies were much used on account of their small stature and a strength quite out of proportion to their size. In Wales it was often the Welsh Mountain Pony or the smaller sort of Welsh Cob. They were known

Underground, the safest form of power was provided by the horse.

as 'pitters' and bred for the purpose. Ponies worked in British mines right up to 1972 when the last five, working at Wheldale Colliery, Castleford, were retired.

Prior to the rail system a network of canals had been established in Britain during the early eighteenth century. Freight and passengers were carried in barges drawn by horses and sometimes by mules or even donkeys. The canals, the barges and the barge horses held their own even after the railway revolution and the barge horse survived into the late 1950s and beyond. There was never a breed or specific type of barge horse, just as there was never an 'industrial' horse, but few horses had so demanding a job and few had to exercise more intelligence and versatility.

For the most part barge horses, 'boaters', were either of a strong vanner type, a light draught horse often of Irish extraction, or they were smaller Shire-type versions of the heavy draught horses. They could not be much above 15.3 hands because of the height of the bridges along the towpaths. Strength was paramount, for boat horses had to shift a load of 50–60 tonnes or so and keep it moving. It was estimated in 1810 that one horse and three men could move as much by barge as sixty horses and ten men could haul over the roads in a wagon. A boater pulled his barge along at a speed of 2mph (3.2kph) but some of the single turnouts when drawn by relays of trotting horses working short stages could cover 50–60 miles (80–96km) in a day. In comparison with the early horsed railway, canal transport was by far the better proposition.

The arrival of the railroads, far from diminishing the role of the horse, in fact created a need for greater horsepower. As more and more goods and raw materials had to be moved to the factories from the railways, so more and more short-haul transport was required.

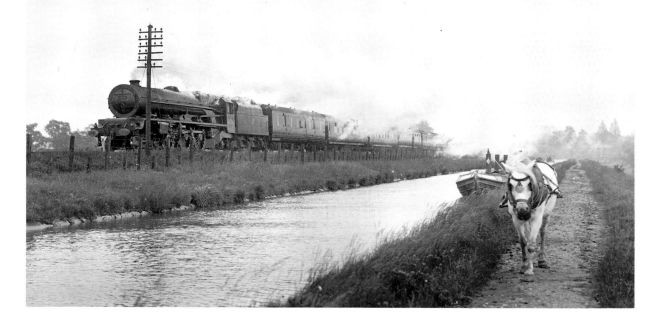

In the mid-eighteenth century barges carrying 200 tonnes were hauled up the Thames by teams of fourteen horses, or they were moved up more slowly and more laboriously by gangs of eighty men straining on the towing ropes. At the end of the same century a form of high-speed passenger and light freight transport, comparable in glamour and status to that subsequently provided by the stagecoach, was initiated on selected canals, especially the Grand Union and the Shropshire Union.

In its day, travelling by the light fly boat must have been an exciting experience, probably more comfortable than journeying by road. The last fly boat only ceased operating just after the First World War, and fly boats carrying urgent freight, up to 17–18 tonnes in weight, remained in general use well after the advent of the railway.

The fly boat was a light, shallow craft, drawing no more than 18in (46cm) of water. It was towed by two horses attached to it by separate lines, one fastened at the stern and one at the bow. On the Shropshire Union a postillion rode the rear horse of the pair, controlling the lead horse with his whip and voice. Once the boat was under way, the pace was a steady, uniform canter which caused the bow to lift and gave a planing attitude to the craft. Since the tow lines were attached fore and aft it was towed parallel to the bank so that the tiller man had to make only minimal corrections of course. On the Grand Union it was more usual for the postillion to ride the lead horse, a method which must have reduced his effective control of the situation but possibly demanded the exercise of less skill on his part.

Fly boats had priority over all others. To enforce their standing their bows were often fitted with sharp scythe blades which would cut through the tow rope of any barge that did not give way with sufficient alacrity. The horses were worked in teams over stages of 3–5 miles (5–8km), and the boats could average speeds of 10–12 mph (16–19 kph). As on the railways, the cost per passenger was a penny a mile. Negotiation of the locks and changes of horses called for a high degree of skill and judgement on the part of lock-keepers and horsemen, but the fly boat operators reached a standard quite comparable to that of the stagecoach ostlers, who could put a new team to a coach in a 50-second change.

In severe weather, when the water froze hard, an ice-breaker often well over 7ft (2m) in beam was used to keep the canals open. Up to twenty horses pulled the ice-breaker and they frequently did it at a gallop. Boatmen packed into the vessels to rock them from side to side in order to clear as wide a channel as possible. Since the canal companies provided 'baiting' (feed) money for the horses and free beer for the boat rockers a good time seems to have been had by all.

The boater had to learn how to cope with the towpath, the bridge and the tunnel if he was to avoid injury or even death. The towpaths on the big canals could be metalled tracks but on the smaller waterways the paths were often neglected and deep in mud. They were, in addition, barred by self-closing gates and stiles which marked boundary fences running down to the waterside. The horses were trained to jump obstacles like stiles, which could be as much as 3ft (0.9m) high. To jump that height out of deep mud or from a slippery, broken take-off and to do so in harness is a feat of considerable difficulty, and many horses were injured when the tow-lines or the harness crossbar became caught on the stiles. Constable's painting *The Leaping Horse* shows a boat horse negotiating just such an obstacle.

As the canals went into decline the condition of the towpaths deteriorated. Henry de Salis, writing in Bradshaw's *Canals and Navigable Rivers* in 1904 when a large tonnage of freight was still being moved on the waterways, drew attention to the danger of these paths: 'often in winter nothing but a slough of mire, and bounded by a hedge so overgrown as seriously to curtail the width necessary for the passage of a horse'. Stiles were still to be found on towpaths well into the 1900s.

Attached to the horse, even the barge could make a lovely picture.

When the towpath changed sides the horse had to cross the canal. This was done by going over a simple hump-back bridge or on a 'roving bridge', a sort of spiral arrangement which did away with the need for unharnessing. Otherwise the boater was ferried over, either in his own boat or on a horse ferry. Or he had to jump into a moving boat from a pier and then jump out from the other side onto a similar pier – a procedure that required both agility and sagacity. Boat horses' lives were full of such hazards.

The canals operated over a series of locks, at which the barge horse had to assist in the opening and closing of the gates, but there were also tunnels bored when the construction of locks and cuttings was not practicable. In Britain there were 45 tunnels in regular use, some being over a mile (1.6km) in length. Some had towpaths but when those were lacking the horse had to be led 'over the top' by children or, just as frequently, had to find his own way to the other end. Bereft of any motive power, the boatmen then either poled the barge through, or lay on their backs on 'wings' (boards placed across the bow) and 'legged' the vessel through against the tunnel's sides.

Boat horses had to respond quickly to commands given from the boat or the bank, particularly when passing or being passed by other horses. They learnt how to apply their weight to the collar or, conversely, ease the force of the pull, displaying a fine instinctive sense of judgement. When men with tractors replaced horses on the Grand Union Canal in the 1950s their lack of 'horse sense' meant they were frequently dragged off the bank into the water.

Falling into the water was, of course, the most common accident that befell the horse as well, and one that could have serious consequences. It was usually caused by a snagged tow-line or by jostling from a passing horse. When it happened the boatman had to go in after his horse without hesitation, in order to get him free of the harness and guide him on to the bank at some shallow spot.

There was still the odd barge horse working when the first man put his foot on the moon, but inevitably petrol- and diesel-driven engines took over, though not entirely satisfactorily. The first engines were not very reliable and took up several tonnes' worth of valuable cargo space. Running costs were not that much different, and the motor barge could hardly travel faster than a horse. If it did, the bow turbulence caused waves which broke down the canal banks, and for this reason strict speed limits were enforced. What an engine could do was to go on working through the night, when a horse had to rest.

Why did barge horses often wear muzzles? It was not because they were vicious, but only to prevent them from grazing along the towpath which in some areas was prohibited by bye-laws. Although the work was hard and often gruelling, there are some examples of very long-lived boat horses. The authenticated record for equine longevity in Britain belongs to a Blackburn boater named, prosaically, Billy. He died quietly in 1972 at the astonishing age of 63 years.

Another transport network was made up of the pack horse and pony trails. These were by no means found only in Britain; pack transport was used extensively throughout the world where there was mountainous terrain and few proper roads. In Britain, ponies and cobs packed slate from the quarries of north Wales down to the harbours at Porthmadog and Bangor. In north Yorkshire, Northumberland and Durham the Dales Pony was used in pack and harness and also in the pits. Versatile and immensely strong, under a pack saddle he carried lead and coal and also worked on the northern hill farms, ploughing, hauling and shepherding in terrain where larger and less sure-footed animals would have been at a disadvantage.

On the northern side of the Pennines and in Cumbria the Dales' neighbour, the Fell Pony, a slightly smaller, lighter type well suited for riding, was used throughout the eighteenth century to cart lead from the hill mines to the docks on Tyneside. The ponies carried about 224lb (101kg) in a pack load and averaged 240 miles (386km) per week over difficult, mountainous ground. They went in trains of twenty or more, following head to tail along the narrow paths and rocky defiles with only one mounted man accompanying them.

Shetlands, the smallest of the pony breeds native to Britain, were used as pack ponies for hauling seaweed and peat as well as for doing farm work on the crofts.

Britain's premier carriage horse, the Cleveland Bay, was also used as a pack horse. It originated in north east Yorkshire, an amalgam of the Chapman horse, the Andalusian and the Barb, the last two being available during the seventeenth century. More correctly, it was the old type of Chapman that carried packs. Strong and short-legged, with the sort of broad, rather long back which is ideally suited to a pack horse, it was the principal conveyance in the North Riding of Yorkshire of farm produce, wool, corn, coal and most other commodities during the eighteenth century. The man leading the horse, the travelling salesman of the day, was called a chapman, which is how the horse got its name.

The other British pack horse was the Devonshire, a bigger version of the Exmoor and Dartmoor ponies. The Devonshire Pack Horse stood just over 15 hands high and in the late seventeenth century was described as 'the ordinary horse of the times used for agricultural purposes'. It was a good trotting horse and was used on the Pack Horse Service running between Bampton, Devon and London in the 1630s and later.

The first railway horses were those which hauled freight and passenger coaches over short and medium distances on what were known as tramways or dramways. (The first line on which horses actually drew carriages was the Surrey Iron Railway, opened in 1803, and connecting Wandsworth with Croydon.) This method of transport preceded the steam locomotive and in some areas it survived for an astonishing length of time. A branch line in Northern Ireland, for instance, which terminated at Fintona Station, was using horse-drawn passenger coaches up to 1957, and on the Continent there were a number of horse-drawn lines which continued well into the nineteenth century.

There was a long-distance horse-drawn railway in Austria which connected the city of Linz in upper Austria with Budweis in Bohemia (Czechoslovakia). It became the principal means of transporting salt from the Saltzkammergut region of Austria to Bohemia, which had none. Prior to the railway, which also carried passengers and did so in some style, the salt had to be shifted in packloads over difficult country either by human labour or pack ponies. The line between Linz and Budweis was opened on 21 July 1832 by the Emperor Franz I, who with his Empress journeyed between Urfahr and St Magdalena in a splendidly opulent state landau with flanged iron wheels, complete with uniformed coachman on the box seat. The total length of the track was 124 miles (200km) and in its heyday the line transported 150,000 passengers each year and 100,000 tonnes of freight, more than half of it salt. The journey took 14 hours and that from Linz onward to Gmunden, a line added later, another six hours. It operated for forty years, closing in 1872.

The Linz–Budweis Line was, perhaps, hardly typical, but it was delightfully Ruritanian. From its inception the management insisted upon a high degree of courtesy being extended to its passengers. Even the warning signs were couched in the most respectful terms. Instead of a brusque 'Private – Keep Out' or 'No Trespassing by Order', these passengers got virtual essays:

> Whereas these rails were not laid for the purpose of accommodating pedestrians, but to ensure the rapid transportation of passengers and freight, we do not wish to deprive anyone of the pleasure of walking along the track. However, we consider it essential to request that all track-walkers step aside when they see the train approaching, as the horses and railcars are not capable of doing so, and to let the same pass unhindered . . .

That was only half of it.

Quaint it may have been, but it was much preferable to the notices issued by the Newcastle & Carlisle Railway operating in the 1860s. They warned that trespassers on railway property were liable to be punished by a term of seven years in the criminal colonies in Australia.

George Stephenson (1731–1848) opened the first steam-powered railway in 1825, when his *Locomotion No. 1* pulled a train of wagons filled with people on the 20-mile (33km) railway between Darlington and Stockton. By 1838 the London to Birmingham line was open and within six or seven years the major cities and towns of Britain were all served by the railway. Isambard Kingdom Brunel (1806–59), engineer to the Great Western Railway, was realising his vision of a regular route between London and New York with his brilliant construction of the line between London (Paddington) and Bristol. Later he designed, with only partial success, steam ships to sail the Atlantic, from the western port, the greatest and the biggest of its time being the *Great Eastern*, launched in 1858.

The railways put an end to the magnificent era of the mail and road coach, which, at its peak, lasted only just over twenty years between 1825 and 1845. But it was immortalised in etchings, prints and then Christmas cards and still remains a popular and potent image today. The railways also provoked considerable opposition not only from landowners but from those involved in the commercial breeding of horses, who prophesied the extinction of the heavy draught breeds. In fact the opposite occurred. Just as the railways acted to consolidate and extend the manufacturing interests which were the products of the Industrial Revolution in England between 1789 and 1832, so their effect upon the horse population was extensive and supportive.

The railway revolution, for it was nothing short of that, acted as a positive incentive to the greater employment of horsepower. Goods and raw materials had to be taken to and distributed from the railheads and passengers required transport. Railways, serving urban factories, contributed to the population explosion in cities, and the whole structure – from the transport of heavy machinery to the provision of foodstuffs for city dwellers – depended upon horsepower.

For well over a century the greatest employers and the largest owners of horses were the railway companies. Thousands of light horses (London alone had a horse population of three hundred thousand in 1890) drew station buses, cabs and single- and double-decker buses. Heavy horses were used in goods yards and for shunting rolling stock: they were cheaper than steam engines, more convenient and more efficient. Goods trucks were fitted with special side bars, known as horse handles, to which the pulling tackle of the shunt horse could be attached.

British Railways used shunting horses in the 1950s and 1960s and the last one, stationed at Newmarket where he moved the horse-boxes in the sidings, was not retired until 1967. (Barely a year later the last steam engine was withdrawn from the railway system.) British Rail

Providing transport of all kinds in the city created a growing problem by sheer numbers.

operated a horse-box service up to the 1960s. During the Suez crisis in 1957, when petrol was rationed, members of the Suffolk Hunt boxed their horses by rail from Bury St Edmunds station to Melton, near Sudbury, in order to hunt.

The early railways also participated in the canal system and the London Midland & Scottish Railway had a fleet of boats which brought goods to its wharves for onward transmission by horse transport to the railway stations.

The majority of the railway horses were employed in cartage and delivery. Teams of Shires were used for heavy transport, such as the moving of boilers, large pieces of machinery and so on; there were 'vanners' used for the lighter goods deliveries, and Hackney-type cobs or Welsh Cobs for the express parcels delivery service, carried at a swift trot at 12mph (19kph). The final design of the express delivery van was introduced just before the outbreak of the Second World War;

it was equipped with electric lamps, pneumatic tyres and disc brakes. These services continued into the 1960s when there were still horses employed at Euston and the London Midland region depots.

In the 1890s, main line companies kept stables of up to six thousand horses in London alone. In 1928 the LMS still owned 9,681 horses, a figure which had only dropped to 8,500 in 1937.

Railway horses were bought at between five and seven years of age. Their useful working life was usually a short one because of the great strain put upon their legs by continual starting of heavy loads. They had also to contend with constant working on the ungiving surfaces of the streets resulting in much wear and tear of feet and joints due to concussion. Horses carting heavy freight in industrial traffic conditions, where they had to keep stopping and starting, lasted only for four years before becoming unfit for service. Vanners working out of London with lighter loads might last twice that time.

The railway companies did, however, maintain very high standards, employing their own veterinary surgeons and sometimes maintaining their own horse hospitals. Of all the companies the Great Western Railway was adjudged the most humane. Horses and teams were allotted to one man, or one man and a boy, and so they had time to get to know them and, indeed, to form strong bonds of affection. Other companies changed their drivers and grooms about according to the need of the moment, a practice which did not allow for the building up of a rapport. 'God's Wonderful Railway', as befitted its nickname, did not sell its old horses, preferring to keep them for light duties and, when they were no longer fit, to have them put down by the company vets.

Omnibus horses (all mares) had a working life expectation on a par with the horse hauling heavy freight. The working life of a tram horse was a good year less because of the weight involved. Both sorts suffered injury to the joints, ligaments and tendons because of the continual stopping and starting.

If the short-lived coach service run in Paris by Blaise Pascal in 1662 is discounted, then the omnibus originated in France in the nineteenth century. Stanislaus Baudry set up a passenger service in Paris in 1828 after experiments in Nantes. There, his terminus had been outside the premises of a certain Monsieur Omnes, who inspired him with the name for the new form of public transport.

The French service was copied by George Shillibear who brought it to London and set up a service there in 1829, running initially between Paddington Green and the Bank. Mr Shillibear went bankrupt but his omnibus service flourished. There were 62 buses running in London in 1839, 1,300 in 1850 and 2,210, excluding trams, forty years later. Eleven thousand men were employed and a total of twice as many horses.

The French retained an interest in the omnibus, and the leading company, the *Compagnie Générale des Omnibus de Londres*, did not change its title to the London General Omnibus Company until 1862. It remained the largest of the companies operating horse buses.

W. J. Gordon, writing in 1893, estimated that the average number of passengers in an omnibus at any one time was 14 (the full complement was 26). On that basis, taking the weight of the bus at 1.5 tonnes, the pair of horses drawing the vehicle had a load of 2.5 tonnes. The average speed at which the omnibus travelled was 5mph (8kph). If the bus was full, however, as it would be on some occasions, the total load including the driver and conductor would have been 3.25 tonnes, which is considerable by any standards.

With a team of eleven horses to one omnibus, each horse worked three and a half hours per day, but it was work of the most severe kind and two out of three horses died in service.

The horses were often Irish, probably of Irish Draught type, but a fair proportion of Clydesdales, or part-bred Clydesdales, were also used. The Irish Draught is capable of doing farm work, pulling a trap or taking his owner across the countryside in the wake of a pack of foxhounds. It is a powerful animal with an inbred ability to jump and generally look after itself when faced with country obstacles. It forms the basis for the Irish Hunter, producing when crossed with the Thoroughbred what many consider the best cross-country horse in the world.

The tram, running on rails, followed hard on the heels of the omnibus. Gordon has this to say about its introduction:

> The tram came into existence to save the horse; it being shown clearly enough that the introduction of the rail meant the reduction of resistance and the easing of the horse's work; but, as a company for merely lightening a horse's labour would hardly be floatable, it was at once proposed to increase the weight of the vehicle, so that the investor might share advantages with the horse. As a consequence, the poor horse is 20 per cent worse off now than he was before the invention of the rail.

The tram, probably because the rail became clogged with dirt as well as because of the weight, turned out to be much harder work to start than the omnibus. A two-horse car when full weighed 5.5 tonnes and the tram horse was soon worn out.

Gordon quoted London as having 10,000 tram horses and 1,000 trams, which operated over 135 miles (217km) of tram line.

The horse-bus era lasted about seventy years, being succeeded by

The colour of the horse was significant in funerals. Some breeders specialised in the production of horses for this purpose.

the electric tram, the trackless trolleybus and finally the petrol- and diesel-driven vehicle.

Many other horses made up the horse population of big cities. In London there were the big, heavy draught breeds, like the Shire, used in the brewers' delivery drays; the Post Office had horses for mail deliveries; there were many carriage horses, some privately owned but most hired from the jobmasters' yards, and there were horses to pull the coal carts, for London in the nineteenth century burned five million tonnes a year. Then there were the curiously named vestry horses, the municipal cart horses which cleared the refuse. The vestries (parochial boards) employed some of the best horses in London, and they had to be able to back easily to take on their loads in narrow alleys and also when their carts were cleared. And there were

Man's inhumanity was not restricted to his fellow men.

the horses of the 'black masters', the undertakers. Funeral horses were almost always showy, black Frisians and no Victorian funeral was complete without them.

London also supported in the 1890s around 11,300 cabs which called for twice that number of horses. Some were well cared for, but many were desperately overworked and cruelly treated. In an even worse state were the cast-offs in every category – worn-out horses taken on by small traders and operators who literally worked them to death.

England may have been 'a paradise for women' (John Florio, 1553–1625), but it was 'a hell for horses' (Robert Burton, 1577–1640). Overloaded horses were savagely beaten; horses were brought down and died in the streets; many were worked in poor condition and were chronically lame. Horses that died in the shafts were moved straight to the knackers' yards by the dead-horse cart, being hauled in by a winch. The sight was commonplace enough to cause little concern to the passer-by.

Largely as the result of the efforts of Richard 'Humanity' Martin, Parliament passed an Act in 1822 to prevent the ill treatment of animals. Martin devoted his life to alleviating their suffering and was a founder of the Society for the Prevention of Cruelty to Animals. 'Humanity' Martin, because of his mounting debts, lived the last years of his life in Boulogne, out of the reach of his creditors, and died there in 1834. By then his Society had become the Royal Society and the work which he had begun in the face of great opposition was bearing fruit.

Few city horses died peaceful deaths. Most finished up at the horse slaughterers and in their deaths contrived still to be of service to mankind. Nothing was wasted: bones were ground for fertiliser after the grease had been extracted for candle-making and for leather dressings; skin and hoofs went to make glue; other bones were for making buttons; manes and tails were used to stuff furniture and make fishing lines and violin bows; hides were for the manufacture of all kinds of leather goods; the meat, in England anyway, was for the cats and dogs. Even the horseshoes were removed to make a new set.

The horse disposal industry as a whole supported thirty wholesale companies in London. It is by no means certain whose lot was the worse – the horse man used for war, or the one he used in times of peace.

Chapter 14

TOOLS OF THE TRADE

From the moment of domestication, the means by which man could control an animal far larger and stronger than he became a matter of urgency. Fortunately, the horse is non-aggressive and does not realise or appreciate the implications of his own strength. Furthermore, the great majority of horses are eager to please and to cooperate with man and by a system of repetition can be taught with relative ease.

Control, however, is basic to the relationship. Thereafter the exploitation of the horse's strength and speed and their effective application to a range of purposes is dependent upon the development of specific pieces of equipment. As the use of horses became more general and more sophisticated, it became necessary to devise ever more items of saddlery and harness.

It is perhaps surprising that the evolution of what might be considered fairly simple items – such as the stirrup, or a form of secure saddle – took so long. In other respects, for example the systems of bitting employed in the ancient world, the technology was well advanced. While bits have been devised in every shape and size, it is a fact that no significant alteration in the basic system has been made in something like three thousand years.

The first people to make use of the horse in a domestic role were already familiar with the handling of cattle or goats or reindeer, and it is very reasonable to suppose that their approach to horses was based on their experience with those animals. There is plenty of evidence to show that when it came to harnessing horses to a vehicle the equipment used was based on that employed with oxen. Initially then, the horse would have been restrained or led from a halter made of woven fibre or a leather thong.

It would not have been long, one imagines, before it was discovered that control was made more effective by the application of increased pressure on the nose by an encircling noose; it is quite possible to ride a horse using just this simple piece of equipment. From there it is only a small step to the fixing of a thong around the lower jaw, which is one way in which the American Indian rode.

The development of a bit, in which a mouthpiece lay over the tongue across the lower jaw, resting on the area of gum known as the 'bars' of the mouth, between the incisor and molar teeth, was

Not perhaps majestic but certainly the most graceful seat of all is that of the lady riding side-saddle. Until relatively recent times, ladies raced in side-saddles and side-saddle show classes now enjoy a huge popularity. On the other hand, when ladies ride astride they frequently beat the men.

relatively swift. Bits were made of hardwood, then bone and horn, and later metal. The Celts were the first horsemen to use a curb bit.

As horses were bred with increasing selectivity to become bigger and more powerful, bitting arrangements became stronger. The mouthpiece incorporated spikes and serrations, and the action was often reinforced by a tight, even a spiked, noseband. By the Middle Ages bits had assumed horrendous proportions. The curb bits of the fifteenth and sixteenth centuries, as well as the fearsome 'ring' bits of Moorish origin which were in use in the seventeenth century and are still to be seen throughout north Africa, were capable of exerting enormous pressures on the lower jaw. The cheeks on curb bits of this period could be as much as 20in (50cm) long and the potential leverage was correspondingly great.

Bits of these proportions – often, once more, with serrations or spikes in the mouthpiece – were made necessary when the use of heavy, protective armour for both man and horse encouraged the use of stronger and heavier horses. These were of predominantly cold-blooded origin, and were in consequence slower-moving and less responsive.

Although the bit helped the rider to obtain control, the full effectiveness of the horseman was limited in the early era by the surprising absence of saddles and stirrups. These two elements have a significant effect. Their use reduces fatigue for the rider and for the horse, whose movement is not restricted by having to carry weight directly on the spinal complex, and it adds enormously to the rider's security. The result, when they did come into use, was to increase the mobility and range of horsemen significantly.

A rider sitting bareback, however strong and athletic, is more likely to fall by losing his balance, and he is easily pulled from his mount by determined opponents. If he attempts to employ the shock tactic of the charge against a solid body of infantry he is again vulnerable, since the very shock of the impact is likely to unseat him. Horsemen without saddles were therefore confined to riding their horses to the place of battle and then dismounting to fight on foot, or they galloped across the enemy's front to throw javelins or fire arrows. They could be enormously effective, but they could not strike the decisive blow which would destroy the enemy line. They could not charge the enemy, to destroy the opposition by weight and impetus, then reform, wheel and charge again to finish him off. They did make use of coordinated charges, but not in the manner or on the scale employed so effectively by later commanders.

The first 'saddles' were probably no more than cloths or animal skins which contributed to the rider's comfort if not to his security. By the time of the Assyrians and Persians the cloth was padded, far more

elaborate, and secured by girth, breastplate and a breeching passing round the horse's quarters.

The Scythians had a saddle much in advance of anything produced by their civilised contemporaries (see chapter 5). It served their purpose very well, but they were horse-archers and their style of warfare did not by any means include the concerted charge. Neither Greeks nor Romans developed a practical saddle, although the Romans were using cloths with a padded roll in front and behind the rider in the second century and probably for a century before that.

It was not until the fifth century that the most significant developments were made in horse equipment, and their effect was enough to alter the practice and even the concept of warfare. The advance came from the Sarmatians, pastoral nomads steeped in an all-pervading horse culture and, as might be expected, great horse-breeders. Their origin was Iranian and their homelands between 600 and 300 BC were the Volga steppes, the area between the Don and the Urals.

By the second century BC the Sarmatians were powerful enough to have overthrown the formidable Scythians and taken over the lands bordering the Black Sea. Within a hundred years these vigorous

Nothing new in the world. The ubiquitous drop-noseband used in our own day to obtain greater control was known to the early horsemen of the pre-Christian era.

barbarians, who thought it beneath them to walk, had extended their influence as far as the Danube.

Alone among the earlier nomadic peoples the Sarmatians were predominantly heavy cavalrymen, a contradiction if ever there was one to the conventional idea of the nomadic warrior as an archetypal light horseman.

Although they did make use of the bow, the weapon which characterised the armoured Sarmatian horsemen was the lance. This and the principle of cavalry operating in close order was to have a profound effect on all the armies of the world. It caused a reorganisation of existing mounted arms and gave rise to a concept which persisted well into the nineteenth century.

The Sarmatian weapon was not a light lance, similar to a throwing spear, but a long, very heavy iron-tipped pole, so massive that the Greeks called it a 'barge-pole'. It was held in both hands, which implies that the horseman must have controlled his mount largely with his legs, or it was couched underarm in the conventional manner, but because of its weight was supported by a hooked bar attachment fitted to the horse's neck. These cavalrymen were also armed with long iron swords. To be used effectively they had to ride in close array, a knee-to-knee affair which created what was virtually the mounted equivalent of the Roman phalanx. Properly handled and acting as a single cohesive body – a sort of armoured projectile launched against blocks of infantry – it proved a nearly irresistible force.

But for a horseman armed with a weapon the size of the Sarmatian barge-pole to remain on his horse at the moment of impact, a padded saddle cloth was of no help, any more than the Scythian saddle would have been. Nor, of course, can a heavy cavalryman, whose strength lies in his acting in concert with his fellows, adopt the forward seat of the horse-archer. He has to assume a more upright posture and he has to have the support that can only be given by a seat shaped in such a way that it is difficult for him to be dislodged by the impact of his lance and horse on a stationary target.

The Sarmatian saddle was therefore built on a shaped wooden foundation, which is called a tree. It had a front and a rear arch fitting over the horse's back, which were joined by wooden bars resting on either side of the horse's spine. Both front (pommel) and rear (cantle) rose to a high peak to make a sort of boat shape in which the rider was positioned very securely, even though he had no stirrups. As he hit the enemy ranks the horseman braced himself against the cantle.

The date of the first Sarmatian wood-framed saddles is put at about the beginning of the Christian era by the Russian historian Sulimirski, author of *The Sarmatians*. His assertion is based on the excavations of the barrow graves of the Kuban Valley in the north-west Caucasus.

Furthermore, he claims on the evidence of the same site that the Sarmatians used stirrups between the years 49 and 193 AD. If so, they were the first to do so.

The stirrup, a seemingly straightforward adjunct to the saddle, not only completed the security of the mounted soldier but also extended the range of cavalry. Mounted men no longer had to be natural horsemen, like the Scythians, Huns, Sarmatians and Mongols. Napoleon's cavalry, for example, frequently comprised nothing much more than uniformed squadrons of cannon fodder. Skilfully led, supported, or exploited, by an élite corps and kept firmly in hand, they obtained remarkably good results (far better than the British cavalry, for instance), but very few were experienced horsemen let alone natural ones. Without stirrups they would have achieved nothing. And, of course, the stirrup improved peaceful communications as well, by opening up riding to the older and less athletic.

There is a surprising lack of unanimity about the stirrup's origin among historians, or it may be that there is simply not enough conclusive evidence. One body of opinion holds that it first came out of the east with the Huns of Attila. A Chinese officer mentions it in his autobiography dated 477, and he says that it was the invention of the Huns. The Chertomlyk Vase of the fourth century BC with its Scythian horse and that hanging piece of rope must be largely discounted. One can hardly imagine that no one else took up the stirrup in the space of seven hundred years.

We are left, then, with Sulimirski's discovery of stirrup irons in the Caucasian barrow grave of a Sarmatian chief. The presence of the irons is indisputable, but others have dismissed the claim on the grounds that the dating is at fault.

There is, however, another tenable theory based on evidence that Indian horsemen rode with a toe-stirrup as early as AD 100–200. A toe-stirrup is a loop of leather or rope big enough to accommodate the rider's big toe. It can be seen in southern India today and boys exercising or racing horses in Malaya and Singapore still use such a stirrup. So it is not unreasonable to suppose that central Asian nomads would in time have become acquainted with such a device. In their case, the loop would have had to have been larger because of the thick felt boots they wore as protection against the cold. From that point on it is only a step to a wooden stirrup, examples of which would not have survived, and finally to one made of metal. In the first four hundred years of the Christian era it is quite certain that the stirrup, in one form or another, spread all the way round the area encompassed by China, central India and the Black Sea. Between the fifth and seventh centuries it was in use all the way through central Asia, Iran,

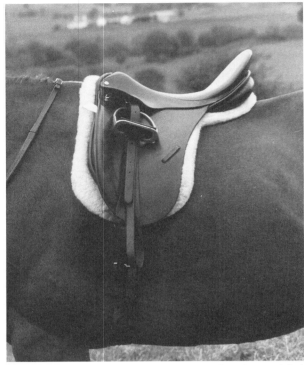

The western saddle *(left)* **retains some of the characteristics of the Spanish saddles which came to the Americas with the** *conquistadores*, **but it is also possible to see the dip-seated European-type saddle** *(right)* **as a stream-lined, adapted version of the knight's saddle.**

southern Siberia, Korea and Japan. The Arabs became familiar with it at about the same time, although it is not impossible to suppose they had used a toe or foot loop for a long time before, since they had contact with India and they also used a rope toe loop for mounting camels. From early in the eighth century up to the ninth the stirrup came into general use in Europe.

By the time the Roman Empire had fallen, the division between the two styles of riding – that of the light horseman, usually of steppe or eastern origin, and that of the heavy cavalryman associated with the western tactic – was becoming quite clearly defined. As time advanced into the Middle Ages the difference became even more accentuated. Both, in basic terms, used the dip seat saddle, allowing for obvious differences in patterns and in the depth of the seat itself, but the posture of the two schools was governed by the position of the lower leg and that in turn was dictated by the length of the stirrup.

The light horseman, still for many centuries to come an archer, rode short with the lower leg drawn back. The heavy cavalryman, who became the armoured knight, rode with a straight leg thrust forward so that he was braced against the high cantle.

In the Iberian Peninsula, occupied for seven hundred years by the Moors, the two schools existed side by side, the shortened stirrup, eastern seat being called '*à la gineta*' and the longer-legged position '*à la bride'*. Iberian horsemen of the Renaissance and after prided themselves on their ability to ride in either style.

The shape of the knight's saddle influenced design right up to the twentieth century. The Spanish *conquistadores* took it to the Americas, where, in an adapted form, it survives as the western saddle. It became, in a streamlined version, the *selle royale* of the Renaissance horsemen and may be seen in that form at the repositories of the classical art, the Spanish Riding School in Vienna and the Cadre Noir at Fontainebleau. It provided the basis for the cavalry saddles of the world and it appears again in the dip-seated saddle of the modern show-jumper, event rider and dressage exponent.

The use of spurs, to encourage the horse forward or to control the position of its quarters, is long established, but just who was responsible for this 'extension to the horseman's leg' is not known. Xenophon knew about spurs and used them, as did the Romans. They were short prick spurs worn on the bare heel. By the fifth and sixth centuries spikes of 4–5 in (10–13cm) long were being used; in the Middle Ages they became even longer and were often fitted with rowels. The knight needed a sharp spur to activate his big, common horse and he needed the length because of his straight leg position. Spurs became central to the ceremony of knighthood in that short-lived age of chivalry, when the knight was seen as the embodiment of the highest Christian virtues. Following a night-long vigil, the knight was awarded golden spurs and was said to have 'won his spurs'. The steppe horsemen never used the spur, relying instead on a whip, which was always carried.

The invention of a horseshoe is attributed to the Celts, renowned as iron workers. Unlike the prototype shoe which was strapped to the foot, the Celt's shoe was fixed by nails after being fitted to the foot straight from the smith's fire. In Europe, where horses' feet grew soft and broke under wet conditions, the invention of the horseshoe was little short of revolutionary. It expanded the use of horses, particularly in draught, by preventing them from becoming footsore and lame.

Horseshoes were in general use throughout the Roman Empire in the first and second centuries and from the beginning they played an important role in every horse culture. The farrier (from the French *ferrier*, in turn derived from the Latin *ferrum*, 'iron') was held in high respect and was the object of many superstitious beliefs. Working with fire and able to hammer out fiery sparks from iron he was thought at one period to be in league with the devil.

The smith was also a subject for deification. Hephaestus, son of Zeus and Hera, was the god of fire and the master of all works in iron, the symbol of strength. At his forge on Olympus, with the help of the Cyclops, he forged the thunderbolts for his father Zeus. In Roman

The devil, voluptuously disguised, here tempts the patron saint of blacksmiths, St Dunstan. He met his match, however. The virtuous (if slightly sadistic) Dunstan inflicted such pain on the forces of evil as to send the devil howling back to the eternal fires.

mythology it was the hooded Vulcan who forged from iron the weapons of war. Thor of the hammer was the Scandinavian god, and the Bantu people believed that they descended from Noto (the hammer), the son of Morizong (the smith).

In England St Dunstan (born in 910) is the patron saint of blacksmiths. He had a forge in his monastic cell where he made bells and sacred vessels for the ceremonies of the church. The story goes that one day he was visited by the devil who asked him to shoe his feet. St Dunstan, recognising his visitor, secured him firmly and then inflicted such pain on him during the shoeing that the devil vowed that

Although the great horses of San Marco may be seen as embodying the whole spirit of the Renaissance, they are probably the work of the Greek Lysippos and were brought from Chios to Constantinople in the fifth century.

Hungarian hussars, descendants of
the Hun horsemen who swept
across the steppes into Europe,
became the model for the light
cavalryman, and their uniforms
were copied in the armies of almost
every European nation.

Murat, the most flamboyant of all
Napoleon's Marshalls was
nonetheless an inspired cavalry
tactician. It should be noted that, in
the best cavalry tradition, he
affected a deliberately casual air.
He leads his troops bareheaded,
brandishing not a sword but a
riding whip.

Levade, the first of the classical 'airs above the ground', demonstrated by a Lippizaner stallion of the four-hundred year-old Spanish Riding School of Vienna. The 'airs' are thought to derive from the manoeuvres performed by medieval knights 'in press of battle'.

Opposite page: Boer troops, adopting the tactics of the steppe horsemen, and resembling them in equestrian skills, contained and frequently ran rings round the conventionally-trained British cavalry. Only when the British operated as 'irregular' bodies did they begin to gain the upper hand.

Deuxième année. — N° 40.   Huit pages : CINQ centimes   Dimanche 1er Octobre 1899.

LE PETIT MÉRIDIONAL

Supplément Illustré du Dimanche

ABONNEMENTS

SIX MOIS | UN AN

France, Algérie, Tunisie. 2 fr. » 3fr.50
Étranger (Union postale). 2 fr.50 5 fr. »

Direction, Rédaction, Administration : Rue Henri-Guinier, MONTPELLIER

ANNONCES

POUR LA PUBLICITÉ S'ADRESSER

A Montpellier : Rue Henri-Guinier.
A Paris : 131, rue Montmartre.

Les Événements du Transvaal.

L'armée Boer.

There was no aspect of life in nineteenth century London in which the horse did not play a part. The London Fire Brigade employed many hundreds of horses.

The sail on this picturesque barge may represent nothing more than an exercise in wishful thinking. Throughout the nineteenth century and into the twentieth horses provided the means of locomotion on the commercially important water routes.

Until halfway into the twentieth century, horses still provided nearly seventy-five per cent of the agricultural power in Western Europe while dependency on horse-power still remains essential in many East European economies.

The age-old appeal of the horse is still a crowd-puller even in the high-tech societies of the New World, and without them there would be no Calgary Stampede to attract huge audiences to the Calgary showgrounds each year.

he would never again enter a place where a horseshoe was displayed.

Horseshoes, whichever way up they are hung, are good luck charms, perhaps because their shape is reminiscent of a crescent, symbol of Hecate, the moon goddess. To the Turks it resembles the sacred symbol of Islam; to the Hindus it is expressive of their phallic symbols and in Sri Lanka it is thought of as the arched body of Nagendra the sacred snake.

Since it is made of iron it is accounted as the best protection against witches and evil spirits. The belief stems in the Christian world from the iron nails with which Christ was nailed to the cross, but it goes back much further than that in the ancient world to the old gods who worked in the metal which was the source of all power.

The carrying of a silver horseshoe by a bride is said to have originated at the wedding of Lars Porsena, King of Tuscany, whose wife's horses were shod with silver for the occasion. The most effective shoe for averting evil is supposed to be taken or cast from the nearside hind leg of a grey mare. In rural areas girls used to count the nail holes in cast-off shoes to find out how many years it would be before they married.

Even Pliny could not resist the properties of the horseshoe. If you found one, he recorded, you were advised to remember the exact spot. Should you thereafter have an attack of hiccoughs the remedy was to recall the place in the mind and the hiccoughs would stop at once.

It is to China that the world owes most for the development of draught harness. Sophisticated wheeled vehicles were used in China by 1300 BC. The Chinese invented the single horse vehicle drawn by means of lateral shafts, and the practice of driving horses in tandem, one behind the other. They had a breast harness supported by a strap over the wither in 250 BC. This design could have originated in the harness used by humans for pulling boats upstream, a matter in which they would have been well experienced.

After that, the Chinese produced the breeching strap and finally the horse collar, claimed as one of the greatest inventions ever made since it allows the most efficient tractive force.

THE WONDER OF THE AGE

Always it was from the steppes, with those successive waves of ravaging horsemen, that the major equestrian innovations came. The nomadic invasions may have been primarily destructive and have left nothing of permanence once the tide had receded, but it was nonetheless the steppe horsemen who were responsible for the introduction of saddles and stirrups and it was through them that driving harness and technical advances in vehicle design were brought into Europe via the Magyars of Hungary and the marauding Vikings.

Wagons, unsprung and with wheels all the same size (not that much different from the ones used by the Romans) were in use all over Europe in the early Middle Ages. In mid sixteenth-century England stage wagons, of similar construction, carried goods as well as members of the public unwise enough to attempt braving the discomfort, while stage 'coaches', of a scarcely improved design, first made their appearance in 1650. Because of the absence of reasonably surfaced roadways and the construction of the vehicles, progress was slow and desperately uncomfortable. The windowless stage wagon of Elizabeth I's day proceeded at no more than walking pace, the waggoner driving his team on foot and getting along on good ground at about 2½mph (4kph). On bad ground the speed would have been half that or even slower.

Leaders in the development of driving and vehicles were the Hungarians, who to this day figure most prominently in driving sports. It was the Huns, from whom the Hungarians descend, who first came into Europe with wheeled transport. Attila had a wagon-laager at the battle of the Catalaunian fields and the Hungarians were operating advanced wagon-train systems to support fighting troops when the rest of Europe was dependent upon pack transport. They had a royal corps of waggoners as early as the twelfth century and the Hungarian pattern wagon and harness was copied and adapted throughout Europe.

The coach, which in its later development was to become the glory of the English roads, was first produced in the late fifteenth century in the Hungarian village of Kocs in the Komorne area, a place famous for the skill of its wainwrights. The coach (*Kocsi*) takes its name from the village.

The early Hungarian coach does not yet have the benefit of springs and it is difficult to see how it could turn in a confined space.

The Hungarian coach was distinguished by having the front wheels smaller than the rear ones, thus allowing the fore-carriage to turn on a very full lock. Like nearly everything else such a vehicle had its ultimate origin in the Orient. The wagon buried with the Sumerian King Abargi in the third millenium BC, for example, had exactly the same wheel arrangement.

Apart from the turning circle which made the vehicle so much more manoeuvrable there were numerous other advantages to the pair of smaller front wheels. The vehicle had a lower centre of gravity, which increased stability and allowed it to be driven faster. It was far easier for horses to start from a halt and the small wheels prevented the poles, to which the horses were attached, from pitching or 'bucking' when rough ground was being traversed. As a result there was greater tractive efficiency. Broquière described the new coaches as being 'very fair and lightly built, so that you would think one man could carry them away, wheels and body and all, on his back.'

Until the invention of the *Kocsi*, it was the custom in Hungary for the driver of the wagon to drive the team mounted on the offside wheel horse (a 'wheeler' is the horse harnessed next to the wheel, while the 'leader' in a four-horse team is positioned, as the name suggests, in front of the wheel horse). The new coach made it possible, and far easier, to drive from the box seat, a position which is much less tiring for both the 'whip' and the horse.

In Hungary, where the techniques and customs of central Asia persisted, the coach was driven either at a walk or at a sharp canter. Coach communications in Hungary up to the time of the railways were swift, particularly as the Hungarians were able to draw on light, Oriental-type horses.

But this was all relative to the country's situation. In terms of industrial development Hungary remained much like the rest of eastern Europe, an agricultural nation operating within a largely peasant economy. Its railway system was not established until long after that in industrial Britain, and there was no comparable growth of urban population and nothing like the sophisticated road network. On the other hand, the impact of the Hungarian coach on western Europe, particularly on Britain, was in the nature of a revolution, for it made possible a whole new system of fast communication and travel which could not otherwise have been contemplated.

The *Kocsi* spread rapidly into Germany and Bohemia and from thence to England in the reign of Elizabeth I, but for all its advantages it was hardly received with open arms. European governments, including Britain, saw it as a subversive introduction which would lead to a decline in the habit of travelling on horseback and subsequently a decrease in the number of horses available for service under arms. Furthermore, it would cause congestion in crowded streets. Laws were passed to restrict the use of coaches and prominent people thundered mightily against what they saw as a 'senseless luxury', a fashion 'to make men effeminate'. It is interesting to compare these views to those often taken in the ancient world, where men of noble birth were advised to drive in chariots rather than ride upon horses.

For all the fulminations, pamphlets and proclamations, the era of the coach had arrived with the invention of the *Kocsi*. In England its influence was to assume massive proportions. Initially Germany obtained a monopoly in the provision of coaches to England, ruthlessly undercutting the native wainwrights. But, as so frequently, the Teutons were heavy of hand. German-made coaches soon lost all the light flexibility that was the essence of the *Kocsi* and became heavier and heavier. Just in time two more Hungarian inventions were brought in: first, the body supported like a hammock on leather slings, and then the final, multi-leaved elliptical springs. During the reign of George II (1683–1760) English coachbuilding became far superior to the German industry.

The advantages of the new system of springing, other than the increase in comfort afforded to the passengers, was, of course, in the vehicle's performance. A sprung vehicle can be driven much faster and with greater safety (it is less likely to be overturned), and it is easier for the horses because of the 'floating' weight load. An unsprung vehicle transmits every bump to the team drawing it, throwing them off balance and making their task doubly difficult and tiring.

The foundations for the 'golden age' of coaching, which seized the imagination of England and became for a short while the greatest source of the nation's pride, were laid in the mid-eighteenth century. Four factors brought about a system of speedy transport more reliable and regular than any other in the world, 'the wonder of the age and the envy of Europe'.

First there was the light, well-sprung coach, made with much improved axle-boxes which largely obviated the broken axles and lost wheels which had caused so many accidents before. Secondly, patterns of harness were devised and superbly crafted from English leather, which was the best in the world. The English climate may have its drawbacks but no country in the world is better suited to the tanning and dressing of leather; the climate allows the leather to mature naturally, with the water of the Midlands being ideal for the purpose. Lighter, stronger and more flexible harness was produced, while improvements in the shaping and fitting of the harness collars and pads made them more comfortable for the horses and less likely to gall.

The most significant factor, however, lay in the availability of horses. The English Thoroughbred was firmly established by 1770. It had by then been bred selectively to a consistent pattern for a hundred years, forming a large national mare herd and a more than adequate stallion band. The situation was, if anything, one of over-production for the purposes of the racing market. There was therefore a surplus of animals which could supply harness teams.

Many stallions, too, were now serving hunter and coach mares rather than being concerned exclusively with Thoroughbreds. The cross with the Cleveland Bay, for example, resulted in the Yorkshire Coach Horse, a breed that was faster than the heavier Cleveland, who could take his place at the plough just as well as at the pole, but more powerful than the Thoroughbred. The breed, although it required constant adjusting infusions of Cleveland and Thoroughbred blood, survived into the twentieth century and had its own stud book. It is now to all intents extinct or, perhaps more accurately, it has been reabsorbed by the Cleveland. Horses of this sort in combination with light coaches and good roads could attain high speeds on flat stages.

The fourth element was, of course, the good road. In Roman Britain there was a time when there were 5,000 miles (8,000 km) of *via strata*, properly surfaced and capable of carrying fast traffic. In common with mainland Europe and elsewhere, the road system fell into decay after the fall of the Empire. In its day the Roman *cursus publicus* operated on those roads as reliably and as swiftly as the post-chaise which represented the most sophisticated form of transport available 1,600 years later.

By 1780, however, road commissioners and the turnpike trusts, levying tolls, had reached that mileage again. But it was largely because of two Scotsmen, Thomas Telford, the bridge and road builder, and John McAdam, whose contribution to road-surfacing is immortalised in 'macadam' and 'tarmacadam', that the golden age came into full flower. By 1830 there were 20,000 miles (32,000km) of good roadways in Britain and the coaching era was well under way.

The incentive for the development of the passenger service which reached its zenith between 1825 and the beginning of the railway age, were the mail coaches. Previously mail had been carried by postboys on horseback, boys who introduced the practice of rising or 'posting' to the trot to ease their fatigue and avoid the worst discomforts of the rough-actioned animals they had often to endure. Later, mail carts, capable of carrying parcels as well as letters, were added to the service. These were marginally more satisfactory than the often unreliable postboys, but they were slow, while the later post-chaises, though very fast and – by the standards of eighteenth century travel –

luxurious, were limited in accommodation and out of the reach of all but the very wealthy.

It was left to one enthusiast, in the face of the usual opposition and even official antagonism, to initiate a mail system which formed the basis of the service we have today. Indeed, in some respects, the system pioneered by John Palmer – Postmaster General, coaching enthusiast and organisational genius – was superior to ours.

Palmer made transport and postal service history by running the first mail coach from Bristol to London, via Bath, on 2 August 1784. It travelled through the night and arrived at the General Post Office, London, at 8 o'clock the next morning, completing the journey in a remarkable 15 hours. The schedule had been maintained exactly, and, just as Palmer had predicted, the time taken was a good hour less than the fastest of the contemporary stage coaches. Much of the success of the mail coaches was due to the organisation of the staging halts, the pit-stops of the age, where the ostlers were drilled to be able to make a change of horses in under a minute.

The mail coach, a development of the early mail carts, carried four passengers inside, in relative comfort, and four on top. The guard sat along a single seat at the back, over the box in which the mail was stored. He was armed with a blunderbuss and carried a long horn, the 'yard of tin', with which he warned innkeepers and tollgate keepers of

This was the end of the trail for many horses who at one time had taken their place at the head of the hunting field.

the coach's approach. Fares were fivepence a mile inside and three-pence a mile for the 'outsiders', which was just one of the words that the coaching era gave to the English language. After 1784, the fares rose to about a shilling a mile and passengers were also expected to tip both coachman and guard. Half a guinea was thought appropriate for a top-class coachman, and two shillings and sixpence for the guard (many of the best coachmen, although paid comparatively low wages, became men of substance as a result of the tips they received).

The beauty of Palmer's system was that the passengers contributed very largely to its cost. The official recommendation concerning their transport stated: 'the advantages proposed for this regulation are various. The passengers will defray the whole cost of the conveyance.' The mail coaches, though the responsibility of the state, were hardly a liability on the public purse. The service was contracted out to private individuals, and coaches and horses were hired. The Post Office maintained its control through the Post Office guard who was responsible for the conduct of the coach, the delivery of mail and the collection of fares. The title 'guard' is still used on modern rail services and is a reminder of the early days of transport.

Encouraged by the success of the mail coaches, private operators were soon setting up passenger coaches which ran to the same standards. As early as 1800 the mail coaches were unable to satisfy public demand and by then the private sector was an established feature, with private coaches operating reliably over all the main routes and keeping so precisely to time that men set their watches by the stage or the mail.

The mails were painted in the royal colours – maroon bodies, scarlet wheels and undercarriages, with the Royal arms painted on the doors, while the guard wore the Royal livery. Private road coaches were painted in every sort of colour, according to the taste of the proprietors, and the names of their stopping places were painted on the doors. They all carried sporting names like *Tally-Ho*, *Tantivy* and *Comet*, and, copying the practice of the mail coaches, their guards wore scarlet livery and carried horns on which many became accomplished performers. Road coaches usually carried twelve passengers, eight of them 'outsiders'. They were cheaper than the mails, but a little slower. For the most part they travelled during the day, stopping briefly for meals at the staging inns.

In 1825, at the beginning of the coaching era, the *Wonder* began the run between London and Shrewsbury, a distance of 158 miles (254km) which was covered at 10mph (16kph) and involved 150 horses. Speeds of this order were pretty uniform over all the routes, but the Royal Mail averaged times of up to 12mph (19kph). To survive in all the competition, private operators had to be as good or better than the Post Office service.

By the 1830s competition was so fierce and costs so high that the coaching business was concentrated into the hands of the biggest coachmasters. Many of them used inns in London and elsewhere as their headquarters and often called their fleet by the inn name, having the inn sign painted on the vehicles. The largest coachmaster was William Chaplin, who ran coaches from five London inns and employed 2,000 men – ostlers, tackmen, coach greasers, cleaners, etc. – as well as 1,300 horses to draw his 60 coaches. Two thousand horses were stabled at Hounslow alone, the first change for coaches going west out of London.

The running of a coach over a 'ground' in stages of 5–15 miles (8–24km), and less than that for the fast coaches , was an organisation of enormous complexity involving hundreds of men and horses, as well as innkeepers and their staff. The coachmaster's 'ground' was divided into three parts. The upper ground was that nearest his base; the middle ground was the centre section and the lower ground the portion furthest away. The 'down' side was from London to the country and the 'up' side was from the country to the capital. We still go 'up' to London and 'down' to the country today.

Expenses were high, particularly in horses, for the wastage rate was heavy. A horse on a slow coach (yet another term which has passed into the language) might last five years, on a fast, 10mph (16kph) coach, the working expectancy was only three years. 'Working to death' was commonplace and was regarded objectively in an industry which held its commercial interests very close to its heart.

To attain the speeds required nothing but 'blood' (Thoroughbred) horses would do and at the prices which the coachmasters found viable any sort of vice as well as some of the lesser infirmities were acceptable. A horse with no mouth and a tendency to bolt would quickly be put right with a carefully chosen bit and a check rein. Even the most troublesome of horses became steady after working in a team for a couple of weeks on a fast coach. For the very unruly there was always the decisive sanction of 'doubling', the miscreant having to work a double stage. Kickers, jibbers, bolters, all had their place. Even blind horses could be usefully employed – 'There's only one eye among us,' said an old one-eyed coachman as he drove his blind team over a bridge in the dark.

Paintings of the era tend to depict teams at full stretch with the wind whipping at scarves and the dust flying from the wheels. In reality, it was not so. Galloping for any length of time would have imposed intolerable strains on horses, vehicle and occupants and would have been wholly impracticable. Coachmen did, of course, gallop or 'spring' a team on occasions – to tackle a slope, for instance, or to make up time on a particularly smooth, straight stretch, but the surface had to be very good.

The western coaches had a galloping ground of 6 miles (10km) between Hounslow and Staines, and there was another of 5 miles (8km) on the Exeter road, which could be covered in 23 minutes at the rate of 13mph (21kph)! For the most part, however, the 10–12mph (16–19kph) which could be covered by a good trotting team was fast enough for all concerned, and far safer.

The coaches of the Royal Mail were forbidden by law to gallop, but that could be got round by including a 'Parliamentary horse' in the team. This was a very swift trotter who would not break his gait. So long as he trotted, his three team mates might gallop and remain within the law.

The most notable feature of the coaching era was the enormous

Driving a team at high speed down to Brighton was a fashionable form of entertainment during the Regency period. Dalmatians, however, were more usually to be seen following a Dog Cart.

interest which the coach and the whole glamour of the road aroused in the British people. London yards were always full of spectators watching the coaches in and out, as people go to Heathrow today to watch the comings and goings of the aircraft. People came not only to admire the turnouts but to pass judgement on the skill of the leading coachmen, who received an adulation not unlike that accorded to modern top-class footballers.

It was a wonderful sight, a unique spectacle. Cobbett, never a man given to fulsome praise, wrote: 'Next to a foxhunt the finest sight in England is a stage coach'. Writing in the English magazine *Riding* well over a century later, Edward Leyhart had this to say:

In its time it was the wonder of the world and even now, long after its passing, the stage coach and the blood teams evoke the romance of the open road. We forget the bitter nights, the fog, frost and

A growing sport today is driving in many different forms.

snow. We see only the good-humoured open faces of the 'outsiders' riding atop the coach with scarves blowing in the wind; the jovial, red-faced, benjamin-clad coachman and the dashing horses who made it all possible. In our minds we hear the clatter of hooves on the cobbles, the rattle of the wheels and the long-drawn note on the guard's 'yard of tin'.

It was probably never like that, but for us it was, and will always be, part of a golden age.

In England 'private driving' by individuals using their own 'private drags' was a direct result of the coaching era. It started a tradition. The exclusive Four-in-Hand Club was formed in 1856, and in 1871 the prestigious Coaching Club. They survive today, when enthusiasm for driving is more popular than ever. As well as coaching there is, of course, the latest of the equestrian disciplines, the Three-Day Driving Trials, operated like a ridden three-day horse trial with a dressage section, a cross-country course with obstacles and, instead of a jumping phase, an obstacle driving test.

On the Continent the coach played a similar role in transportation but it never reached the heights nor approached the standards attained in England. Coach design was not so advanced, roadways not so well made and there was no supply of horses equivalent to that available in England. There were, of course, a great many coaching breeds on the Continent, but they were the legacy of Europe's slow, heavy war-horse of feudal times. The only horses comparable to the English were those bred in eastern Europe where fast, active horses of the light cavalry order were traditional. But eastern Europe, less intensely industrialised than Britain, had no need of such an extensive transport system.

The American equivalent of the peak of the English coaching era started at about the same time, 1825. The best known coaches were those made by the Abbot–Downing Co. at Concord, New Hampshire, which became famous as plain 'Concords'. A feature of these tough, hardwearing and very practical vehicles was the supporting leather 'thoroughbraces', several inches thick, on which the rounded body was suspended. This arrangement proved most effective over rough roads and some of the Concord coaches, often drawn by six horses, could travel at 15mph (24kph). By 1849, the time of the Californian gold rushes, Concords were in use on most of the American long distance routes.

The same coach was introduced to Australia by Cobb & Co., a firm founded by four Americans at Victoria in 1853 when the Australian gold rushes were at their height. Cobb & Co. prospered, adapting and improving the basic Concord to suit Australian conditions, and its factory at Charleville did not close until 1920.

Australian coaches at first used six-horse teams, but Cobb & Co. later devised a method of harnessing five- and seven-horse teams, with three horses in the lead and two or four hitched to the pole. In the 1880s they had a stage coach network in New South Wales and Queensland which extended to over 6,000 miles (9,655km).

In all countries, the driver of a coach or horse-drawn vehicle sits on the right of the box seat. However, in countries with open land, like America and many parts of Europe, where enclosure took place late in history, drivers drove on the right-hand side of the road so that when passing another vehicle the drivers' whips, carried across the body but inclined upwards from the hand at an angle of 45 degrees or so, should not become entangled. In Britain, where high hedges and trees marked the boundaries of often narrow roads, it was more sensible to drive on the left so that the whip did not become fouled in the hedge or an overhanging branch. It was held across the body, from right to left, to reduce the danger of entanglement with the whip of a driver coming from the opposite direction.

The side of the road we drive on today is a lasting legacy of the coaching era. In mainland Europe, the USA and Australia cars are driven on the right of the road, in Britain they are still driven on the left.

Chapter 16

AN AGE OF EXTENSION

At the end of the First World War the cavalry had become virtually irrelevant in warfare, while in agriculture horse-power was fast being replaced by mechanised farming. Nonetheless, the horse continued to play an important role in Europe.

Horses were still used for short-haul transport and in commerce; ponies worked underground in the mines. London's milk and that of almost every British city, town and village was delivered by horse-drawn floats – many of them, particularly the London ones, drawn by a spanking Welsh Cob in the shafts. The butcher, the baker and all sorts of other tradesmen used a horse turnout; horses hauled timber in the woodlands, barges on the canals and shunted wagons in railway sidings, while most farms still had a working horse or two.

Right up to the Second World War the majority of the world's countries maintained cavalry and horse transport formations. On the day in 1939 that the British Prime Minister declared a state of war existing between his nation and the Germany of Adolf Hitler there were still British cavalry regiments, and a number of Indian ones, which sharpened swords in accordance with King's Regulations. In fact, both horse and mule transport was used extensively by all the protagonists in almost every theatre of war between 1939 and 1945.

Today, in the less agriculturally efficient countries of Europe, notably those of the Eastern Bloc, horses remain integral to the farming system, while in large areas of the USSR sizeable horse-based industries exist. In Southern Kazakhstan and the regions of Gurev and Kzyl-Ordin, which are the habitat of the Kazakh pony, large horse factories have been established to provide meat, milk, hides, horsehair and other associated products. Such factories also exist elsewhere in the Soviet Union.

The Dzhabe pony, a strain within the Kazakh breed, is calculated to produce a total carcass meat yield of 570–620lb (258–281kg), while in the period between May and November mares may have a milk yield of up to 4½ gallons (17 litres) per day. Even in the climatically severe southern foothills of the Urals, the hardy Bashkir mares produce as much as 550 gallons (2082 litres) during a seven to eight month lactation period.

In Northern Siberia the ancient Altai breed and the even older,

Dressage is the most rapid growth area of horsemanship today and possibly causes more arguments than any other discipline. One of the world's most successful partnerships has been that of Dr Reine Klimke and his horse, Ahlerich.

'primitive' Yakut, existing in the Yakut Autonomous Republic which extends beyond the Arctic circle, are both used to further the economy of their regions and to provide valuable sources of food. In these areas such ponies are better able to survive and are more easily managed than most other animals.

For all that, it would not have been unreasonable to imagine that a sharp decline would take place in the world's horse population once the battlefield and the needs of agriculture, the two prime incentives for breeding, were removed.

Remarkably, not only did that not occur, but the years after the Second World War marked an extraordinary phenomenon in the history of the man-horse relationship.

Until that point, horse-ownership had for the most part been within the prerogative of the well-to-do, as it had been since the very beginnings of an equine-based aristocracy. In Britain, between the wars, those who kept horses for recreational purposes were concerned very largely with their use for hunting between November and late April/early May. By the early 1950s that had changed. With the breaking down of the old 'class' barriers and the advent of a more affluent society, with greater opportunities for leisure at its disposal, riding and horse-ownership extended to many more classes of society. Riding became the sport of the urban and suburban dwellers, as well as that of country folk. The influence of television, bringing show-jumping to the attention of the public as an exciting spectator sport, was a major factor in popularising the recreational aspect of the horse.

Although hunting, the traditional British preoccupation which still provides a basis for light horse breeding, increased in popularity in the post-war years, the emphasis shifted towards competitive sports. These allowed all-year-round participation and provided riding opportunities for horse-owners who by reason of their employment or their geographical situation found hunting inconvenient, impossible or just insufficiently attractive.

However, it was the hunting field that inspired the first youth organisation based on the use and care of horses and ponies. The Pony Club was founded in 1928 with just three branches, which were attached to individual Hunts. This association, which persists today, provided a convenient geographical coverage of the country, but there are also modern urban branches which are not so connected. There are now over 365 branches of the Pony Club in Great Britain and 1450 overseas branches. Membership in the UK alone exceeds 40,000. The Pony Club organises instructional rallies, with the accent placed firmly on correct equitational methods and horse management; it grades by examination; branches hold annual camps and there is a full

programme of competitive events. It has become a vast reservoir of talent from which the country draws its international riders.

For adults, there is the ever-expanding riding club movement, which, like the Pony Club, operates under the benevolent aegis of the British Horse Society, the governing body of the British horse world. There are over four hundred clubs in the UK with a total membership exceeding fifty thousand and others exist all over the world. By far the greater number of riding club members are people who hold down regular nine-to-five jobs and there is a good percentage of housewives who contrive to look after a horse as well as their human family.

In all, a quarter of a million households in Britain alone (excluding Northern Ireland) include someone who owns a horse or a pony.

Far from declining, the horse population is often in danger of exceeding the worldwide demand. Britain, apart from its Thorough-bred racing industry, has no fewer than forty breed societies, all intent upon the improvement and promotion of their particular horse or pony.

Overall, the emphasis in Europe is towards the 'competition' horse and pony, which will compete successfully in the major sporting disciplines. On the mainland of Europe the Dutch, the Danes, the Germans and the French have been particularly successful in produc-ing an athletic half-bred (warm-blood) horse very suitable for show-jumping and dressage, by introducing Thoroughbred blood to the indigenous stock, much of which was originally evolved for carriage work and light draught. Notable among the warm-bloods are the Hanoverians, the Trakehners and the Holsteins. The Dutch have developed a remarkably effective performance horse and so have the Danes, while the French, inclining always to the lighter blood horse, continue to produce their tough Anglo-Arabs, on which so much of their breeding history is founded.

Britain and Ireland favour a larger percentage of Thoroughbred blood in their crosses. While British breeding is impossibly frag-mented in comparison with the controlled and often state-assisted industries in the rest of Europe, it does nonetheless continue to produce a stamp of horse which has a greater potential for versatility than the stronger continental sorts. The best of them make superla-tive hunters and eventers and may also be capable of winning point-to-point races and hunter chases, while not a few go show-jumping successfully.

America, Australia and New Zealand, all with established Thor-oughbred breeding industries which produce top-class stock, also favour the Thoroughbred and the Thoroughbred cross for high-level competition.

The principal equestrian sporting disciplines are show-jumping, horse-trials and dressage, all three of which are included in the

The greatest race over big fences in all the world and the most thrilling is the Grand National Steeplechase at Aintree, outside Liverpool.

The player who fails to turn his knee into the saddle while playing this particular shot is likely to make a rapid exit from the plate.

Nearly in the steps of the Master, Caprilli would not have been too displeased.

Olympic Games. However, there are other disciplines, outside the Olympic ones, which are just as important.

Carriage-driving, with events based on the three-day horse trials system, are hugely popular, with European and world championships being held regularly. Driving, either in competition or privately, is a continually expanding sport. In one aspect at least, there is an echo of the Greek and Roman circus: 'scurry' driving, in which a pair of ponies is driven through a course of obstacles against the clock, seems very reminiscent of the chariot sports of the ancient world.

Polo, of course, continues to thrive throughout the world. There is a large and growing interest in the demanding sport of long-distance riding, in which the Arab horse and his close derivatives excel. (Although the pure-bred Arab cannot compete against bigger, faster horses in the major disciplines, Arab racing, confined to pure-bred and Anglo-Arab horses, is firmly established and breeding is conducted on a worldwide basis, with America having the largest Arab population in the world.)

Long distance or endurance rides are often held over courses of 100

Horse-gunners of Britain's King's Troop, Royal Horse Artillery performing at their favourite pace – the gallop. Horse artillery was first introduced to the battlefields by Frederick the Great of Prussia.

miles (161km), involving difficult country and the modern sport now carried on at international level is strictly controlled and under veterinary supervision.

The modern horse is, for the most part, the partner of man in the latter's pursuit of sport and recreation. Most of these sports have their origin in war or as training exercises for that purpose but there is one activity which has no such connection and has a very special therapeutic value. This is the movement known as the Riding for the Disabled Association. The notion of disabled people carrying out therapeutic exercises on horseback was born after the 1947 poliomyelitis outbreak which affected so many children. It was the brainchild of Miss S. Saywell at Winford Orthopaedic Hospital in London (a Norwegian hospital had the same idea at almost the same time).

In 1964 the Advisory Council on Riding for the Disabled was formed with groups of volunteers working in cooperation with physiotherapists and doctors to provide ponies and riding all over Britain. In 1969 it became the Riding for the Disabled Association and there are now some three hundred groups in operation.

Riding, which can add a new dimension to the lives of disabled people, has been proved to effect a general improvement in their health as well as specific gains in mobility, coordination and balance. It can act to stabilise the emotionally disturbed and seems to encourage a broadening outlook and ambition in both mentally and physically handicapped persons.

On 20 July 1969, Neil Armstrong landed the lunar module Eagle on the surface of the moon as the final stage in the American Apollo II mission. Standing on the ladder in preparation for the first step that a man would make on an alien planet, Armstrong said that for a man at that moment it was a small step to take, but for mankind it was a gigantic one.

Some three years after the American landing on the moon a disabled spastic boy belonging to a Suffolk group of the Riding for the Disabled Association struggled out of his wheelchair. Watched by helpers, he took two unsteady steps towards the pony he was going to ride. They were his first steps. They were small steps, but for him, and perhaps for us all, they represented an enormous achievement.

Both his steps, and those taken by Neil Armstrong, were made possible by the horse and his relationship with mankind over five thousand years.

GLOSSARY

À La Bride
The term is concerned with the horsemanship of the Iberian Peninsula where two styles are recognised – *à la bride* and *à la gineta*. *À la bride* describes the long-legged western seat with which was associated a high degree of collection.

À La Gineta
The seat derived from the Moorish invaders of the Peninsula in which a shortened stirrup and a consequently bent knee is employed. Spanish and Portuguese horsemen prided themselves on their ability to ride in both styles.

Aids
The signals made by the rider to indicate his wishes to the horse and by which the horse is trained and guided.
Natural aids are the legs, hands, body, weight and voice. *Auxiliary* or *artificial* aids are the whip and the spur.

Airs Classical
The movements other than the normal walk, trot and canter that form part of High School riding. These include *piaffe* and *passage* as well as the 'airs above the ground'.

Airs above the Ground
These leaps do not form part of modern dressage riding but they are looked on as being an extension of the advanced movements in collection, the *piaffe* and *passage*.
 The Spanish Riding School recognise and perform three classical leaps: *levade, courbette* and *capriole*.

Alfalfa
Also known as lucerne, *alfalfa* has the highest protein content of any of the grasses. It is, therefore, highly nutritious and may be fed either as hay or when freshly cut.

Amble
See pace.

Bars
The area of gum between the molar and incisor teeth on which the mouthpiece of the bit lies.

Bars (Stirrup)
The metal bar on the tree of the saddle to which the stirrup leather is attached.

Bay
An equine coat colour. The body is a chestnut-brown while the lower limbs and mane and tail are black.

Bell-mare
An old, quiet mare which will lead the herd, the horses following the sound of the bell fixed round her neck.

Blood-horse
A Thoroughbred horse (see also half-bred, warm-blood, cold-blood).

Breeching
A broad strap fastening low round the quarters of a harness horse and which is attached to the shafts. It helps the horse to take the weight of the vehicle and to hold the load when going downhill.

Capriole
One of the classical airs (or leaps) above the ground. Derivation from the Italian *capra*, meaning 'goat'. The horse leaps from all four legs simultaneously, striking out with the hindlegs while the body is virtually suspended horizontally in mid-air.

Careta
A noseband fitted with spikes or metal studs that gives the rider a greater degree of control and helps obtain a desirable head carriage. The horse is virtually ridden on nose pressure. Nosebands of this type were used by the ancient Persians and also in the Renaissance schools. It is still used in Spain and Portugal as part of a sophisticated system of bitting.

Cavesson
Derivation of the French *caveçon* and Italian *cavezzone*, meaning a halter. The modern cavesson is either a noseband used with a riding bridle or it is a schooling cavesson, which is a stout, padded noseband fitted with rings on the sides and centre nose. To one of these rings is fastened a rein and the horse can then be worked on a circle with the trainer standing at its centre. The exercise is called lungeing.
 (Classical training frequently involved riding the horse from the cavesson rings as a prelude to riding from the bit.)

Chaff
Hay, or a mixture of hay and oat straw, cut into small lengths and fed together with concentrates, such as oats. It is one method of providing roughage and it prevents horses from bolting their feed.

Check Rein
A short rein attached to the bit of the harness horse to fix the head position.

Cold-blood
Heavy horses, descendants of Europe's Diluvial horse, are termed cold-bloods. Thoroughbred and Arab horses represent hot-blood and crosses between the two are thus called warm-bloods or, in Britain, half-breds.

Collection
A shortening of the outline of the horse and of his base. The head is carried high, the poll being the highest point of the neck, and

the face is held in the vertical plane. The croup (just behind the saddle) is lowered and the hindlegs carried well underneath the body.

Counter Canter

A schooling exereise inducing better balance and demanding obedience to the rider's aids. Instead of leading with the inside foreleg, i.e. left fore on circle left, the horse is asked to perform the circle with the opposite leg leading, i.e. right fore on circle left.

Courbette

A classical High School leap. From the *levade* position the horse makes a series of equal forward bounds while maintaining the bent posture of the forelegs.

Curb Bit

A bit made in the shape of an H, the horizontal bar being the mouthpiece and the verticals the cheeks. A chain passing behind the lower jaw and attached to the top of the cheeks permits a lever action. The longer the cheeks the greater the leverage that can be applied. Its object is to obtain flexion of the lower jaw, a retraction of the nose and a lowering of the head.

Dawn Horse

Translation of the Greek name Eohippus, the name given to the horse whose remains were discovered in America about one hundred and fifty years ago and which forms a direct line with the modern horse.

Dish

A horse is said to dish when the forelegs are swung outwards in an arc before returning to the ground. The action, because it is not straight, is judged to be uneconomical and mechanically inefficient.

Drop Noseband

A noseband which fastens tightly below the bit. Its object is to close the mouth so that the horse is unable to evade the action of the bit. It also provides the rider with greater control. Used with a snaffle bit.

Dun

A coat colour caused by yellow pigment in the hair. Usually this yellow colouring is accompanied by a dark dorsal list and sometimes bars of black hair on the legs. Otherwise the lower legs may be black. The mane and tail are black. A variation is a blue dun which will have a black mane and tail and possibly a dorsal list and dark legs as well. Dun is a characteristic colour of the 'primitives'.

Ewe-neck

A horse is said to be ewe-necked when the muscular development of the under-side of the neck is noticeably greater than that on the top-side. A pronounced bulge is apparent and this causes the horse to carry the head close to the horizontal plane. Such a carriage of the head and neck is usually accompanied by a hollowed back which, in turn, will prevent the full engagement of the hind-legs under the body.

Extension

The opposite of collection in which the base of the horse is shortened. In extension the stride in each of the gaits is lengthened.

Feather

Name given to the long hair growing on the lower limbs of heavy horses like the Shire, Clydesdale etc.

Flying Change

When the leading leg at canter is changed in the air without the horse being brought back to trot and being asked to strike off on the opposite leg.

Frog

A leathery V-shaped pad on the sole of the foot, which is sufficiently elastic to expand laterally as the foot takes the weight of the horse. It acts as a shock-absorber and is also an anti-slip device.

Gaits

The natural gaits of the horse are the *walk*, which is a gait of four-time; *the trot*, a gait executed in two-time, the horse using the legs in diagonal pairs, i.e. right fore and left hind, then left fore and right hind; and the *canter*, a three-beat gait in which the horse 'leads' either with the right or left fore according to whether it is circling to right or left. The sequence of footfalls for the canter with the right foreleg leading is: left hind, left diagonal pair, i.e. left fore and right hind simultaneously, and then the leading right foreleg.

The *gallop* is an extension of the canter and becomes a four-beat gait, but there may be variations in the sequence of the movement according to the speed. In the riding school phraseology of European countries, other than Britain, *galop* is used instead of canter. See also *gaited horse* and *pace*.

Gaited Horse

The term is applied to those horses using gaits outside what are considered to be the natural ones. Pacing (see pace) is one such gait but it can occur naturally in a number of breeds. With the exception of the *tölt* (rack) of the Icelandic ponies most gaited horses, however, are to be found in the Americas. Principal exponents are the American Saddlebred, the Tennessee Walker and the less well-known Missouri Fox Trotter. In addition there is the South American or Peruvian Paso. The supreme example of the pacing horse is the American Standardbred harness racer.

The Saddlebred may, in addition to the basic walk, trot and canter, performed in a distinctive elevated style, be shown in an additional stepping pace (a slow rack) and the 'single-foot' rack. The former is a slow, brilliant and exaggerated action, and the latter, still in four-beat, is very fast while retaining the brilliance of movement. In both the back is held level and as a result the rider sits easily and in great comfort. A horse performing in all these gaits is termed 'five-gaited'.

The Tennessee Walker uses a four-beat running walk and can obtain speeds of up to 15mph (24kph) at this gait.

The Fox Trotter produces a very smooth pace that can be sustained over long distances and rough terrain at speeds of up to 8mph (13kph). Essentially the horse walks rapidly with the fore legs and trots behind with the legs being slid forward well underneath the body.

The Paso employs a lateral gait unlike any other, the forelegs arcing outwards in a high paddling action while the hindlegs take very long straight strides which take the hocks well underneath the horse. On rough going the horse can cover long distances at between 10–11mph (16–18kph) while for short bursts on good ground the speed may increase to 15mph (24kph).

Gelding
A castrated male horse. Stallions are sometimes described as 'entires'.

Girth
The strap attached to both sides of the saddle which keeps the latter in place.

It is also used to describe the barrel of the horse, the girth being the measurement round the body taken from a point just behind the withers.

Half-bred
A horse bred by a registered Thoroughbred out of a mare of unknown ancestry, or one other than Thoroughbred. Primarily, this is a British term and is extended to three-quarter-bred or even seven-eighths bred. A three-quarter bred, for instance, would be by a Thoroughbred out of half-bred mare.

See also warm-blood and cold-blood.

Hand
A hand is the unit by which horses are measured and is of medieval origin. The hand equals 4in (10cm) (the approximate breadth of a man's hand). A horse is measured when he is standing square on level ground from the highest point of the wither to the ground, the resultant measurement being described in hands high, i.e. 16 hands high equalling 64in (163cm). On the mainland of Europe the metric system has been adopted and height is expressed in centimetres.

High School
Also termed *Haute École* and sometimes *Dressage Académique*. It is the highest level of training in the classical art and includes *passage*, *piaffe* and the airs above the ground as practised at the Spanish Riding School and in the Cadre Noir.

Hock
The joint connecting the tibia and metatarsal bone in the hind leg, i.e. the joint between the thigh and shank.

Horse Trials
This sport, which may be divided into one-, two- or three-day trials or events, derives from tests designed to prove the stamina, fitness and versatility of cavalry mounts. It was first introduced to the Olympic programme in 1912 and for a long time this type of competition was called 'the Military'.

The competition consists of three phases: a dressage test to show the obedience of the horse and its level of training. A speed and endurance phase involving a section of roads and tracks and a steeplechase and then a timed cross-country course over large obstacles. The third phase, to confirm the horse's fitness to continue in service, is a relatively straightforward course over show-jumping fences.

It is sometimes referred to as Combined Training and in common European use is the phrase, *Concours Complèt d'Équitation*, which is possibly the most accurate description.

Jibbing
A vice usually concerned with harness horses. The animal refuses to go forward and often runs backward.

Leader
The leading horses in a team of four or the lead horse in a tandem where two horses are harnessed one behind the other.

Levade
The first of the High School (classical) airs above the ground. The horse, tucking up the forelegs, raises the forehand from the ground sinking down onto deeply-bent haunches.

Limber
The attachment connecting the gun in a gun-carriage with the team.

Martingale
A schooling device used to control the position of the head. It comprises a strap fastened at one end to the noseband and at the other to the girth, passing between the forelegs. This is termed a 'standing' martingale. Another variety, running martingale, is divided at the breast, the straps thus formed terminating in rings through which the reins are passed.

Mule
Offspring of a mare by a jackass (male donkey). A *Jennet* is the offspring of a female ass or donkey by a horse sire. These hybrids are considered sterile.

Napping
A horse that refuses to obey the aids, i.e. it will not leave the company of others, it may refuse to leave the stable yard or to turn down certain roads. Usually the horse resists by swinging away from the direction required of it.

Neck Rein
A method of turning used when the rein is held in one hand. The rein carried against the left side of the neck causes the horse to turn right and vice-versa.

Nisean
The supreme horse of antiquity. Based on the introduction of the steppe horse some time after 2000 BC they were bred in western Iran on pastures which were conducive to the breeding of big, substantial horses. Selectively bred for 1,500 years and crossed with indigenous stock, they dominated the Middle Eastern scene as the ideal cavalry mount.

Pace
The two-beat trot accomplished by the movement of lateral pairs of legs. It is sometimes termed 'amble'.

The American Standardbred races in harness at this pacing gait and can reach speeds of up to 30mph (48kph).

Passage
A classical air, it is developed from trot. The steps, in two-time, are lofty and cadenced and are executed in a state of high collection with a brief pause as the horse moves from one diagonal to the other.

Piaffe
Passage executed virtually on the spot.

Pillars
A training aid in the High School. The horse is secured by reins to pillars placed some 5ft (2m) apart and is then urged into motion from behind. It is used in teaching *levade*, *piaffe*, etc.

Pirouette
A small circle made on the pivot of one hind leg. It can be ridden at walk and canter.

Points

Usually used in conjunction with a colour to qualify the latter, i.e. bay with black points means a bay horse with black lower limbs and black mane and tail.

Points of the Horse

Synonymous with *parts* of the horse. The various parts, i.e. thigh, fetlock, hock and cannon are all termed *points*.

Pole

A central timber on each side of which a pair of horses can be hitched to draw a vehicle.

Pony

Officially, a pony is a male or female horse not over 14.2 hands in height. There are, however, differences of conformation, particularly in relation to scale and character between horses and ponies.

Posting

The practice of rising to the trot. The rider sits to one beat of the trot and raises the seat for the following beat. It is less fatiguing for the rider than sitting throughout the movement.

Shoulder-in

A suppling exercise in which the horse, with the head inclined away from the direction of movement, moves sideways and forwards in the direction of the convex side.

Snaffle

A bit with a single mouthpiece, which may be jointed at its centre, operated with a single rein from rings on the ends of the mouthpiece.

Stirrup

The shaped metal device, usually with a flat tread, which supports the rider's foot. The full name is 'stirrup iron' often abbreviated to 'iron'. The stirrup is fastened to the bar of the saddle by an adjustable stirrup leather.

Tack

Stable word for saddlery. It is an abbreviation of tackle (harness). A room in which saddles and so on are kept may be known as a 'tack room' and a man employed to clean tack as a 'tackman'.

Tree

The wooden frame on which a saddle is built.

Volte

A small circle ridden in the classical school and as a training exercise.

Warm-blood

The European term for half-bred horses. Hot blood, or full-blood, is recognised as being either Arab or Thoroughbred. Cold-blood horses are the heavy horses descended from the Diluvial horse of Europe.

Whip

Apart from the whip carried in the hand to encourage or correct the horse, the word is also applied to the driver of a horsed vehicle.

Wheeler

The horses in a team of four (or more) hitched next to the wheel of the vehicle.

Withers

They lie at the end of the neck and just in front of the saddle and arise from the superior spines of the third to ninth dorsal vertebrae. Prominent withers are preferred to low, flat ones.

PICTURE CREDITS

The author and publishers are grateful to the following for their help in supplying photographs and for allowing their copyright pictures to be used:

Front jacket Top: Michael Holford; Bottom row, from left to right: University of Reading, Allsport and National Railway Museum.
Back jacket Ronald Sheridan
Endpapers Ronald Sheridan

Black and White photographs
Arxiumas, 120; Gunner R. O. Allen, 212; Beamish North of England Open Air Museum, 170; BLV Verglagsgellschaft Harrap Ltd, 50; British Museum, 32 (bottom), 48, 65, 71, 202; Brooke Centre, 159; Clydesdale Bank plc, 203; Danube Travel, 56; Alan Dennison, 32 (top), 54, 190; Dover Publications (New York) Ltd, 178, 179; Edinburgh District Council, 110; Fores Gallery Ltd, 42 (top left and right and above left), 173; French Tourist Board, 10; Harrap Ltd, 194; Michael Holford, 51, 111; *Horse and Hound*, 13; Kit Houghton, 29, 45, 136, 166 (top and centre), 206, 210, 211; Hulton Picture Library, 70, 78, 112, 115, 122, 143, 171, 192; Imperial War Museum, 148, 150; Bob Langrish, 27, 132, 166 (bottom), 184; Library of Congress, 131, 163; MacQuitty International Collection, 109; Mansell Collection, 46, 76, 82, 94, 96, 97, 98, 100–101 (top), 102, 153, 156, 181, 199; Marwell Zoological Park, 22, 24, 25, 26; Muschamp Stud (Mrs Diana Lorch), 37; Peter Newark, 8, 12, 15, 30, 34, 38, 58, 66, 79, 88, 105, 116, 118, 124, 129, 130, 133, 154, 182; Newmarket Racing Museum, 42 (above right), 43; Novosti Press Agency, 16, 28, 49; Photoresources Colour Photo Library, 53, 73, 74, 90; Pitt Rivers Museum, 11; Miriam Rothschild, 57; Ronald Sheridan, 52, 60, 134; University of Reading, 160, 162; Wilton House, 137; Xinhua News Agency, 106.

Colour Photographs
Bridgeman Art Library, 6; Mary Evans Picture Library, 17, 18, 29, 30 (bottom), 31; Fores Gallery Ltd, 4 and 5; Michael Holford, 10 (top), 14 (top); Kit Houghton, 7, 28; Bob Langrish, 32; Mansell Collection, 24, 26; Peter Newark, 12, 19, 20 and 21, 22, 23, 27, 30 (top); Novosti Press Agency, 3; Photoresources, 10 (bottom), 13; Planet Earth Pictures, 1, 2; Ronald Sheridan, 8, 9, 11, 14 (bottom), 15, 16, 25.

Line Drawings
Maltings Partnership, 40 and 41; Lorna Turpin, 18, 63.

SELECT BIBLIOGRAPHY

Anderson, J. K., *Ancient Greek Horsemanship* (Berkeley, California, 1961)

Anderson, J. K., *Hunting in the Ancient World* (University of California Press, 1985)

Barclay, H. B., *The Role of the Horse in Man's Culture* (J. A. Allen, 1980)

Bokonyi, S., *The Przevalsky Horse* (Souvenir Press, 1974)

Brereton, J. M., *The Horse in War* (David & Charles, 1976)

Chenevix Trench, C., *A History of Horsemanship* (Longman, 1970)

Chivers, K., *The Shire Horse* (J. A. Allen, 1976)

Colledge, M., *The Parthians* (Praeger, New York, 1967)

Cooper, L., *British Regular Cavalry 1644–1914* (Chapman & Hall, 1965)

Creel, H. G., 'The Role of the Horse in Chinese History' (*American Historical Review*, xx, no. 3, 1965)

Daumas, E., *Horses of the Sahara* (University of Texas, Austin, 1968)

Dent, A. and Machin-Goodall, D. *The Foals of Epona* (Galley Press, 1962)

Ewart, J. C., 'The Derivation of the Modern Horse' (*Quarterly Review*, no. 411 1907)

Ewers, J. C., *The Horse in Blackfoot Indian Culture* (Smithsonian Institute, 1955)

Fei, Hsiao Tung and Chih-i-Chang, *Earthbound China* (Routledge & Kegan Paul, 1948)

Fox, R., *People of the Steppes* (Constable, 1925)

Froissard, J. and L., *Horseman's International Book of Reference* (Stanley Paul, 1980)

Georgano, G. N., *A History of Transport* (J. M. Dent, 1972)

Gianoli, L., *Horse and Man* (Allen & Unwin, 1969)

Gordon, W. J., *The Horse World of London* (1st edn., 1893; reprinted J. A. Allen, 1971)

Gryaznov, M., *The Ancient Civilisations of Southern Siberia* (Cowles, New York, 1969)

Gurney, O. R., *The Hittites* (Penguin, 1954)

Haines, F., *Appaloosa* (University of Texas, Austin, 1963)

Hartley-Edwards, E., *A Standard Guide to Horse and Pony Breeds* (Macmillan, 1980)

Hartley-Edwards, E., *Country Life Book of Saddlery* (Country Life, 1981)

Hartley-Edwards, E., *Encyclopaedia of the Horse* (Octopus, 1977)

Hartley-Edwards, E., *Saddlery* (J. A. Allen, 1963)

Herbert, I., *Horseracing* (Collins, 1980)

Herbert, I., *Steeplechasing* (J. A. Allen, 1963)

Hope, C. E. G., and Jackson, G. N., *Encyclopaedia of the Horse* (Ebury Press, 1973)

Howard, R. W., *The Horse in America* (Follett, 1965)

Jancovitch, M., *They Rode into Europe* (Harrap, 1971)

Lamb, H. *Genghis Khan – Emperor of All Men* (Robt. M. McBride & Co., 1927)

Machin Goodall, D., *Horses of the World* (Country Life, 1965)

Mirov, N. T., 'Notes on Reindeer Domestication' (*American Anthropologist*, XLVII, 1945)

Mohr, E., *The Asiatic Wild Horse* (J. A. Allen, 1971)

Morgan, M. H., *The Art of Horsemanship – Xenophon* (with notes) (J. A. Allen, 1962)

Phillips, E. D., *The Royal Hordes: Nomadic Peoples of the Steppes* (Thames & Hudson, 1965)

Rees, A. D., *Life in a Welsh Countryside* (University of Wales, 1961)

Rice, T. T., *The Scythians* (Thames & Hudson, 1961)

Royal Academy *The Horses of San Marco* (1977)

Rudenko, S. I., *Frozen Tombs of Siberia* (J. M. Dent, 1970)

Russell, V., *Heavy Horses of the World* (Country Life, 1983)

Santini, P., *The Caprilli Papers* (J. A. Allen, 1967)

Simpson, G. G., *Horses* (Doubleday, 1961)

Spuler, B., *History of the Mongols* (Routledge & Kegan Paul, 1972)

Sulimirski, T., *The Sarmatians* (Praeger, New York, 1970)

Trew, C. G., *Accoutrements of the Riding Horse* (Seeley Service, 1951)

Tylden, G., *Discovering Harness and Saddlery* (Shire Publications, 1971)

Villiers, G., *The British Heavy Horse* (Barrie & Jenkins, 1976)

Varolo, F., *Typology of the Racehorse* (J. A. Allen, 1974)

Waley, A., 'The Heavenly Horses of Ferghana: A New View' (*History Today*, v, 1955)

Walrond, S., *Encyclopaedia of Driving* (Country Life, 1979)

Wentworth, E., *The Authentic Arabian* (Allen & Unwin, 1962)

Wentworth, E., *Thoroughbred Racing Stock* (Allen & Unwin, 1962)

Willett, P., *The Thoroughbred* (Weidenfeld & Nicholson, 1970)

Willoughby, D. P., *Empire of Equus* (A. S. Barnes, 1974)

INDEX